Embrace the
Chaos in your life.
Sometimes it can
be funny :)

♡ Suzy
2020

Sunny Day Publishing, LLC
Cuyahoga Falls, Ohio 44223
www.sunnydaypublishing.com

Vacuum in Squares

Illustrations by Kyle D. Traum
Edited by Ruth Beach
Photography by Stacie Gerrity

ISBN 978-1-948613-10-1
Library of Congress Control Number: 2020921834

Printed in the United States of America

To my loving husband for his infinite patience with almost every aspect of my life.

To my sons for their unwavering love and wicked sense of humor.

To my twin sister, without whom this journey would have been significantly less interesting.

And to my beautiful mother who taught me grace, humility, and determination.

"There is a thin line that separates laughter and pain, comedy and tragedy, humor and hurt."

–Erma Bombeck

Vaçuum in Squares

Suzy Remer

preface

"It is possible that when a person is troubled with mental anguish, know not which is the right or wisest road to follow, his mind has got to play peculiar tricks on him or his emotions may bring out things in him that are not true to his real self. It may happen that there are several important and vital things he may desire, or want to achieve or some things he desires to right at the present and cannot do all of them at once. He cannot decide which to do and being confused does not do any of them but still has them on his mind and keeps thinking and often worrying about them (even though he shouldn't worry about them but look and reason things out to a logical conclusion) but is not so often as easy as that. Perhaps he derives some pleasure by just dreaming about the pleasant things he wants to have and do and pass over his more serious troubles, thinking that in time everything will right itself. He could believe too strongly in the old adage—'time heals all wounds' or something to that general effect or that the future will take care of itself to his own satisfaction without his help and things will come nicely for him and he won't have to work for them and that will just fall right in his lap. Wishful thinking, but all people aren't that lucky. Arguments are often brought about as an outlet for pent-up emotions or desires and wants. If people would find an outlet for these things, even if they are not in the field they want them to be, it would help use some of this latent energy and would tend to forestall an argumentative state of mind because they can't have or do something right at the moment, which they have a great yearning for. An argument most often is a convenient outlet for these feelings of frustration and if they find someone who will give an argument, this allows the ill-feeling person to let go with all the spite and hate in his system, if you wish to put it that strong. He may use an innocent person as the poor goat for his stinging remarks. You might say this is a poor control of the will. In fact, it means the will controls the individual and he exercises no restraint over his sometimes ill-tempered moods and takes this out on the first convenient, innocent person who will listen and take it. Perhaps they should listen and then show the other person up by not getting angry in return or ask him to listen and talk back to him in the manner and tone of voice which the ill-tempered one so childishly used."

— Louis F. Remer (June 28, 1942)

Our father Louis was a very troubled man, but not in a way that was immediately obvious to anyone. I am not certain he was fully aware that he suffered from narcissistic, paranoid delusions. However, as evidenced in a handwritten letter he wrote when he was 23 years old, he seemed aware of what a nuisance he was. Louis knew from a young age that he would always and forever seek out far weaker souls than himself. He was cunning and cool and used people his entire life. Who would be the poor little goat he would kick? Who could he fight with to alleviate his stress and quell his torment? It took my sister and me until our mid-40s to really come to terms with the sobering fact that our father was a sociopath with a major personality disorder. He had a personality flaw that created discontent, frustration, sadness and confusion wherever he went. As his children, we were angry and discouraged and cried all the time. Other people just turned their backs on him or simply ran away. We never could. Our sweet mother never could. So guess who was his goat? Who would be left to swallow his venom day after day? Life has a funny way of showing you exactly why you were put on this earth and some of those reasons are not glamorous or good.

I don't wish to come off as sounding entirely negative, as our lives were filled with many good things. But it's the bad things that seem so wrong, so strange that our friends and the people we know continually ask us to share more. When you look at my sister and me, none of the stories make any sense. One might imagine we would be highly dysfunctional people. I can assure you, the opposite is true. I believe we are who we are in spite of our father's attempts to drag us down into his quagmire of self-doubt and pity.

Living a life with our father Louis was troublesome and frustrating but it wasn't until long into our relationship that my sister and I realized how sick and anxious he really was. So much was abnormal compared to everyone we knew that we rarely had friends over because we were never certain how our father Louis would behave (or whether or not the number and sheer size of our dogs would offend them). Needless to say, we kept our home life fairly private.

Everyone has a story. Some stories are sad. Some are funny. Some are tragic. Some are scary. I don't know which kind of story my life with my father makes. What I do know is that I cannot help but tell stories about my life and that of my twin sister in a funny, sarcastic, in-your-face way. I won't apologize for one word or action. You didn't live with this guy. We did. This book is not a series of sequential events. This is a book of anecdotes about our relationship with our father, Louis Franklin. These aren't tragic stories with horrible endings. These are stories about my life with my father and all the "what the fuck" moments that started long before I was born and continued until he passed away.

Throughout this book I alternate between telling stories from my perspective (using "I") and our perspective (using "we"). The people that know me also know us: "the twins," Cindy and Suzy. We are identical. It's more difficult than you can imagine, trying to separate yourself from someone who looks and acts exactly like you. We speak the same, look the same, dress the same (many times by accident which is why we have to check with each other before we show up at the same event wearing eerily similar outfits). We have the same friends, went to the same college, have had similar jobs and our kids look alike. Our hair is the same, we wear the same size clothes and shoes (which is very handy) and we are always mistaken for one another. We share everything except tennis shoes, wedding rings and husbands. Those you have to get for yourself.

I am confident once you've read our story you will rethink your own upbringing, so much so that you will either slit your wrists with a cheese grater or start writing your own stories. I hope you choose the latter. Life is about all the good and bad. More importantly it is about the curve balls life throws at you and how you handle them. You can catch them, dodge them or get hit square in the face. It is at these times when our character is measured. The only consistent thought should be to get up every day and tell yourself you are ready for whatever happens.

This is a story about why Cindy and I could never run away. This about how we survived to tell our story of crippling emotional abuse that lasted 52 years. Cindy and I—“we”—have traveled together from the time our egg split in two and we haven’t separated since. We try to laugh more than we cry when we talk about “Lou.” We have to laugh otherwise we might curl up in the fetal position, drool, and repeat “why me” over and over again. Seriously, what’s the point in that? We faced many challenges with our father with a “kill or be killed” attitude and of course, with some humor thrown in for levity. It’s simply how we are wired.

— Suzy (and Cindy)

the chapters of my life

During my adult years I frequently contemplated my relationship with my father Louis. I have spent hours, which turned into days, months and years thinking about why people end up with certain parents. Specifically, I wondered why I ended up with this man as my father. I believe that things happen for a reason and that the reason would present itself sooner or later. In my case, I am still waiting for a giant burning bush. I have no clue why I was born Louis' daughter.

Over the years, from childhood through adulthood, I found myself feeling confused and empty. There were many "why me" moments: feeling sorry for myself, my mother, the dogs and my siblings. I could never really pinpoint why I felt blue. I wanted the kind of father who might scoop me up in his arms and swing me in a circle for no other reason than to hear me giggle. I wanted a father who would gaze upon me with paternal pride. I wanted a father whom I knew above all else that I could go to with any problem big or small and he would say just the right thing to put my mind at ease. All of those things would have been ideal but I think it became more important to understand what I didn't want.

He would look at us, me and my family, and talk to us, but not like you might think. He was gazing, all right, but it was with a critical eye to zero in on our imperfections. Lou was much more critical of my sisters and me than of our brothers. He watched closely and frequently made remarks on how we looked, walked, talked, smiled and ate our food. He never talked to us. He talked at us. There is a huge difference between the two. So, eventually what I didn't want was for him to look at me or talk at me at all. Eventually I got my wish and he just started ignoring me, ignoring my sisters, ignoring my mother. At least until he thought he had something profound to say that would "fix" whatever was currently wrong with us. Our life in his house was nerve wracking.

Through all of this, I don't recall ever hearing stories about how our mother ever won an argument about any of her five children. Her first three children were fathered by her first husband who died tragically. Mike was her eldest child followed by Greg two years later and then Debbie eight years after that. Cindy and I were born six years later after she married our father Louis.

I know my parents fought frequently about Mike and Greg, the second eldest son, but I am sure she never got her way. She would sneak cigarettes with my older sister Debbie and help her lie about the smell. They would sit in the bathroom on the edge of the bathtub and blow smoke out the window.

The boys hated the strict atmosphere they were subjected to and their lack of freedom. My brothers, along with Cindy, Debbie and me, worked like dogs. Through all of this, Cindy and I watched closely. We soon realized that our home life was intentionally oppressive with a lot of lying and sneaking around occurring regularly.

Greg made the mistake once in asking, "How do we get out of this chicken shit outfit?"

Lou had an answer. "The same way you came in. Bare ass naked."

Greg was as insubordinate as his older brother. The difference was that Greg confronted Lou regularly where Mike said, "fuck you" under his breath and disappeared. Greg's experiences with Lou, whether good or bad, rank as high as any of ours. He too managed to graduate from college and move on to adulthood. Our real mutiny was getting married much too young. For Mike, Greg, Debbie and me, we all married and left the house by the time we were 23. We left with a job and our clothes. We could not leave with a bedroom set, housewares or linens unless we paid Lou first. He only provided us with what he thought was well-meaning advice. He was always full of that.

He would begin and end his lectures with advice but it was always in the form of some weird proverb. His words almost felt like they came from somebody else, like he had read them in a book. Words to him were a tool. We never got hugs or pats on the head with words like, "It will be OK" or "Try harder next time" or "I love you no matter what." He would say things like, "a bird in the hand is worth two in the bush," or "the early bird gets the worm," or "useless as tits on a boar," or "colder than a well-digger's ass," or "sucking hind tit," "wish in one hand and shit in the other and see which one fills up first" and "it depends on whose ox is being gored." Usually he used the most vulgar he could think of. I am middle-aged now and one thing is certain. When I was little, I never knew what the hell he was talking about.

In an effort to make some sense out of his nonsense, I pondered the idea of writing a book. The only thing I knew enough about to hopefully fill a few pages was growing up in my house or the eleven years I spent working for McDonald's. The story I had in mind about my life would be filled with controversy and humor. There was nothing funny about getting up in the middle of the night, dressing in a bow tie, penny loafers and leisure-wear to trek across town to make coffee and eggs. I was left with no other choice than to explore the more unbelievable golden nugget which was "my life with Lou." There was really nothing I wanted to fill page after page with about how many trucks of product I unloaded, the number of second-degree burns I got cooking all that food or the number of people I hired and fired. Here is that story: It was a job I hated. The end.

In my twenties, I started to think about what it was really like to eat a meal in front of my father or to try to watch television without him telling all of us, including our mother, to "shut up" all of the time. Even chewing gum irritated him. I thought about all the big dogs we had that made an even bigger mess and how many hours my sisters and I spent cleaning up after them. I could only ever recall that doing anything in our house was always a major production and we usually walked away from whatever we were told to do in tears.

When Cindy and I recall our "life with Lou," our recollections are one continuous blur of rolling eyes, guttural sighs and name calling. Of course, none of this happened as long as he could see or hear us. That would have gotten us a well-placed slap to the head. Under our breath though, we called him an asshole many times and uttered "Oh my God. What the fuck! Is he crazy?" I wish I could say that by his 93rd birthday we didn't find that necessary any longer, but the truth is I think my father was an asshole up and until he died. He had his moments of kindness, but they were few and far between.

Cindy and I thought he was an "asshole" before we graduated from elementary school. This was mostly due to his treatment of our mother. We hated him for his sarcastic cracks and disregard for her as his wife and wished he would just shut up and leave her alone or drop dead. What was sad was that all Cindy and I really wanted was to be able to love and admire him. As more time passed, that idea seemed impossible and entirely improbable.

Our thoughts weren't a matter of disrespect. It is what he inspired in all of us, all of the time. Just as any of his children or grandchildren might start to warm up to him, he would correct the pronunciation of some word, tell you to stand up straight, stop scowling when you spoke or don't flail your arms when you speak.

A few years ago I was feeding him dinner with his favorite martini and he matter-of-factly announced, "You're getting fat, kid." I was 46 years old. I felt my knees get weak as I turned around. I had that fight-or-flight response. I should have cracked him upside the head with a skillet. Instead I decided to ask him what part was growing too big for my delicate frame. "Your ass is getting big." He was looking at me so matter-of-factly, so detached it was scary. I guess he just felt like carving me to shreds for a second and couldn't control himself.

This is how it was and always would be. Louis was an uncensored human being; cruel and unforgiving. His words could be more painful and shocking than a punch to the gut. And he thoroughly enjoyed the emotional pain he could inflict. As I got older I became more confident, so it was not difficult to shift from "Should I write this book?" to "I will write this book." I became committed to writing one chapter after another until I might suddenly surprise myself with an entire book. In the end, I will have hopefully gained enough insight into what made him tick and never tell my sons their cheeks were looking chubby or hand them a tablespoon-size shovel to pick up a pile of dog poop.

funky monkey

I did not write this story on behalf of Cindy or myself to evoke a mountain of sympathy from the masses of people who themselves think they were screwed up by their parents. I did not write this so that she and I could reap a collective "sigh" of pity from our friends for our less-than-perfect childhood. I wrote this so other people could see that life goes on in spite of all we perceive as "bad." There is humor and heartache in every chapter of my life with my father. I am certain that I survived only with the support that my twin gave to me. Our older brother offered us stability by listening to what seemed like never-ending complaining. I am eternally grateful that he could do that with impartiality and compassion.

My four siblings and I managed to grow up, get jobs and keep them, get married (in my case three times), have children, fall in love, fall out of love, take vacations, laugh and make friends. We fell down a lot but we always got up and kept moving

The best part of writing this story is that I found humor in a lot that was thrown my way. I am sure that humor was simply a well-disguised defense mechanism. Whatever it was, it worked for me. The worst part of writing this story is that I hate why I wrote it. Deep down, I loathe the words that spill out of me when I talk about Lou, my father. It is surreal when I say out loud that our lives, although affected positively by him in many ways, would be better now had he died the minute each of us hit voting age.

I am a decent person. I am kind to my friends, love animals and am charitable with my time unless you ask me to join the PTA or some women's club. Those groups are full of too many people suffering from an egregious amount of self-importance with poor time management and shitty people skills. Anyway, when I speak about him, my father, I am actually shocked at the words I use and the manner in which I use them. I find that I frequently tell people that I just wish he would die. I despise it even more when someone says, "Good for him." I am not happy that he lived to be over 90. I cannot breathe when I hear people living to be well over 100 years old. The oldest person on record just died at 114! "Not him," I would mutter. Please.

None of what I so deeply wished for was really true. It wasn't untrue either. I do not know what to think other than he was who he was and I didn't like him very much. There was something seriously wrong with my father and it would take me many years to realize what kind of sick person had made such an impression on my young mind. I often wondered what happened to him that made him incapable of showing love and affection. What made him a joyless human being who seemed to lack a conscience? Why did he prey on the weak and seek out to inflict emotional duress? He was some kind of funky monkey that's for sure; sick in the head but not totally deranged. Simply put, he was peculiar in a slightly psychotic way.

The reality was that my life with "him," my father Louis and those of my siblings was scary. We were always unsure of how to behave and what to say which is exactly how he wanted it. The house was always closed up and dark. Big heavy drapes covered most of the windows so even at two o'clock in the afternoon the inside of the house looked like ten o'clock at night. No wonder my mother wanted to sleep all of the time. She never knew what time it was. There was a chill that hit you on the back of the neck and ran down your arms the minute you stepped inside. Except when it was the middle of July and it was 95 degrees. The only thing that ran down your neck and arms then was sweat. When my mother became too ill to bake and cook from scratch their house started to smell like a combination of wasp spray, wet dog and old people.

Our big house on Lake Avenue never felt cozy except when mom was cooking, the radiator was on and all four dogs were sleeping under our feet at the kitchen table. It felt nice to run your feet over the St. Bernard's back and feel how warm he was. If I didn't think I would have caught fleas, I might have crawled under the table with him. Cindy and I could relax in the kitchen and color or talk because Lou was never in there unless it was time to eat.

If we couldn't hide in the kitchen where it was warm, we always had our upstairs bathroom. Cindy and I frequently hid in there with our mother and older sister so we could talk. He never followed us in there unless he thought we were using too much water to wash our hair. In that case, without warning, he would turn the water off while you were standing there soapy and wet. He repeatedly reminded us to turn off the water while we soaped up and then turn it back on to rinse. My husband made the ill-fated error of coming into the bathroom when I was 50 years old and told me to turn the water pressure down because I was wasting water. I said, "If you value your life, get the hell out of here and NEVER tell me that again."

Any other part of the first floor in our house was off limits to just simply relax. We were never permitted to throw ourselves on a couch or chair and put our feet up. He always insisted that all of us sit nicely and put both feet on the floor. We were never allowed to jump on the beds either. We couldn't tip back in our chairs or put our elbows on the table. We could not lean on the sink to wash the dishes, drag our feet when we walked or chew gum. My parents had a lot of really nice antiques so I can appreciate now as an adult why children should not abuse the furniture. Even though I have rules in my house, the atmosphere doesn't seem as stiff as it was when I was growing up. And I could give a shit if my kids chew gum or jump on the beds. However, I have to admit that I never let them drag their feet while walking or put their elbows on the table while eating.

Lou never seemed happy to see us when we came home from school, a sporting event or a friend's house. He never really picked his head up from the paper or whatever he was working on to greet us. We usually just said "hello" and kept on walking. We beat it to the kitchen to eat or upstairs to our rooms. There was a weird, pervasive politeness that existed in our house; like when you meet people for the first time and aren't sure of their sense of humor, religious background or education so you keep your mouth shut and smile a lot until you get a feel for the situation. In our case, it lasted more than 20 years.

Looking back, I would characterize our adolescence as a series of hazing events. The hours we had to spend caring for his dogs, cleaning his big house to white-glove perfection and preening his rental properties (which now don't even pass a Section-8 inspection) were horrible. Even simple stuff like doing homework, speaking (even if it was only at the dinner table) and walking across a room drove all of us to a level of frustration where running full-blast into a brick wall would have been less painful. Even while we were trying to do normal everyday things the sound of his voice made all of us look up at the sky and say, "What the fuck."

Cindy's and my older siblings were actually our half-siblings. Tragically, they lost their father, our mother's first husband, at a very young age. Our mother was a widow at 34 years old. Debbie was a baby when he died and the boys were under ten years old. Our mother had to make quick adjustments to her living conditions given that she had three young children to care for and no feasible way to earn a decent wage. She dropped out of high school at 16 and available jobs for her would take her away from her children who desperately needed her. Income from life insurance and social security back in 1958 would do very little to ease her daily financial commitments. She knew full well that her money would run out. But my mother was beautiful and kind and would no doubt attract attention from many men. She would only be left to choose another mate of her liking.

Less than a year later, she met Louis, who quickly filled the void left by her deceased husband. Understandably, her sons questioned his very presence and were resistant to another man replacing their own father. Debbie had no idea who this man was or what he would represent in her life. The boys were suspicious and resisted every attempt he made to infiltrate their lives. Four years later and admittedly by accident, my mother was pregnant with twins at 38 years old.

Our older sister was six when Cindy and I were born, forcing the entire household to make adjustments. At six, she was left to fend for herself with the help of her older brothers. Sometimes she stayed with her new grandma. Although Lou's mother was a little eccentric and a bit of a kleptomaniac and might have fed our sister too many M&M's, she did take her to movies and kept a good eye on her. I always felt Debbie was resentful of Cindy's and my mere existence. Our older sister wanted her mother-daughter relationship the way it was before her father died and before we were born. Mom did what she could but was exhausted from nursing two babies non-stop for six months. Mom needed help any way she could get it even if it was from a woman more inclined to teach her daughter how to shop lift than knit a sweater.

Lou's affection toward Mike and Greg was simple tough love. They were 14 and 16 years old when Cindy and I were born and Lou was hell-bent on making men out of them as quickly as possible. His monologue to them once he latched onto our mother was startling. He proudly announced, "Your mother is no longer your nigger maid." This meant that they would assume every chore and duty and would be working as soon as the law allowed it. They knew right then they were screwed when they got their "you have no rights in this house" speech.

The boys hated the transition from one father to another and they openly showed their contempt. Sometimes they rolled their eyes at him and one time gave him the finger. That was a huge error in judgment because I don't think Greg saw the left hook that caught him across the mouth. Mike and Greg did what they were asked, although not willingly. It was usually the threat of punishment from Lou or feeling sorry for mom that kept the boys in line. They turned into the family's landscapers, babysitters, drivers and housekeepers. I know how much they must have hated losing their father and then having to adjust to new surroundings just as they were making the transition from boys to young adults.

I've been asked how I would describe my father and many words spring to mind. Mostly, I tell people he was a nasty prick. A more refined and accurate word is "sociopath." It has taken me a very long time, a lot of reading and hours of watching talk shows to finally figure out that there was something clinically wrong with him. He lacked a conscience and simply wanted everyone around him to feel sorry for him. Pity from others. That was one of his prizes and he nailed his landing perfectly when he met our mother. He used her pity for him to stay married to her for 50 years. When I asked her why she stayed with him after all he had done to her she said, "Because no one else would have."

The way he treated us and our mother on a recurrent basis made it impossible however, to feel love for him. Yes, Lou provided. We never went hungry and we always managed to have what we needed—school supplies, clothes, food, shelter. What we all craved was love and affection. Even when we had hurt ourselves badly and he would demand the ER doctors get plastic surgeons or orthopedic surgeons because we managed to mangle ourselves, it just wasn't enough. It didn't feel like love to me. Forget that he didn't hug any of us or tell us not to worry or that we would not be scarred for life. The worst part of getting hurt wasn't the pain from a split skull or broken bone. It was the ensuing lecture about how defiant Cindy and I were and the reason we got hurt was because we did not listen to him. Accidents never happen. You bring it all on yourself. We were supposed to feel guilty for not listening and sorry for him because we just cost him more money.

Hugging him was like trying to hug a perfect stranger. It felt weird and you just knew you didn't really want to do it again. When Cindy and I were little, we would get up next to his green leatherette chair while he smoked a cigar, reading the newspaper, just to say goodnight. It wasn't really terrible. We'd usually kiss him on the cheek and he'd pat our buckets and we'd leave the room. He was expressionless, though, most of the time. I just always wanted to be able to sit on his lap, get a big hug and for him to tell me he loved me. At the very least, for him to smile at us once in a while. Living with him was like living with a stranger. We lived a parallel life and his lack of involvement was creepy.

I have wished many times that my father had been a well-respected member of the community, popular with the neighbors and loved by my friends. Instead, he sat low in his car, never acknowledged our friends and never socialized with anyone. He did this on purpose because he liked to come across as someone not to fuck around with. He always looked like he was ready to flip you the bird or take a crowbar to your head. In fact, he could give anyone a hair-raising look; even his own kids. Only a few of our friends were unaffected. Most everyone else got the message.

Cindy and I have been told by many people that we are lucky Lou lived so long that our children are blessed to actually know someone from the "greatest generation." Maybe that's true—on the surface anyway. For many years, we thought our father was the smartest, most clever man we knew. All children think that in the beginning. Many children grow up and continue to foster a healthy two-way relationship with their parents. For a lot of people, their relationships with their parents get better. In our case, our opinion of Lou over time slowly deteriorated and our relationship became almost unbearable.

All of Cindy's and my conversations with him were one-sided. He lectured, we listened. Talking to Lou was never a lively two-way banter but an endless diatribe. He shouted. We listened. We shouted over him. He enjoyed giving a never-ending monologue of purposely confusing phrases and expressions. It was inevitable after five or ten minutes of trying to have a conversation that I would demand, "What is your fucking point?" However, somewhere along the way Cindy and I had to learn to shut our mouths and make him believe we agreed with him or we could never move on. We could argue with him forever. This was a sport for which I wish I could somehow have gotten paid.

He believed everyone around him was meant to simply validate his opinion at the sacrifice of their own. If he wanted our opinion, he would give it to us. Unfortunately for him, as Cindy and I got older, we became less interested in his outlook on life, so conversations turned to arguments with each side ramming his/her opinion down the other person's throat. Arguing soon became a sport with no one ever winning. I hate not winning. Always feeling like I had to concede to his bullshit was maddening. However, I am now at a point in my life that I see what a terrible waste of time it was. Although, I have to admit that it was sometimes entertaining to watch him stomp his feet, throw papers, swing his cane and turn shades of red and purple like a three-year old trying to get his way.

I have friends who love to seek out the help of their parents. A woman I know told me, "Oh, I just adore my father. I can't bear the thought of him dying. I could ask him for anything. I will miss him too much when he's gone." I realized I must have had the dumbest expression on my face, looking at her thinking, "This kind of human being exists? Why wasn't he my father?" I was jealous of someone I hardly knew just because she said she really loved him. How sick is that?

I stopped asking for his advice before I graduated from high school. We were all above-average students and had a network of mentors elsewhere. Fuck him. We got so sick and tired of him making us feel like shit, which explains why four out of the five of us married and got the hell out of there before we were 23. The sad thing was that I felt guilty leaving Cindy and my mother behind. Somewhere deep inside me it was about self-preservation. Mom would have to learn to argue on her own and Cindy would have to find her own husband. Just like my three older siblings, I got the hell out of there.

We all did what we did and hoped somewhere along the way that he would acknowledge our accomplishments, however big or small. What would a shrink say about our constant search for his approval? I am certain he would say that it shouldn't matter anymore. It just pisses me off that we tell ourselves he was just sick in the head as our way of justifying the fact that he withheld his affection in so many ways.

It was so stupid that for over 50 years my sister and I never stopped seeking his validation and approval. This is where crazy starts. There are a hundred people out there who think we're above average. The truth is that maybe all he ever thought was that we were all nothing more than idiots, average humans who didn't deserve his attention and validation.

I wanted to hear from him that I mattered. Cindy wanted to hear from him that she mattered. I wanted him to admit that we made it, that he loved us and that he was proud. I heard him tell me he loved me—once, and that was after he drank a half of a bottle of Jack Daniels. This was some Christmas back in the 90s when my oldest brother tried to tell me, "That was real." Bullshit.

Besides trying to get my mother to tell him to "fuck off," I only recall one time when she was brilliant. His way of insisting that he is not stupid was to say "I wasn't born yesterday ya know."

To my mother's credit she said, "No, you weren't born yesterday. You were born 90 years ago." Amen, sister. Other than that, she was pretty quiet. I believe she was quiet because she wanted to be the one person who did not pick on him. He told her so many stories about being bullied and how hard his life had been that she couldn't see how he had manipulated her. Telling someone who really has it coming to "fuck off" is freeing. She wouldn't have meant it though.

Lou didn't teach any of us how to make and keep friends or how to get good jobs and keep them. He taught us how to be vindictive, racist, argumentative, quick-tempered, and foul-mouthed. He was a petty thief, pathological liar and conscienceless bastard who bragged incessantly about his "accomplishments." This was a great education if you wanted to be a member of a "gang," but it didn't do much to help you succeed in the real world. I take that back. Congress is full of people just like that. I just never wanted a job in politics.

So, when does a human being become unhinged? Go a little

insane? I have been wondering for almost my entire life if I will suddenly lose my mind. Did my father know he was crazy? Reading the letter he wrote to himself in 1948, I think he knew something was wrong. But instead of seeking any kind of help, which was out of the question for his generation, he spent a lifetime suppressing his fears and insecurities. He believed that other people's reaction to his behavior and personality quirk was a dysfunction in them. He was fine. It was the rest of us who were weak and stupid.

I might have no idea I've gone off the rails, left the reservation or come completely unglued. It might happen at a traffic light, at my kid's baseball game, playing golf, eating dinner, having sex, washing my hair, or walking the dog. Had my father put me through enough emotional turmoil to cause my mind to spill over with confusion, denial, depression, regret, guilt, stress or hatred to the point where I go bat-shit crazy? Don't get me wrong. I feel those things all of the time. But I function. I don't steal and I am certainly never mean to my friends. I try to accept people and their differences or opposing views. I don't do drugs and I have a job. I function in society. My father never could.

Although I may be hanging on by a thread, I am still hanging on. He is not going to drive me to the nut house. He will not do that to me and do you want to know why? The reason is simple. Spite. And the fact that I vow daily not to use people or be hateful and vindictive. We all have bad days and I have regularly dropped the ball. I guarantee my kids have wondered if I was alright after watching me cry or lose my temper for no apparent reason. I would then apologize profusely for my behavior and tell them, "Mom is just tired." They accepted whatever reason I gave and never judged me. It was during those moments that because I knew how bothered I was at my own behavior and that they assured me things would be alright that I knew I wasn't insane.

One day I may not have a choice and will unknowingly lose all control. Today is not that day.

i smell bullshit

My father Louis served in World War II and the Korean War. He survived the depression and lived without a father (who died when Louis was seven of a burst appendix). A lot of kids grow up with one parent but unfortunately for him, it was probably the beginning of the end. He was raised by his mother, whom he openly hated. She didn't care for him much either, as I found out. He disliked her primarily because, as I understand it, she was hoping for a girl instead of a boy and she only had one child. She let his hair grow long and put him in dresses when he was an infant. She picked at his character and his desires and God only knows how else she tried to emasculate him. She was hard on her son simply because she wanted a daughter. As a result he developed a powerful stubbornness that served him well throughout his life. His mother may have tried desperately to keep him in check but failed miserably and eventually let him do as he pleased.

I think that people are predisposed for certain kinds of mental illness and just need the right circumstances to flip their mental switch. After all the years of watching and listening, my guess is that his issues stemmed from not having a father after the age of seven and a mother who wished her kid had a vagina instead of a penis. One of his cousins told me a story of walking in on him while he was banging his mother's head against the floor. God only knows why. Maybe she threatened to cut his dick off.

He had it tough but not as tough as a lot of people. There are stories out there of kids getting chained to toilets, sexually abused, beat, starved, sold and otherwise neglected. Kids today complain when they don't get the newest cell phones, $80 Abercrombie jeans, Xbox 360 and a Lexus when they turn 16. My parents were happy to have a few toys, shoes that didn't have holes in them and something more for breakfast than dry toast and black coffee. But Lou used any inconvenience, however large or small, as an excuse to brood, slack off, bully or steal.

His mother Mary was a little quirky. She loved sugar and ate it right out of the bowl. She collected dolls and rhinestone jewelry and danced the "grapevine" across the living room floor. She didn't seem so awful to me, but I wasn't raised by her. He said he was teased by his uncles incessantly which caused him to roam the streets alone. Unless I am missing much of his story though, I can't think of one concrete reason why he was a joyless human being. Something had to make him happy, but I will be damned if I know what it was.

Part of his life story makes me pity him. He had a joyless expression on his face most of the time. The way he talked, you would think he was some kind of victim of some awful crime. He came across as a person who was unappreciated, undervalued, unloved and basically disregarded as a human being. I know his life could not have been so bad that he spiraled into a world of unrecoverable self-loathing. Maybe he had a legitimate chemical imbalance and truly suffered from some kind of psychosis and that is why he could never find the joy in anything. When he was 93 his doctor said to me "You know your father has a major personality disorder."

I said in return, "No shit. Stop giving him cholesterol and thyroid medication and prescribe him something else. Doesn't anyone make an anti-asshole drug? Give him that."

On a clinical level, maybe I just don't know what the hell I am talking about. What I do know is that whatever his problem was, he sure did a good job trying to pass it along to his wife and kids. It was all of us who daily ingested some kind of mood-altering substance because of the enormous pressure we were under just trying to be his kids. In his opinion, our depression and anxiety were nothing more than a result of our over-active imaginations. According to him, "It's all in your head. Deal with it. You don't need pills or a shrink. You need a foot in your ass." Well, the reality is that it was the words that came out of his mouth that made all of us shovel pills and alcohol into ours.

So he hated himself and his life. I hate my big arms, the fact that I didn't have the balls to go to law school, my intolerance for stupidity and that I can never stop worrying about money. I don't throttle my friends and family with insults and mind games. Did this give him a license to be a bully? When I say "bully" I mean a person who is a never-ending nitpicker; a person who raised his voice for the sheer pleasure of shock and awe and then withdrew into a world of silent self-pity.

I suppose in many ways he had an excuse for his behavior. When you're sick, you're sick. But if he claimed he was unloved then why would he treat his wife and children like an inconvenience? Maybe he felt ripped off by the system, ripped off by his family and ripped off by society. If that was the case then to his thinking, everyone owed him something and he could go through life bitching and moaning and stay joyless. I think he did it for attention and wanted all of us to whirl around him and tell him "Poor baby. You must have had it so hard. You're a great dad. You always know the right things to say. You've always been there for me." He wanted a giant pity party. I refused.

He was drafted for WWII and served his time. I am sure he saw some pretty ugly things during his tour, but he was not injured and came home in one piece instead of in a body bag. Perhaps he would have preferred to lose a limb than come home with demons in his head. Maybe it might have been easier to adjust to a physical disability rather than a mental one. I know for him neither disability would have been preferable. He certainly would have never conceded to suffering from post-traumatic stress under any circumstances. Whether or not that was brought on by his father's death, his mother's idiosyncrasies or the war was irrelevant. To him, everyone else was bat-shit crazy. I am convinced his disability was a short circuit to the brain. The kind of faulty wiring that manifests itself as conscienceless.

After WWII, he barely settled into a regular life with a job, housing or relationships when he was drafted into the Korean War and had to leave again to serve his country. He did not see active duty this time and spent a great deal of time pushing papers and driving generals around. Still, this interruption derailed him yet again from pursuing his dreams. He never spoke of what his dreams were and like a lot of men from his generation, he knew he had to somehow earn a living and pay his way in whatever way he could. That generation was not about doing what you loved but doing what was necessary. For my father, digging ditches, driving a school bus or working at a local hardware store was not on his radar. He was in search of a meal ticket. Little did my mother know what and who was waiting for her in ten years.

During the 18 months my father was away serving his time in the war, his mother gave away many of his treasured possessions that he managed to hang onto from his childhood. She had no right to discard his bike, baseball glove or trinkets even if they were something she thought he had outgrown. If I had to guess, this was when he was found trying to flatten her skull with the kitchen floor.

I am sure that no one, especially our mother, knew any real

details about our father, her soon-to-be husband. It would take years before she figured him out and it would only be because she watched him closely and listened even closer. The problem was that no matter what she may have seen or heard, she quickly suppressed her fear and anger. Without much experience and even less education, our mother figured that as long as someone was paying the bills and putting food on the table then she could ignore the rest. For the most part, Louis put on a great act in the beginning and would continue his charade for the rest of his life. He was a superior bull-shitter and managed to con our mother, his friends, insurance agents, tenants and most of his family.

In 1960, he married our mother Marie. She was introduced to him by a friend who told her on their wedding day, "If he treats you as well as he treats his dogs, you've got it made." What an odd thing to say to a beautiful bride. That comment should have made her run for her life. I wonder if she had second thoughts even if it was for a split second. Maybe she believed he would spoil her rotten and impartially love and adore her three children from her first marriage.

The sad fact is that he never did treat her that well. In fact, I don't think he treated his dogs all that well either. The dogs lived a meager existence of Pick-n-Pay brand dog food and nights on a hard tile floor. I give him credit for saving every scrap of food, food by-product, and grease from bacon, roasts or chicken and cooking up this slop and dumping it all over their food. It actually smelled pretty good and they gobbled it up from their cast iron food pans faster than a pack of starving hyenas.

When Marie was introduced to Louis, she already had three children. She met and married Lou 18 months later out of duty, desperation, fear or some widow-induced insanity. She said she loved him and has a handful of love letters to prove that he loved her; at least the letters said so. I read one of those letters and could not believe what I was seeing. His words were like poetry and I am sure my mother was smitten. She must have been infatuated because she married him less than a year later. She never knew what hit her. She never pondered why a 40-year-old man who still lived with his mother, would want to marry a woman with three children.

Lying in a hospital bed in 2009, she cried as she said, "I'm sorry. I thought I married a gentleman. He's nothing but a prick. That's all he's ever been." She accepted her sacrifice and her burden because without him, Cindy and I would not be here. However, Cindy and I begged her many times to leave him for the sake of her well-being. We well knew as teenagers that he would steal her life. He would steal her self-esteem, her energy and her money. Her final "fuck you" though was to tell him on her death bed that she wanted to be buried with her first husband Mike. He sat there with his mouth hanging wide open.

Although she said he never complained about her pregnancy with Cindy and me he must have been shitting bricks at the thought of two more mouths to feed. Maybe he was thinking, "My mother should have chopped my peter off. I wouldn't be in this fucking mess now." Regardless, he was happy to be cashing social security checks from her other three children, benefiting from her dead husband's life insurance policy and her house.

Whether or not he meant it, he said to Cindy and me just before our mother died that he made two stupid decisions in his life. He said, "My mistakes were marrying your mother and having you two. You are the worst things that ever happened to me." He didn't mumble and Cindy and I didn't even flinch.

We were thinking, "Fuck me? Well, fuck you right back." One of us should have said, "I wish I would have been raised by wolves." Instead, we kept our mouths shut. The last thing we wanted to do was start a fight in front of our dying mother.

Cindy and I looked at each other and then looked at his wrinkled, sagging, miserable fucking face and wished he would drop dead.

On second thought, I believe he did mean what he said. He lacked compassion and empathy and a conscience and was a criminal at heart. The day we were born was the day his little scheme got thrown into reverse. I am certain now his plan was to hang on to whatever my mother brought to the table and use her for as much personal gain as possible. Good. I hope we ruined his life.

We often asked mom why she stayed with him and for her the answer was simple. "If I don't, who will?"

We always thought, "Who gives a shit?" but she felt it was her duty or her will to stay married with him. She did it out of pity. Honestly, she never wrote a check or paid a bill. Not once in her married life. She always had a roof over her head and food to eat. He made sure everything was taken care of including paying all her medical expenses. He might have complained about how much it cost and tormented her in the process, but she could go to sleep at night and not have to really worry about where the money came from. He would finagle, steal, cheat and lie to get it and she knew it. He had all of the control and she had to live with a miserable prick.

So, thank God we're all normal, whatever that means. All five of us (Cindy, me and "the other three") came out the other end with impeccable table manners, perfect postures and well-maintained lawns. We can carry ourselves in all social situations, throw like boys and shovel shit better than any cowhand. We graduated from college, never went to prison and between five of us, managed to have 14 children. We all own homes, cars, businesses of our own and not one of us ever moved back home once we left. That was because struggling financially and figuring out our own way in life was a better alternative than going back and having him say, “I told you so.”

At the end of the day a child should go to sleep knowing they are loved. Our mother wrapped her arms around us like a warm blanket. She smoothed over every rough spot with just a few words, warm cookies and handmade clothes. She stayed true to herself in spite of feeling like she married a “walking, talking, poke in the eye.” It was Lou who made us feel unsteady, unworthy and unloved. He was why we cried ourselves to sleep.

It turned out that there was really a difference in how he treated his dogs versus his kids or his wife. So, I say, “Up yours” to the guy who said we all might get treated better than a dog. We didn't. Lou spoke to his precious pooches sweetly and loved them unconditionally. He would say, “What's the matter baby” as he patted their heads. It made me sick that I could be jealous of a dog. Life with my father was a nightmare and I am anxiously waiting for the post-traumatic stress to kick into high gear.

I don’t know when I figured out that my father was really nothing more than a pathological liar and sociopath. He was full of shit all day, every day. I think I was in my teens when I finally pushed that thought to the front of my brain and said, “What the fuck is with him all of the time?” I really started to think about him and realized that nothing he ever said made any sense. I began not being able to tolerate the sound of his voice, much less his opinions. It was a constant battle of logical versus illogical and reasonable versus unreasonable. It was nonsense, which is why all of us got out of there as soon as we had the ways and means to take care of ourselves.

He stretched the truth about his childhood, his time in the Army, and his relationships with his family just so Cindy and I and everyone around him would feel sorry for him. He told his stories and somehow, he was the one always taking it in ass at the end of the day. This included everyone from his kids and wife to the people at AARP, the IRS, Medical Mutual, his doctors, his dog's doctors, neighbors, tenants, auto mechanics, single mothers, drug addicts, blacks, congress, Santa Clause and the fucking Easter Bunny! Life was a huge conspiracy and he got screwed at every turn. Well, there is a reason why a guy doesn't have any friends. My advice is "Don't be a parasite. Don't be an asshole. Don't be a lying sack of shit." Why don't any schools in this country teach kids how to avoid people just like him? This should be a required course before teenagers head off to college. It is a lot more useful than learning a foreign language.

He mumbled often, "no one understands." "Understand what!?," I say. His biggest prize was to gain your pity. After that, he wanted anything he could get for free even if he had to bend the truth to get it. I gave up trying to empathize, rationalize and understand his behavior a long time ago. The truth is that I just don't give a damn anymore why he was so misunderstood. We were all his victims and he was one of them too.

mr. manners

Lou always said that a person was judged by three things; appearance, friends and table manners. This, I believe, is very true. I tell my two sons the same thing. It's just that I go about their training differently than he did. I did not loom over them and watch for every tiny infraction. I concentrated on their looks and behavior as a whole. How they presented themselves to the world and the first impressions they would make motivated me to carefully choose my words to inspire each of them to eventually face society and all of its petty criticisms with confidence.

We had a large family. One might imagine that mealtime was filled with laughter and light conversation. Wrong. At a very young age, like six, eating at the table with Lou soon developed into the seven circles of hell. Cindy and I were silly kids and found humor in any deviation from the norm. Food on someone's face or the dog farting under the table sent us into uncontrollable laughter. My sister Debbie was much less inclined to the giggles at the table because she simply wanted to eat and be excused to her room. Even when he wasn't looking, he was seeing all that we did.

Not Cindy and me. It took us forever to eat. We simply could not have cared less what our father seemed to give a shit about at any particular moment. It was a moving target. However, at the worst possible moment, like when our food was hot, we would notice something, anything, that would immediately induce hysteria. This usually got my mother started. Talking and, especially, laughing at the dinner table was for some odd reason forbidden. So all one of us had to do was get started with that quiet, shoulder-heaving laughter and everyone else except Lou joined in. Of course he thought we were being impolite or picking on him so he would call our silliness to a screeching halt. Laughter and loud conversation resulted in Cindy and me being sent away from the table many times.

In the midst of trying to control our giggles, our table manners were scrutinized every second. We felt like circus animals. Instead of cracking a whip to get us back in line, he had his spoon, or any other utensil that he had just licked clean. At any moment he would remind you not to eat like a hog, slurp your soup or slouch at the table.

We could never fucking relax and just eat. It really was exhausting to think about the process. Did I have one hand in my lap? Was I sitting up straight? Did I cut only two pieces of meat at once? Did I put my knife down between bites? Did I spoon my soup or stew from the front of the bowl to the back? Did I spread butter on a bite of bread instead of the entire piece? FUCK! My cereal would get soggy or my dinner ice cold before I could remember everything and get through a meal. I don't know how he even managed to eat, watching us non-stop like he did. However, Lou was always the last one finished, so he made sure you did it right and ate everything on your plate. Period. Every meal, every day.

If you were unlucky enough to get caught with your elbow on the table, you might take a direct hit on the offending body part with a United States Navy spoon. He wielded this thing like a Chinese star. What's funny is that he was in the Army, not the Navy. That was my Uncle's spoon (his brother-in-law.) Anyway, that was his whip. When he couldn't reach an elbow, he caught you on the forehead. That thing was forged steel and it hurt like a bitch. My kids think it's funny for me to tell their friends the "spoon" story. "Mom, tell Joey about the time grandpa hit you in the face with a spoon!" These poor kids looked at me like I lost my mind. "Are you kidding me?" they would ask. "Absolutely not. Anyway, didn't you get hit with a spoon?"

His elbow was always resting comfortably next to his plate. We had spoons and could reach across the table. All is fair in war. Why didn't we reciprocate? Because we lived in the house of "Don't do as I do, do as I say." He held all of us, even his wife, to a higher standard than he was willing to attain for himself. He often said that table manners tell a lot about a person. This is true. However, I doubt that Miss Manners recommended hitting family members with cutlery to make a point. And the worst part was that you never saw it coming.

The worst foods to eat in front of Lou were cereal or soup. Come to think of it, fried chicken was no fun either. He required all of us to cut it off the bone and eat it with a fork. It was bad enough that none of us could lean forward towards our plates to meet a utensil full of food. It became a balancing act that we failed miserably. Three things had to happen when eating cereal or soup before you actually got it into your mouth. First, do not drip. Second, do not lean forward. Third, do not turn the tip of the spoon into your mouth. Eat off of the side of the spoon. What? I want you to try this the next time you sit down to eat and tell me you aren't ready to throw the whole fucking bowl across the room. By the time you got half-way done, your cereal would be unrecognizable, or your soup would be ice cold.

We had to sit in front of him until we were done eating. He never left the table before we did, so there was never a chance to relax and eat or try to feed what we did not want to our St. Bernard, Thunder. The dog was obnoxious. He always sounded like an alligator that just swallowed an entire goat in one bite. Three "gulp, gulp, gulps" and whatever was in front of him disappeared. You could never quietly feed this animal. He didn't mean to get you into trouble, but he did if you tried to hand him food under the table.

Our brother got caught trying to cover up a handful of green beans with his napkin and get away from the table. He made it as far as the kitchen sink. He forgot to feed them to the dog to get rid of the evidence. Instead, he put his plate in a dishpan full of soapy water. Lou found his plate and the beans and made him eat them covered in soap.

Of course, we were thinking he was an asshole. Our mother was just hoping we could get through a meal in one piece. We just wanted to eat. Try cutting fried chicken off the bone and eating it with a fork when you're nine years old. Try sitting at the table until 9:00 pm. because you aren't allowed to leave the table until you eat everything on your plate.

What kid likes green beans with almonds or giant slimy tomatoes in vegetable soup? Cindy hid in the bathroom more than once hoping that whatever she decided was uneatable would disappear at my mother's hand or be sucked off her plate by the St. Bernard. Neither would ever happen. My mother would overload our plates because we were skinny children and Lou would make us eat it. Forget the fact that our stomachs were the size of a tennis ball. If we didn't finish every scrap, short of licking the plate clean, he said it would be there for breakfast. (That never happened but I do remember sitting at the kitchen table past my bedtime once or twice.)

Try eating a meal with nothing to drink. Not even water. I know families that had pitchers of water or milk on the table and their kids could fill up on whatever they wanted. Lou would tell us that "If you have room for water, you have room to finish your food." What he didn't understand was that I used the water to wash down whatever I was choking on. Until Cindy and I were in our teens, our father never wore his false teeth, so he insisted that mom overcook everything. Many times dinner had a weird, mushy consistency and water was the only way to rush it down your gullet. So we had a glass of water on the table but were forbidden to touch it until our plates were clean.

If it was your lucky day and you could have a glass of water, you got it right out of the tap. We never wasted our time putting ice in it. Day after day Cindy and I watched him fill his rocks glass full of ice cubes and then pour gin, vodka or bourbon over them. He would stop us in our tracks after two ice cubes. He told us that the refrigerator used more electricity to freeze water to make more ice. Was he serious? I believed that bullshit for a while and finally gave up trying to understand him. I think I was probably 20 years old before I realized the refrigerator ran 24/7 regardless of whether we needed to make ice or not.

We only ever got two shitty ice cubes and gave up asking him to explain to us over and over again his justification for why his drinks got to be just above freezing and why ours had to be room temperature. Anyway, two was all we needed and was all we ever got. Asking for anymore was wasting electricity. All you could do was roll your eyes and take it. As an adult any time I was at his house I made sure he saw me force a whole tray of ice into a glass, fill it with water, take a few sips and throw the whole goddamn thing down the drain when I was done. I was secretly hoping he was stupid enough to utter one syllable about the amount of money it cost to make that single tray of ice.

To this day I panic a little bit when I sit down to eat a meal, especially if it's in a restaurant. I make sure I sit with my back straight, my feet planted firmly on the floor, that I cut only two pieces of meat at a time and don't lean over my plate. I keep one hand on my lap, never speak with my mouth full and eat my peas with a fork. I keep a small glass of water or wine with me and take small sips. No gulping allowed. I am sure my table manners have impressed enough people to get or keep a job over the years or had my in-laws thinking I was English royalty.

I also make a point of not finishing everything on my plate and, no, I will not eat it for breakfast. I feed my dog from the table and let my kids laugh and talk during dinner. I put ice in my milk, my beer, a martini, or a glass of wine because I have an ice maker that never ever stops making me ice cubes. I never realized how truly magical an ice maker could be.

I instruct my children to use proper manners and etiquette while eating a meal. If you were to ask them, they'd tell you they aren't afraid to eat in front of me or tell me they can't finish what I have put on their plate. They may be afraid to tell their stepfather that but not me. I watched my older son vomit up a pile of mashed potatoes he was forced to eat by his stepfather, who thought it was ridiculous to have some weird aversion to certain food consistencies. I sat back and watched with the best "I told you so" look I could manage. After that, I was the ruler of all things food.

My sons put their napkins on their laps and don't hunch over their plates. At this point I don't give a shit if they eat their peas or corn with a spoon as long as the food makes it to their mouths and they aren't flinging it across the room. They ask me if they may be excused when they are finished and thank me for their meal. The miracle in all of this is that I have managed to teach them how to eat like polite little humans and I never once hit them with my spoon.

I figure my sister Cindy and I spent the better part of 17,520 hours of our childhood sitting in the breakfast nook in the kitchen. We ate, drew pictures and taught ourselves everything from math to biology sitting across from one another. While we were in there, our father watched television from his precious green vinyl chair. He never sat anywhere else in a room that was thirty-one feet long and fifteen feet wide. If he wasn't in his office swearing about some resume he just fucked up, then he sat in his throne—a pale green vinyl chair that smelled like cat piss. Frankly, the kitchen was the warmest part of the house in the winter. The radiator was right under the table and the dogs with their warm bodies and hot breath were right under our feet.

Dad had a strict rule about school nights. In a way, he should be respected for being able to enforce this rule for twelve years. There was no TV on school nights. Period. Cindy and I might have tried to sneak an episode of *Dark Shadows* or *Speed Racer* right after school. Occasionally we got away with it. However, until we had straight As, we had to hit the books. We'd ask, "Can we watch *MASH*?" and he would say, "Do you have straight As?" The answer was no. We were close to straight As but close didn't count to him. He always trumped us by asking that single question and with that we would turn around and walk away defeated.

However, Sundays didn't count as a school night. Sunday evenings at 6:30 was time for *The World at War*. My earliest recollection of being forced to watch this show was in 1974. This was a documentary about World War II. Instead of our father telling us of his personal experience, we had to watch a show narrated by Sir Laurence Olivier. His quiet, depressing narration offered a front seat to the true images of war. There were corpses everywhere, explosions, terrified citizens and broken soldiers. Yes, this is what we wanted to do at 12 years old, especially if we'd been outside playing with friends. "We have to go inside now to watch men get blown to bits! We'll catch you later for that game of kick the can." Some of our friends must have thought we were nuts.

go back to the preface

As young children, Cindy and I were happy that there were shows he allowed us to watch. It was during these moments that we all openly laughed out loud. *Benny Hill, All in the Family* and *MASH* were staples in our television diet. These shows helped shape our young psyches. So did *The Love Boat*, *Happy Days* and *The Brady Bunch*. We appreciated the life lessons you could scrape together from shows such as these and preferred them over some televangelist begging for money. For that matter, thank God we weren't forced to watch *Polka Varieties* or *Lawrence Welk*. I would have hung myself in the shower. My great Aunt Frances thought Billy Graham was the second coming and sent him money regularly to fill his coffers. Thank God our father wasn't some religious fanatic. Can you imagine what life would have been like? Does David Koresh, Jim Jones or Warren Jeffs ring a bell?

Dad watched a lot of TV and never sat with us to work on homework or school projects. We did not have an "open door policy" in our house. Not only did our parents never talk about sex or drugs, but they never talked about our schoolwork either. Seriously, I don't know how we did it. One of the hardest things Cindy and I ever had to do was to ask our father for help with something. I can't think of a time when he actually put his fucking newspaper down and took five minutes to keep us moving in the right direction.

Cindy and I both have school-age children and I can tell you that it has been our daily mission to keep our boys organized and encourage them to get good grades. Cindy spent so much time with her oldest son that I asked her frequently where "they" were going to college.

We struggled for hours until we summoned the courage to go into the living room. Our mother tried to help but once we got out of elementary school, she could not really remember enough to be helpful. God bless her but unless we were asking for three dozen cookies for the next day's bake sale, Cindy and I would have to ask "him."

One or both of us might sit huddled in the warmth of the kitchen and wish whatever answer we needed would appear before us. That never happened and if we wanted to get to bed at a decent hour, then the only alternative was to go ask for help. Fuck. I don't know why we kept doing it. We always got the same response. It was like banging your head against a wall but not being able to stop yourself from doing it.

As was usually the case, he had the television on from 6:00 pm until 11:30 pm. He would sit in his favorite chair, in his favorite corner of a thirty-foot living room with the newspaper and a cigar. I felt like I was tip-toeing up to a sleeping giant. He was usually expressionless so you could stand there for what seemed like an eternity with no one saying a word. Except someone had to break the ice. It wasn't that interesting to look at the wrinkles on his forehead for four hours or the cigar smoke hanging over his head like thunder clouds.

We slithered up to his side and tried to get his attention by simply saying, "Dad." He ignored us until we said his name a few more times. "Dad." "Dad." We always waited patiently thinking he somehow didn't see us or hear us. Ultimately, we just figured he was ignoring us. How can a person disregard a child like that?

We might be three quarters of the way through a school year

and it made no difference. His response was always the same when we were brave enough to ask a question. "Dad, can you help me with something?" He would say, "What." "I don't know how to find the value of X." His response was, "Did you read the preface? Go back and start at the preface." Go back to the beginning in an algebra book? Was he really serious? Reading the preface of any book, let alone an algebra book, was useless. A preface only existed to make the author feel important about his or her own work. A preface set up what the book was about and maybe included a "thank you" to some distant friend or relative who might have helped get the book published.

So, that was it. The advice we got was to go back to the very beginning and start over. I would turn and leave with my tail between my legs. I could not stand him not helping us. It was cruel. So, Cindy and I taught ourselves everything from algebra to English composition. I tried to do that too with high school biology and college calculus and got Ds for my troubles.

The only plausible reason for why he always sent us away to start from the beginning was because he didn't understand it himself. It was some of the most ridiculous advice I have ever received. Period. It wasn't because he was trying to teach us the bigger lessons in life like the satisfaction that comes from figuring something out on your own. That's just too deep. The only other reason besides the fact that he didn't know what the hell he was doing was that he was trying to torment us.

Getting through school was excruciating. All five of us grappled with our homework, which I think is what he wanted. Ultimately, it was because he struggled and as long as we knew less than he did, he had the upper hand. There was no reason for him to send us away each night to answer our own questions. He could have helped somehow. I felt frustrated and ashamed because I believed my father thought I was stupid because I couldn't figure out how to find the value of X or conjugate my verbs. He made Cindy and me believe we weren't trying hard enough and that if we just stared at our work long enough, the answer would appear before us.

I recall many times sitting with my own kids trying to help them figure out their homework and asked more than once, "where is your textbook"? They would tell me they didn't have one and that they worked from a computer. I could not believe that the internet was replacing history and math books. I was trying to help and needed a book because I had no idea how to use Google docs. They would roll their eyes much the same way I did at my own father. But at least I sat with them for hours learning the lattice method. They knew I was at least giving it a shot. They stopped asking for help with math shortly after when one of them came home and told me I got all the answers wrong.

There is a point in parenting when you have to be more willful than your child. As parents, we do this so we can feel good and show them who is the boss. We make them eat different foods because it's what some doctor said we should do. I doubt though that many parents get some twisted pleasure from forcing their will upon their child to the point that he or she wants to vomit just to show them you have power and they don't. It's difficult to make a point and stand by it. It's hard to demonstrate good parenting by setting good examples. If you lived in my house, you did what you were told and hardly ever asked questions. Louis would simply say, "Because I said so."

Whether or not you believe it yourself, you have to tell your children to try new foods. What we as parents do is try to get them to eat a few bites of a new food so that hopefully they grow up wanting to eat more than McDonald's. Many docs say that a child has to try something at least ten times before developing a taste for it. My father had all kinds of tools and machines, knives and screwdrivers all designed to perform a specific function. There was one that he possessed that made my chest tighten and my knees weak each and every time he dragged this thing out of the cupboard on Sunday mornings. I bet all I would have to do is show my sisters the juice maker our father owned and they would get sick to their stomachs.

When I was little, under the age of ten or so, I would just be waking up wanting to eat a bowl of sugar-coated cereal and watch *Big Valley* or *Bonanza*. My sisters and I would quietly come downstairs in hopes that we could sneak our breakfast into the living room. Most times our father beat us to the kitchen and sat there with the newspaper spread open and a dog-food-sized bowl of oatmeal at his fingertips. He'd say, "Oatmeal is hot. Eat it." Of course it's not at all what we wanted and we were not really permitted to voice an opinion on the subject either. It was breakfast, who gives a shit? But he always did. So we would usually say, "no thanks" and leave the kitchen hungry. It was only when he was done reading the paper, two hours later, that we could go back to the kitchen and quietly get our cereal.

i think i'm going to puke

On the unfortunate mornings our father felt like pushing his nutritional agenda on to three little girls, and when carrots were on sale, he would put a big gray and white juicer on the counter. I hated that thing. They are all the rage now but when you're eight or ten years old, you want chocolate milk, not carrot and celery juice. I know he thought he was doing something wonderful and meaningful, but this was not a father-daughter bonding moment I cherished. No one did. I don't remember our mother ever drinking anything from this monster, but we would each have to stand and wait our turn, holding out our juice glass and wait for the orange sludge to drip from the juicer. I gagged with every sip and it was only six ounces. I just could not make my mind swallow liquefied carrots without wanting to puke. I just wanted to eat my carrots right out of the ground like every other kid.

What's worse is that we not only had to try it, but he made us drink the whole glass. It wasn't good enough that we took a sip and said, "No thanks." Have you ever said to your kid, "it won't kill you. Now eat it." Every time I think I should make my kid eat something he doesn't want or finish everything on his plate, I am reminded of what growing up in my house was like. I just tell them, "One day you'll like the taste. Or not. It doesn't matter to me."

Lou thought he was a terrific cook and he drove my mother nuts. He would get himself in the middle of her cooking to tell her how to use knives, peelers and pressure cookers. Or he would unnervingly stand and watch her. Cindy and I might be sitting in the breakfast nook coloring while she was working and thinking as she rolled out homemade biscuits or dropped homemade dumplings into soup. She wore a flowered apron every day and always seemed to have flour on her hands. Every single thing my mother made us to eat was from scratch and she was so thoughtful about getting a meal just right. It was relaxing to watch her move about a kitchen. She knew what she was doing.

And then, out of nowhere our father would somehow just be standing in the doorway watching her. He would impatiently push her aside and tell her, "Give me that before you kill yourself." I watched my mother in complete disbelief hand over the knife and watch him do her work. I can't remember if he was literally schooling her, but she stood there with her arms folded and waited until he had done enough to prove he was more skillful. I felt badly for her as she stood there patiently and waited until he was done showing off. The only thing he did was ruin dinner and made a bigger mess to clean up afterwards. He should have worried that she would repeatedly impale him with a potato peeler.

So when he got near a pot of soup, you knew the outcome would be questionable. He really didn't think she was going to kill herself making dinner. He just wanted to make it his way. A bowl of vegetable soup turned into an episode of Fear Factor. Children do not have sophisticated taste buds. Kids don't want weird-tasting food or odd textures. I know what I'm talking about. It took my one son 11 years to eat mashed potatoes and in 18 years one of my sister's kids has never eaten an egg or a bite of macaroni and cheese and still wanted the ends of his hot dogs cut off. When my son's stepfather thought this idea was ridiculous and tried to make my oldest son eat mashed potatoes, I laughed my ass off when my son gagged on them like a cat puking up a hairball. Leave a mother alone when it comes to feeding children. Please.

My mother was always careful to finely chop vegetables and trim all the fat off the meat. Not him. He left the chunks of meat extra-large, fat included, and I know he purposely put whole canned tomatoes in his soup just to watch us gag. You could gnaw on a piece of meat for minutes before you gave up and swallowed it whole. When it came to the tomatoes, swallowing those was like taking down an egg yolk. Big and slithery. I almost puked. We had to eat string beans with almonds, cooked spinach and liver with onions. He sat and watched us until our dinner was gone. I would look at my plate and only ever wanted to eat the potatoes.

My sweet mother always tried to make our dinner the way we liked it and just let time and maturity around the table take care of itself. But our father practically made us lick our plates clean. At least a few times a week I tried to convince myself I could swallow everything that my mother put on my plate. When I was given overcooked carrots or liver and got tears in my eyes knowing I would have to sit and eat everything I was given or I wouldn't be permitted to leave the table.

As a joke one time, dad had Cindy, Debbie and me line up in front of him. He said he had a surprise for us. Of course we were excited. Maybe he was going to give us a trip to Disney World or something. Maybe he was going to order us our first home-delivered pizza. We all closed our eyes and waited. Before we knew it, he took a finger full of Limburger cheese and wiped it under all of our noses. Have you ever smelled that cheese? It's the same smell that has to come from a bum's six-month unwashed ass. It's like the cheese from the bottom of someone's belly button. Only a sociopath thinks of doing something like that. He laughed his ass off. We were horrified. When you're ten years old are you allowed to ask your father, "what the fuck is the matter with you?"

If we wanted sugar coated cereal, mom would have to sneak it into the house. My father only ever ate Wheat Chex and oatmeal. Only a few times did we have to eat his oatmeal. It looked like wallpaper paste. Extra brown sugar and milk please. That was funny because we dumped more sugar on our cereal than would have ever been in a serving of Frosted Flakes. He let us sugar coat our oats simply because he thought the oatmeal was better for us.

Good luck getting any young child to eat anything slimy, stinky or grizzled. You may think you're getting somewhere but you aren't. Every adult who has read Dr. Spock or watched Dr. Phil and thinks he/she has their shit together will do their best to be willful and make a point, but a kid wants what a kid wants. If you see a kid racing through the house with an Uzi or a flame thrower shouting at his brother, "You're fucking dead this time you little cretin!!," then that's the time to exert your parental rights. Otherwise, pick your battles wisely and let your kid eat Lucky Charms, Corn Pops and Cocoa Puffs. If they only want corn or peas, don't make them eat lima beans. If they only like American cheese don't force them to try Swiss. Let them have chocolate pudding instead of yogurt. If they want a hamburger instead of meatloaf, why do you give a shit? Meat is meat. Make life easy on yourself for a while. I promise you they will still graduate from college and you won't raise children with eating disorders.

get your own knife

Memories of Christmas. We had rituals and traditions like every family. Putting up the tree, hanging the wreath on the front door and getting an occasional visit from Santa. We had lights, the tree and lots of presents. It seemed as though my mother Marie was mixing and freezing cookie dough for the big event back in July. She made three different kinds of pinwheels, a mountain of butterballs and kolaches with apricot and nuts. When she baked them, the house smelled like a pastry shop. We were, however, forbidden to eat a single cookie until Christmas Eve.

We all shopped for one another and spent hours wrapping presents. As youngsters, Cindy and I shopped at the local mall or drug store. We bought mom jewelry and dad typical dime-store items. Although one Christmas gift he kept was a large piggy bank that looked like a sergeant in the Army. He had a scrunched-up face with a cigar shoved between his teeth. It was the spitting image of our father and it still sits in one of Cindy's china cabinets. I think Cindy still has a cat-shaped bottle of perfume I gave her when I was nine or ten years old. It was pretty close to a Norman Rockwell painting. We really took our time to pick out presents and then wrap them carefully.

Although our father really decorated nicely and was dedicated to creating a beautiful Christmas scene, there was one ritual that ranked as one of the most bizarre in our childhood. After having to wait on the stairs for what seemed like an eternity, we all gathered around the base of the tree. Every year, Christmas falls on the same date. The same thing usually happened on Christmas morning. Everyone knew the routine. Kids up at dawn, take pictures while opening presents. Done. The entire experience should have been over within seven maybe eight minutes. Not in our case. Opening a gift, let alone 20 of them took an hour or longer.

There are two reasons for this. The first was Lou's camera. A Leica that he did not know how to use. He threw the flash attachment so hard in frustration one year that he put a hole in the wall. It was impossible to focus. You needed a PhD to take one picture and trust us, no one was qualified. The second reason getting started to open gifts took so long began when Cindy and I were maybe eight or nine years old. We were too young to know any better and old enough to follow his instructions

Cindy and I were in charge of handing out the gifts. Everyone watched in anticipation as each person took his or her turn opening a present. Only, this took slightly longer than it did for most families because of the way we had to open presents. Lou would hand us his pocketknife to slice through the tape so we didn't ruin the paper. The big sheets were folded neatly and saved for the next Christmas. My sisters and I soon realized that we should just all have our own knives so we weren't still opening presents on New Year's Day. So Lou kept his pocketknife and the rest of us had kitchen steak knives. We sat there slicing and folding for the next ten years. All I really wanted to do was rip something wide open, crumble the paper into a baseball-sized wad and throw it right at his head. But when you're a little kid, you just do what you're told. My mother sat there like this was completely normal. As I look back at it, she was too afraid to rock the boat so she got her own knife too.

Flash forward 35 years. Our parents were still living in their gigantic house. Over the years, all attempts to get them to downsize proved futile. Lou had made half-assed attempts to lighten their load by offering us a few trinkets here and there. He was not going to offer up any item that he thought had value. It was even difficult for him to throw out empty coffee cans and plastic bags. At the age of 90, he shredded 50-year-old checks and a lifetime of tax returns. It took him a week. Why shred? Guaranteed, the bank he used in 1955 doesn't exist. At the time, it was 2008. He also got rid of the receipt that he had from when his mother was cremated. Who the hell keeps that for over 30 years?

This kind of thinking really stumps me. I am a person who cannot wait to crumple, tear and shred anything just so I can get it out of my house. The only papers I still have are all of my report cards from kindergarten through high school and a few tax returns in case the IRS comes calling. And for the record, I only possess the report cards because he kept them for so long. But I guarantee you that those too will find a burn pile very soon.

Our father called either me or my twin every few months and asked us to come and "take a look at this stuff and see if you can use it." There was always a knee-jerk reaction in us when he said those words that said "run." Any trip to Lou's house was a trip back in time. Not the kind of trip that awakens cherished memories. It was the kind of trip that woke up the undeniable need for a trip to the dumpster.

December 2007, Lou would not let up about wrapping paper and gift boxes. We had to come and look at the paper. We finally relented and made our way across the street, from the protection of Cindy's house, grumbling and swearing the entire time. Lou proceeded to walk us up two flights of stairs to the attic. We followed him begrudgingly. Why did he always call us? Our other siblings should have endured this as well, but he only picked on us.

We knew what waited for us up there. It was garbage. His garbage that he could not part with. Everything he put in front of us was some pile of crap he couldn't throw out. It never mattered why we thought we were there. Lou always tagged on something else. On this day, it was stuffed animals from when we were kids and an old mattress he thought we could somehow use. If you saw the condition of the attic, you'd understand why none of what he'd stored up there was useful to anyone. The mattress looked like a dead body had been lying on it for decades. I would not have let my dog sleep on it.

We started to cough from the dust and probably asbestos poisoning. Cindy and I should have been wearing ventilators and HAZ-MAT suits. The ceiling was half falling down and you just knew that some kind of cancerous breeze was wafting through the air. Cindy and I stuffed things into garbage bags as fast as possible while he yelled at us "Not so fast!" We refused to go down memory lane with him so taking our time was not an option. We just wanted out of there. When our backs were turned, he pulled out the golden goose. The stuff he had really asked us to come and look at. It was 2007, it was colder than a well digger's ass up there and we were out of patience and we had only been up there ten minutes.

He handed us a box of folded Christmas paper! He was serious. "Take what you can use." Cindy and I looked at each other, dumbfounded. We read each other's minds. First, we knew that the only use for it was to line a bird cage or start a fire. Second, we knew just to say, "thank you" with outstretched arms. We had gotten a little smarter over the years and realized that the only way to get rid of this stuff was to tell him, "Thanks" and take it with us. It was a little pathetic that he began to explain that some of it was very brittle and not of much use. We nodded our heads in agreement while gritting our teeth thinking, "No shit, Captain Obvious."

Cindy and I fought the temptation to look in the box, but we failed. We were drawn to the contents of the box and the musty dry smell like a moth to a flame. We looked at each other, then started pulling paper out of the box. One folded sheet at a time. I saw snowmen, poinsettias, Santa Claus and snowflakes. I could almost recall the presents that had been wrapped in these sheets. For a brief moment, I was back in 1972 and it was a nice feeling until I remembered why this paper was sitting before me. The knives. With that thought, I balled it all up except for a few sheets. Those were used to wrap his presents that year.

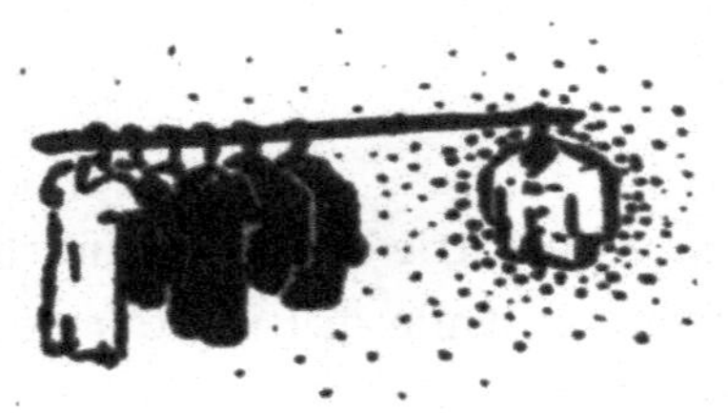

what's yours is mine

Lou always managed to get his hands on our stuff, people's stuff, tenant's stuff and make it seem legitimate. The more Cindy and I dug around his life, we came to find out that the truth was a little different. He would find a better use for something or figure someone wasn't using something so he would take it, assuming no one would miss it. He got some of our stuff by making deals that we could not live up to. He took stuff from his tenants when their backs were turned or when they just died and left their shit behind. He would tell my husband or Cindy's husband that he would "store" something for them, like tools, until they needed them. When that time came, he developed amnesia and no one ever got their shit back. The only way to get anything returned to you was to steal it back.

It perplexes me to this day when I think of how hard we tried for his approval. To get a pat on the head from Lou meant his mother, his kids, his wife, his insurance agent, his auto mechanic or his tenants for that matter had to conform to his ideas and sense of entitlement. In addition to his warped ideas of possession, we all had to agree to his deals. Which meant simply that if we wanted "this" we had to give "that." He was a score keeper.

He learned early on the value of a deal. He was not an agreeable child which meant his poor mother Mary probably showed him just how profitable a deal could be. It is difficult to imagine his personality wrapped up in a child's body. She must have wanted to jump off a bridge. I imagine he wore the poor woman down to a stump just so he could have his way. He was relentless. His ultimate deal with her came in the 1970s when he told her, "I will help you with your house, but you have to sign it over to me first. Then when you can't live alone any longer, you can come and live with me."

He took his mother's house and she eventually came to live with us. It wasn't very long after she dropped anchor in our house on Lake Avenue that my mother was waiting on her hand and foot, changing her diapers and lifting her on and off a bed pan. Mom washed her bed clothes and the cut-up blankets she had to use as diapers. We all listened to grandma scream for help in the middle of the night. She wailed for "Marie" in a high-pitched scream that gave me chills. She never asked for her own son. Ever. When my mother couldn't take the sleepless nights and the smell anymore, our father put his mother in the nastiest nursing home Medicaid would pay for.

His mother Mary died in 1978 at the age of 82. Mom told me that the nursing home called to tell him that she was pretty weak and didn't have much time left. You know what he said? "Call me when things get worse." What a coward. He was too afraid to go sit with his own mother for fear that the guilt he was suffering might force him to say something nice to her on her death bed. He never got the chance. The next phone call was to tell him she was dead. I remember the call. We were sitting in the living room in the evening and Lou walked past mom, Cindy and me and said, "She's dead." He didn't look very upset. Even then, at the age of 15, I could not show any sympathy for a man who hated his mother. I felt bad for my grandmother who died alone in a nursing home. I did not feel anything for him.

He got her house and all the "stuff" coveted for years.

He organized her jewelry by color and kept her clothes and bed pan well into the next century. Cindy and I were never allowed to look through her jewelry—even if it was just for fun. There were times when he wasn't home that Cindy and I would sneak into this secret room and look at his "stuff." I opened the cabinet many times and stared at grandma's jewelry. She had pink, blue, green and yellow earrings, bracelets and rings. As I admired her things I often wondered where she got all of it. Did she ever get to wear it anywhere? I didn't really know her at all so I would imagine she could not have been too bad. Her taste in jewelry was OK.

He kept it locked away in his "den" where he kept his other prized possessions. He kept it simply because he believed whatever he had would increase in value. Cindy managed to take a few pieces like a bracelet or a broach. Other than that, we have nothing to remind us of her except her gold wedding band. Cindy found it in a small box with some very nondescript things. When Cindy showed it to him a few months before he died, he said, "Your name isn't engraved in it. What do you want it for?" We were her only biological grandchildren. Since then, Cindy and I take turns wearing it.

Anytime dad did a favor for someone, you better believe he kept track. My mother's Aunt Frances was a regular fixture in our lives for as long as I can remember. She lived in her own house on Lakeland Avenue until it became too difficult for her to live on her own. Since mom had just finished nursing her mother-in-law, she didn't feel it out of line to ask if Frances could come live with us. With total acrimony, Dad agreed.

She had her own room and stayed away from him whenever possible. He was unbelievably rude to her. He shot her dirty looks if she washed her breakfast dishes and he thought she was making too much noise. He made fun of her because she talked about what was for lunch at the local senior center. Overall, he was just a complete dick and made sure she knew that her shuffling, clanging, talking and breathing irritated him to no end.

She couldn't take it anymore and decided to move into her own apartment just down the road. This suited everyone because you could cut the tension in our house with a knife. Instead of dad driving her to her to appointments and to the store, my older sister made a point of taking mom and Frances out every Saturday. This went on for years. If Debbie couldn't get her to the store, she took a bus to the grocery store. Frances was really a very sweet little old lady and hardly asked for any help. Other than mom, Frances only had one nephew whom she talked about often.

When she was in her early nineties, she started showing signs of advanced congestive heart failure. Talk about a vulture—Dad could already smell the decay of her dead body when he decided to pressure mom into making sure Frances had all of her paperwork in order. What he really wanted to know was what her will said and it became my mother's job to find out.

I have no idea how he did it, but he somehow convinced mom to convince Frances to give them a copy of her will. Lou figured that since he was her personal taxicab and let her live with us for like five minutes then mom should get everything she had left. He must have put a gun to my mother's head or my mother was so weak she couldn't tell him to "eat shit and die" when he asked her to forge Frances' signature on a "new" will so that only Mom was the beneficiary. To be honest, I do not know for certain if my mother was the sole beneficiary or not since I never saw the will. On this particular subject, my mother refused to speak. He might have forced her to carry out some dastardly deed, but I will never know for sure.

Cindy and I would not have not known this much except he

could never keep his fucking mouth shut. He bragged that Aunt Frances left our mother a "tidy sum." I am certain he believed that Cindy and I would have thought that whatever means he took to secure my mother as the beneficiary to her Aunt's estate was pure genius. I can only imagine how much it might have been. Paying our mother's final medical expenses 20 years later was a hefty burden so I am sure it's all gone and then some. But this I know for sure; She never got to spend one red cent of her inheritances on anyone or anything while she was still alive. He took it and kept it.

Lou liked to make deals. Any arrangement usually meant, "I'll give you this if you give me that." For example, a tenant might get lower rent if he or she performed maintenance on his property. Although he thought he had the upper hand, deals with his tenants usually backfired. No one ever painted or cut the grass and they were usually gone within three months.

When it came to his kids, a deal was something that he could easily default on because he held us to an almost unachievable standard. Making deals wasn't only so we might be taught some kind of life lesson; it was also a way to get us to comply. It was one of his ways to get anyone to conform to his way of thinking, living or doing business.

Lou hated that Greg started to smoke. He was 16 when he started to light up and only had to ask an older friend to purchase them. His friend John was in his band, "The Eight Balls," so it was simple to roll a pack in his sleeve and be like everyone else. Mike probably was already on his way to lung cancer so if Greg couldn't get them from John then he could get them from Mike, who was already 18 by this point.

It was almost impossible not to pick up this deadly habit since Mom smoked a pack or two per day and Dad alternated between stogies and cigarettes. In the 1950s and '60s no one gave a shit either. There was no such thing as a surgeon general's warning. There were advertisements on television and in Life magazine espousing its coolness. Lucky Strike claimed it would help keep a slender figure. Every enlisted man who was a bad ass supposedly smoked Camels. Babies were begging their mothers to smoke Marlboro's. And, if James Dean and Frank Sinatra did it, then it had to be all right.

A person could smoke in movie theaters, airplanes, schools, restaurants and stores. It was socially acceptable. Well, screw all of that. Dad zeroed in on something that would allow him to make Greg miserable. He caught Greg smoking and insisted that since he wanted to smoke so badly, then he would make Greg smoke like a man. Lou made Greg smoke an entire pack of unfiltered Camels out behind the garage, one after the other. Greg inhaled so deeply that when he finally got away from Lou and into the bathroom, he puked all over himself in a tub full of bubbles. My mother watched my father torture my brother and then watched him puke. Unbelievably, my mother didn't stop my father from trying to kill her son.

However, this abuse did not result in Greg giving up his habit. It made him sick as a dog and probably almost killed him. I can only imagine how I would have felt as his mother watching my kid's stepfather hand down this type of punishment, but Mom did not say or do anything to stop it. She only hoped Greg would survive so she could clean up his puke and try to convince him that Lou meant well in trying to teach him a lesson.

Over time, Lou figured out that this form of child abuse had not worked so he decided to hang Greg's brand new, cherry red sparkled Leedey drum set right over his head. Greg was in a band with his friends and if Greg didn't have drums, he was out of the band. Lou told him that he either quit smoking or he was taking the drum set. Greg had to agree to the deal because the drums were a gift from Lou but in all likelihood, Greg knew he was screwed. Greg couldn't do it. I am sure he felt like a failure and hated his stepfather for the rest of his life. A deal is a deal and by God, Lou was going to bend Greg's way of thinking.

Maybe Greg thought he could bullshit his way through the deal, smoking in secret and trying not to get caught. Forget about it. In the end Lou took the drums, Greg was out of "The Eight Balls" and he never played his Leedeys again. Lou had to have known that Greg could never hold up his end of that deal and that was how he would get them back. They stayed in my parent's attic for almost 40 years when Greg somehow got them back. Greg put them in his garage and left them there. It was probably too painful to try to ever play them again. Taking Greg's drums never taught him the lesson Lou thought it would. Greg continued to smoke well into his forties and finally quit on his own terms. Two heart attacks later his brother Mike thought smoking wasn't such a good idea either and quit at 42.

Around the same time (1964) Greg borrowed money from a preacher's kid named Rick. Rick was a nice kid who steered clear of trouble and was generous to a fault. It did not matter whether or not Greg could pay him back. Rick recognized that his friend wanted something so he gave him the money. It was that simple. Greg marched right up to Radio Shack and bought a reel-to-reel tape recorder. It was a James Bond type that when closed, looked just like a suitcase. He wanted it simply because it was new wave and very cool. Back then something like that had a pretty heavy price tag. It cost him like $79.95.

I thought the recorder belonged to my father because I saw it in our house for years. When Greg explained how he bought this cool gadget and then said he never really knew what happened to it, I told him I looked at it almost every day in Dad's home office for 40 years. Greg was shocked. He said Dad told him that someone stole it from his car. The truth is that Dad took it from Greg before he could move out so he could keep it for himself as a sort of payment for keeping a roof over his head.

The point is it was never of any concern to my father what his relationship was with you. If the opportunity was there, you were screwed. When George and Cindy purchased a new house, they ended up living directly behind my parents. When they took possession, the house was empty except for a few tools left in the garage. One of the items was a relatively new pickax and a box of Snap-On sockets for a socket wrench. The sockets were in a new red, shiny metal box just like the day they made their way out of a Sears department store.

George asked Lou to put these items in his garage until he and Cindy were completely moved in because the garage didn't lock and they didn't want to risk them being taken. A few months passed and George wanted the pickax for some yard work and asked Dad to walk it over. Lou proudly did but returned one with a broken handle. George looked at him, burst out laughing and said, "What the hell happened to it?" Of course Lou was going to try to convince him that this was the very same ax that George asked him to store. Did he think everyone on the planet was stupid?

George saw what was happening and knew that he had to get his Snap-On sockets back too. He ordered Dad back through the gate to get what belonged to him. That's the thing about George, he can laugh in your face one minute and then tear you a new ass the next. Dad was walking on the edge right between a humorous oversight and death. What could Dad have been thinking as he walked back home? He should have been thinking what a sneaky, underhanded cocksucker he was for trying to screw his son-in-law, but I am sure he was lamenting over how George could tell the difference between a new ax and the busted-up piece of shit he tried to pawn off.

Dad walked back to George's yard just as cocky as before. Dad did not learn his lesson five minutes prior and not only did he hand George the "new" ax but a rusty box full of rusty sockets. George could not believe what he was looking at George was laughing so hard that he could barely make his words heard. "Are you fucking kidding me?" he said. George took the box and let the issue drop like a lead balloon. It was becoming too much trouble to hang onto something that was free in the first place. Fifteen years later they were still sitting on a table in Dad's garage. George knew he would get them back. When Dad died.

who is growling in there?

We were young at a time when people could take a bus downtown at night and shop at department stores. There was very little fear in the late ’60s and early ’70s. People could leave the house for hours on end and never check in or find the need to make a phone call for any reason. A woman could navigate her local community with confidence. Our mother Marie and her Aunt Frances did this frequently. The two together would leave the house and disappear around the corner and there was never a thought that they might never return.

It was even more fun to watch them walk around the corner, heading home with shopping bags full of clothes. This usually meant we had new outfits to wear, even if they were sometimes too big (meant to last at least two school years). That was the best part of their shopping experience.

The hard part was watching my mother leave, knowing Cindy and I would be home alone with Lou. Debbie was older and usually out with friends and by 1972 our brothers were married and gone. The time we spent with our father was usually quiet. Often, we were left to our own devices. This usually meant coloring or doing homework in the kitchen.

On rare occasions, we ventured out into the dark side. Dark is exactly what it was. Peeking our heads around the kitchen door was like a foreign film without subtitles. Cindy and I knew something was going on in other parts of the house but without any words to explain it, we were simply left to our own over-active imaginations. The dogs stayed in the kitchen with us and even they did not want to venture into a dark house full of uncertainty.

What the hell were we supposed to do now? Our mother was gone for one reason or another and our house was huge and there weren't there any lights on! More importantly, goddamn it, where was Dad? He must have been sitting off in the dark watching and listening to us because at the exact moment we opened the kitchen door and timidly said, "Dad?" someone or something started to growl. We knew there wasn't a wild animal in the other room and our own dogs were in the kitchen with us. So what twisted fuck hides from his young daughters, growls to scare them and then denies the whole thing? Lou did this shit more than once.

We spent our lives wondering what motivates someone to do what they do. It's like with Ted Bundy, Adolf Hitler or Charles Manson. You want to send their head to Columbus to have their brain matter analyzed to find out what makes them tick. We never really saw our father openly laugh at our discomfort, but there was a definite smirk. He enjoyed making us uncomfortable, keeping us off balance.

Lou knew us three girls were chickens at heart. We were afraid to go anywhere in the house without company from somebody. We'd take a dog with us if we could get away with it. We all had to do the normal stuff like go to bed alone. When any of us gave mom the look that said, "Come tuck us in.," he said, "You don't need your mother. Go by yourselves." Ugh. At least Cindy and I had each other. Our sister, from the time she was six, had to go up and take her own bath and get in bed. Mom said she looked terrified. She should have marched right up the stairs after her while simultaneously telling Lou to mind his own fucking business. But she was as afraid of him as the rest of us, so she never reacted and just sat on the couch like a mute.

So, Mom sat there handcuffed and we marched upstairs feeling abandoned. We can recall at least one time when Lou sent my older sister to the backyard at night armed with only a flashlight to look for God knows what. She looked at us to come with her. Nope—not allowed. He frequently sent either me or Cindy to the basement to look for a screwdriver or some such useless item. He'd ask us to do this when he was watching television and smoking a cigar. It wasn't like he was trying to fix something. When the kid who was assigned to run the errand said, "Come with me." He'd say, "Go alone." Why would it matter to him if we went together and dragged all five dogs with us? Why?? So he could stay in control and watch us squirm.

I asked him many years later why he sat in a dark living room and tried to scare us like that. He said, "I have no idea what you are talking about. I never did that to you girls." I really believe that he didn't remember making guttural noises in the dark or sending us into a dark basement just to scare us. He only did it a few times, but it was enough for us to realize that we could not trust him. The bottom line is this—a child should go to sleep knowing they are loved. Which means, we should be valued as people and protected from the dark, scary realities of life. Life is hard enough without someone in your own family pulling twisted pranks.

I never gave much thought as to whether or not I had monsters hiding under my bed or in my closet. Although I can tell you that I slept with the closet door shut and a night light on for many years. The monster I was afraid of was the one who sat in his green vinyl chair.

leftover pancakes

Did it ever cross your mind to have your kids steal for you? No, probably not. Have you ever thought about taking something that didn't really belong to you because you thought you could get away with it? Yeah, maybe. Maybe you thought about it because what you wanted wasn't tied down and no one was really looking. Besides, who would miss it? Of course, you might steal if you had no food to eat or needed money to buy booze or drugs. I know I would.

Cindy and I got our first job when we were 16. The date was April 19, 1979. We were paid $2.90 an hour to hustle fast food at our local McDonald's. The most unforgettable thing about our first day was the smell. I remember the two of us looking at each other when I said, "What the hell is that? Rotten meat?" It was a mixture of rancid grease and hard-boiled eggs. It stunk like shit and I could not imagine anyone wanting food from this place. "What the hell" we said and knocked on the back door. The store manager, Tony and his first assistant Jim greeted us with smiles and escorted us along with the other new hires to the basement for our orientation. This was the beginning of a love-hate relationship and the beginning of an 11-year career for me.

That first day, I sat there with a mixture of excitement and anxiety. This was our first real job with a uniform and everything! I wondered two things as I checked out the other recruits. Would Cindy and I be able to get all of our hair into those tiny hats and does McDonald's make uniforms small enough for our 112-pound frames? The most important part of the uniforms was that everyone wore name tags. Thank God because for once people would stop asking Cindy and me, "Which one are you?" With all of these fragmented thoughts, we punched our first time clock and entered the work world.

The slogan in 1979 was "Nobody can do it like McDonald's can." The ad had fresh-faced employees cooking and cleaning and looking deliriously happy while doing it. There wasn't a speck of dirt on the floors, the wall-to-wall stainless or the uniforms. If they could do it, so could I. The problem with my thought process was that I conveniently forgot that the ad was full of actors who were paid to act like they gave a shit. We would all have to do the same thing for considerably less money and for considerably longer periods of time.

I realized I was not able to concentrate on what was being said at the orientation because Jim, the first assistant, was shoving a quarter-pounder-with-cheese into his face as he extolled the virtues of being able to list McDonald's on one's resume. He ate and talked simultaneously and I could clearly see the food stuck to his teeth. I was so distracted by this troll eating like a hog at a trough and giving us his less-than-thought-out lecture I could barely pay attention. I wanted to run. I was going to make $2.90 an hour to work side-by-side with this animal for eight hours at a time.

Jim was what I would consider a "little person" because I was 5'8" and he was considerably shorter than me. He was no taller than 5'4." It's difficult to take direction from someone shorter than you. Try it. You will see what I mean. I just wanted to give him a step to stand on so we were at least face-to-face. On top of that, he was a total slob. His shirt and tie (which was too short and sat just at his belly button) were filthy and he smelled like he hadn't showered in a week. Tony wasn't much taller. He was just meaner and smelled only slightly better. Of course, by the way the smell wafted through the back door, they probably picked up that indefinable stench before they hit the time clock. Great. This would now be our smell. Cindy and I would smell like rotten eggs, reconstituted onions and salty beef every weekend for years to come.

Cindy and I were only 16 but we believed we already knew more about getting a job, keeping it and looking like professionals than these half-wits. Pretty arrogant considering we had never had a job with a paycheck until this moment. Given our work history with our father and the competition we were facing, our assessment seemed reasonable. We gave each other a comforting, "No sweat. We got this" look from across the room.

I can tell you some of the most useless facts about the golden arches. For instance, Ronald's shoes are a size 14, there are supposed to be three different-sized French fries in every order and each fry is 17% fat. There are 160 slices of cheese in a "brick," a pancake should be 4¾" wide and no one should wait at the drive-in window for their order longer than 30 seconds. McDonald's was named after two brothers who owned a small walk-up burger joint and met Ray Kroc who was trying to sell the brothers multi-mixers for their milkshakes back in the 1950s. And yes, there is a Hamburger University, from which I graduated with honors. I could go on and on but that's not what this book is about.

Cindy and I worked for at least four years every Saturday and Sunday from 6:00 am until 2:00 pm. We showed up tired on some days, hung over on others but always performed like well-oiled machines. We shoved our long hair into those tiny hats, securing it with large hair pins which, after eight hours, gave me a migraine. Mom always made sure our uniforms were cleaned and pressed although they were 100% polyester, so I don't think she ever had to iron them. We worked like dogs for our $2.90 an hour and were pleased when we got our $0.15 an hour raises each year. The managers would have told you we were invaluable as they counted on us for their weekend rushes like flowers needed the sun. In fact, I think the sun did rise and fall in our perfect fitting McDonald's uniforms.

As the months passed, Cindy and I were trusted with managerial duties. One such duty was to count "waste." This was their word for food that had been cooked and not sold. Sometimes there was a lot of waste and sometimes there was not. If what we had cooked had not been sold in ten minutes, it was discarded into a waste bucket. These were just regular garbage cans for waste and not paper garbage. The transition from breakfast to lunch was tricky so the managers usually had extra breakfast cooked to hold off the customers while we prepared lunch.

Usually Cindy and I caught a break at the end of breakfast by being able to do some managerial duties or "dive," which meant to do the dishes and stock for the next day. In the midst of this, we had to mark down all of the breakfast waste which could amount to 20 or 30 different muffin sandwiches, pancakes, sausage and hash browns.

We were proud of the responsibility that the managers bestowed upon us and couldn't wait to tell our parents. Mom was pleased by giving us her best "I'm a proud parent" smile. Dad on the other hand was curious about this "waste" thing. "Are you just throwing this food in the garbage?" he asked. "Yes, after we have counted it and given the list to the manager" we said. In our heads, we immediately thought, "Ah, fuck, here it comes." He then asked us if we could bring the food home. He was so predictable. At some point we were trusted to count money. Thank God he didn't ask us to pinch that too.

It was made clear to us from our orientation that any food that left the building that had not been paid for was considered stealing and would result in our immediate termination. Taking food that was considered waste was also considered stealing. Dad, therefore, actually left it up to us to figure out how we would get bags of leftover pancakes and eggs out the smelly back door and home to our freezer. He didn't give a damn whether we got fired. He just wanted something for nothing. His head-hunting business wasn't doing very well, and he was a crummy landlord so maybe he figured we could do our part by stealing food and helping feed the family. A better idea would have been for him to go get a real job and stop leaving it up to everyone else to fix his problems.

Cleaning up after breakfast meant that we had to haul the garbage out to the dumpster. This was the last task before we were once again shoved onto the floor taking orders or cooking our "12—6 rotations." The dumpster was conveniently located in the back of the parking lot surrounded by an eight-foot gate. Right behind the dumpster on the other side of a six-foot-high chain link fence was a set of railroad tracks.

As we counted the waste, we carefully placed the food wrapped in either paper or in Styrofoam trays in a garbage bag and set it by the back door. Either Cindy or I took the garbage out back and when we thought no one was looking, we tossed a giant bag of food over the fence into the weeds that lined the tracks. What the hell were we thinking? We would have been totally embarrassed had we been caught stealing. The twins with the perfect hair and teeth who lived in a big rich house were petty thieves. Teenage girls should be stealing lip gloss from the drug store or vodka from their parents' liquor cabinet. We couldn't get a date now so getting caught would have just kept us single and the brunt of our rich friend's jokes—forever. If someone found out, we would have had to leave town.

After our shift was over, we went home and told dad what we did. If my kid told me he did something like that, I would have beat his ass and then sat down contemplating where I fucked up so bad that my child believed he could steal and then come home and proudly tell me about it. Dad was giddy and couldn't wait to get us in the car so we could collect our loot. He also couldn't wait until we could do it again. This was a major WTF moment in my life.

There was a side street close by where you could literally pull your car right up to the tracks. There was no fence stopping anyone from getting on to the railroad tracks. Dad parked the car and we got out, walked about 200 feet to our garbage bag. We picked it up and walked it right back out to his car. He drove away and it was clear no one gave a shit what we were doing. I was secretly hoping a train would come by and flatten me. I couldn't stand the sense of betrayal I felt from him putting our jobs, pride and reputations at risk. Even worse was the utter guilt and embarrassment I suffered from just this one single act.

When we got home, we pulled out all of the food, most of which was still in good condition. We stacked hotcakes with sausage and muffin sandwiches in the freezer. Dad saved some of the eggs for the dogs. I seriously cannot believe we ate that food over the next several weeks. I should say, he ate it; not me. I don't think Cindy or I touched it. He thought this was genius and probably believed he was moving his children into a profitable life of crime. It's like a drug addict telling his/her kids to steal and then acting surprised when they get caught. He would not have done a thing for us if we got busted and subsequently fired.

Thinking about taking the food makes me sick. I am so ashamed that he somehow convinced us to steal. We might have done this one or two more times before we finally said we had had enough. Cindy and I simply said everyone was being watched too closely and it was too risky. That was a lie, of course, since we did not have the nerve to tell the truth. The truth was that no one watched us because we were trusted employees. The truth is that we thought he was a selfish asshole for putting our jobs and reputations on the line.

What kind of father puts his child at risk and convinces them steal for no apparent motive? A demented psychopath, that's who. Fuck him. Let him steal and get caught. We didn't need left over pancakes all that much. Besides, we got a free meal for each shift we worked. If he wanted free food, he should have gotten his own job. In the part time jobs my sons have had, I never once encouraged them to pad their time sheets or take food that they hadn't paid for. I made sure they knew there was no honor in that kind of behavior. To this day, Cindy and I are mortified by this one single act of taking something that didn't belong to us even though it was going in the garbage regardless.

We stopped taking the food and eventually became managers of the restaurant. I know that he was probably disappointed that he wasn't getting anything out of us anymore and he never once asked us if we could get in trouble for what we had done. Cindy and I just moved on from there to pay our own medical bills, car insurance and buy our own clothes. This, I am certain, was a far superior deal than getting a few eggs and leftover pancakes for nothing. We kept our dignity and our jobs and paid all of our own bills. He could figure out another way to fill his freezer and feed his dogs. Ten years later our mother got a part time job at the same McDonald's and I wonder if he ever suggested she do the same thing. He must have found another way to feed his dogs because I never saw one piece of sausage or a pancake after 1979.

barefoot in the grass

I love dogs. If I had a farm, I would take in all the unwanted, crippled, ugly dogs that come my way. I would feed them, clean their beds and pick up their crap. I would do it because it was my choice. Not because someone said, "Go clean up the shit." I loved all of the dogs Lou had too. It's just that he had too many of them. The dog's names were Curly, Duke, Thunder 1, Thunder 2, King, Prince, Baron, Mitzi, Ben, Max 1, Max 2, Sam and Luba. Every one of the male dogs took a bite out of another dog, a cat, or one of us. Mitzi and Luba never did.

It served him right one day in the summer of 1972 or so when Thunder 2, the St. Bernard, snarled at King and Lou kicked him in the ribs. That kick sprained Lou's ankle and did nothing to the dog. All of these animals were huge except for Curly so you'd have to be crazy to fuck with them the way he did. He had St. Bernards, German Shepherds and Mastiffs. We'd often sit back and wish one of them would have the courage to take a big wet bite out of him. What's pathetic is that instead of going after him, they went after us, including our mother.

In 1963 or 1964, Duke, the collie, had mom pinned to the floor by her neck. Lou pulled the animal off, slapped the shit out of him and helped mom off of the floor. Marie was dazed and physically unharmed. She must have been terrified and Greg watched in horror. Greg thought for sure that the dog would be dead by morning for having betrayed his owner. Little did we know that this would become a pattern with Lou and his ill-mannered canines. His dog's bad behavior would affect us all one way or another over the next 20 years. Mom may have loved his dogs, but they didn't care for her. Mom was screwed.

The smallest of the bunch was a cocker spaniel named Curly. Lou talked about this dog like he gave birth to it. You know how you think of your first love as you gaze into the sky? That was it. Curly had been a mouthy little shit and was dead before Cindy and I were two.

Greg was the only one who knew how Curly died. Lou, in one of his prouder moments, decided to mess with this little dog. I guess he thought it was a good idea to put a laundry basket on top of Curly. A dog who, we understand, was a little nervous to begin with. Good idea until the dog dropped dead. Right there.

Now since Lou was never wrong about anything and nothing was ever his fault, how was he going to explain this one? "Geez, Marie, I have no idea how the dog got under there and why his eyes were bugging out of its head." He loved this dog and he fucking killed it. He broke out his shovel and buried him. Live with that.

We didn't live on a farm or have a house with sprawling acreage. We started on a small side street until Cindy and I were about four. All five kids, two German Shepherds and a collie. There were a number of cats sprinkled throughout the over-populated clutter through the years, but it was the dogs that shaped the chaos. Prince, one of the shepherds, looked menacing. A black Belgian shepherd that looked like a wolf. Lou loved this one in particular because he was tough looking and growled at every person that wandered by.

In fact, he encouraged that behavior out of all of his dogs. He always had a "beware of dog" sign hanging on the gate, meant to warn intruders, including our friends, that they might be eaten if they dared try to see what life was like on the other side. Hardly any of our friends ever came through the front door because of the snarling teeth and the slobber. Tons of slobber that hung out of their mouths like cooked spaghetti.

I can remember one particular day like yesterday, right down to what I was eating. The raisins were warm and chewy and the sunshine felt good on my 2-year-old skin. I was sitting on the back porch when my older sister Debbie's friend stopped by. His name was Herbert. Herbert was an easy-going child, small in stature. He was only eight years old. As he started to open the gate, I opened the back door to get Debbie and that's when Prince made a run for the kid. Prince was an impressive animal. He was jet black, had pointy ears and could get from 0 to 40 mph in four strides. Herbert was going to be lunch.

Lou quickly did what any parent would do in a situation like that. He ran around with a glass of saltwater looking for this kid's lower lip on the sidewalk. I felt helpless and I was shocked. I was sure Lou would blame me for this wolf-dog escaping. Surprisingly and fortunately for Herbert, we found his lip and the doctors sewed it back on. Thankfully Prince didn't swallow it and this time, we were in the clear. After that, Prince started hiding in the basement.

Not long after, Prince became a guard dog at a hardware store or used car lot. That time, Lou did the right thing by getting rid of a vicious animal. Vicious or not, it didn't stop him from making one last visit to see if his pet really was ferocious. So that neither he nor my mother would be devoured, they tossed Prince my mother's scarf. Her scent took Prince back to happier times. He softened his demeanor for a few seconds but started to snarl and that was it. They backed out of there and never returned.

The kids at school were cruel and blamed Debbie for poor Herbert's lip being torn from his young face. She was only eight when this happened and as long as we continued to live in that house, no one would ever stop by again. This broke Debbie's spirit as she was happy at having a young boy interested in her. The only solution to this predicament was to move. My mother knew it. Lou's reason for moving was that he wanted to get away from the Puerto Ricans that were invading his quiet piece of suburbia. Debbie always believed that it was because he was ashamed of what his dog had done to an innocent child. I think he was more bothered by the "spics," as he called them, than his own conscience.

By the time Cindy and I were four, we moved to a much grander house. It had a huge back yard. The smell of honeysuckles and roses permeated the air. It even had a cement pond with a statue in the middle. It was beautiful, until we moved all of the dogs in and Lou gave them free reign. By this time we had Thunder, King and Baron. They were two German Shepherds and a St. Bernard. We soon adopted Mitzi, a black poodle/Airedale mix. Someone saw our affection for pets and dropped her in the yard one day while we were gone. Lou had put a padlock on the gate to keep people from letting the dogs out. It didn't occur to him that someone may want to get one in.

It didn't occur to my parents to have Mitzi spayed so it wasn't long before she was pregnant, compliments of Thunder, the Saint. She had nine puppies. My brothers were married and gone by the time Cindy and I were six, so this left Debbie and her little sisters to help clean up the mess. The birth of these dogs was the beginning of years of shoveling tons of dog shit. My parents managed to sell all but three dogs. We ended up with five dogs. Our kennel would never get any larger, thank God. King had since been put down from bad hips and old age. "Crazy" was just building up steam and no one knew what the next 12 years would bring.

Cleaning up after these dogs, whom we loved, was repulsive. Each weekend brought the chore from hell when Lou bellowed at us to get the yard cleaned, which had to be done before we could pull weeds and cut the grass. We were probably ten or so when he added this job to the list of farm duties we were already required to do. Over our lifetime, Cindy and I cleaned up enough dog crap to fill a swimming pool. Debbie helped with this chore for a while, but the job primarily belonged to Cindy and me. We each had our own small gardening shovel and a bag. The bag was an empty 25-pound dog food bag. We filled it. It made us sick. Lou sat in his office in the back of the house and watched us out the window. He worked from home which meant he could watch us all of the time.

It took him years to put up a fence to keep the dogs on the driveway instead of shitting in the grass. He was in no rush to make it easier on us because it was our job. To this day Cindy and I cannot walk barefoot in grass. Anywhere. The fear that we might step in dog crap or what had been dog crap is, I believe, a legitimate stress disorder from years of picking up wet dog shit out of the grass. Even if we both know that it isn't even possible, we cannot do it. We don't talk about this anxiety, but I assure you, it is absolutely real. I bet you never thought of it until just now and I may have just ruined your life.

When Lou finally put the fence up, cleaning the mess was only slightly better. If he wanted to go anywhere, he would tell us to go "shovel up the shit" so he wouldn't roll his car in crap. Nothing says "hillbilly" like mashed-up dog shit in the tires of a station wagon. No wonder my friends never played at my house. They'd have to dodge these steaming land mines. We hated it. It was easier to go somewhere else. Cindy and I had nothing to say about wanting these dogs so cleaning up after them built up massive resentment. He never fucking helped us.

As time went on, something awful happened to the dogs. Thunder was put to sleep as a result of hip dysplasia. The day we put him down, I fed him a giant bologna sandwich and watched Greg help carry him to the car. We had Thunder's offspring and their mother Mitzi left. Max, Ben and Sam. All were sweet dogs but as time passed Max and Sam developed a hatred for each other. It became impossible to keep all the animals together. Lou's solution to this was to simply separate them. Max and Mitzi got to stay in the house and Ben and Sam were relegated to the garage or the back hall. We didn't save newspapers for the paper drive at a local school. We used the newspapers to cover a portion of the garage floor or back hall to keep Ben and Sam warm when it was cold.

So the trick in all of this was to get Max and Mitzi out. To do this, we locked Ben and Sam in the garage so the two from the house could get out. There was always snarling and growling through the garage door. This was Max's "fuck you" to Sam, who was eventually going to make him pay for his smart mouth. This went on for many years. Of course, our timing wasn't always right, and a few times Max and Sam were nose to nose. Allowing this to happen, which was surely an ill-timed accident on our part, turned out badly.

The first time they tried to kill each other, Cindy and I were about 14 years old. A dog with murder on his mind will fight to the death. On this particular sunny Saturday afternoon, you couldn't make out one dog for the other. They had each other by the throats and didn't acknowledge our pleas to stop. Of course, Lou stomped outside to yell and command his dogs, whom he always thought were well trained and obedient, to knock it off. Those were his words and many to that effect. Was he kidding?? Nothing short of a fire hose or a gun was going to get them to separate. My father is a large man so it surprised us that he couldn't just pull them apart. My mother was screaming in her high-pitched fashion, so much so that we couldn't think. We stood there helpless and thought, "What the hell are we going to do now?"

His weapon of choice to put them into submission this time was the hose. After getting bitten two or three times by trying to get between them, he crammed the hose down Sam's throat. We both stood there staring. Cindy and I were in complete shock. Who lives like this? You'd think our house was in a slum somewhere. We lived on the most premier street in my city with people who had club memberships and sent their kids to private schools., while we had dog fights. I don't think we ever really talked about this to our friends. How could you work this into a conversation as a teenager? While our friends were taking ski trips, going on boats and hanging out at their country clubs, we were bandaging chewed-up dogs and cleaning up shit.

As Sam puked up about one gallon of water, he let go of Max. That was it. It was over. There was blood all over the dogs and Lou. We took Max into the house to lick his wounds. My father would treat these injuries and other maladies by dumping peroxide on wounds and coating them with antibiotic ointment. He even did this to himself. It didn't matter that he and the dogs all needed stitches. There was no explanation for any of this and he was not about to answer to a doctor of any kind.

Family slip-ups with the dogs as to who belonged in or out happened many times. My brother Greg happened to cause one such fight while Lou was not home. Greg, not being used to the shit we lived with and not knowing the rules, opened the back door and the party started. Max went after Ben and all hell broke loose. I am certain Greg was thinking "What the fuck is this?" and grabbed a metal rod instead of the hose and split Max's skull for him to get him to stop.

I know Greg felt terrible. He must have wondered what we had to endure and what the hell was wrong with the dogs. I, on one occasion, contemplated using one of Lou's guns just to shoot the poor bastards right there. Where were the neighbors in all of this? Why would somebody not report it? We wish somebody had. Anyway, Greg couldn't wait to get out of there before Dad showed up because even though he was married and had a life outside the seven circles of hell, he would still get his ass chewed for being so stupid.

The cops finally showed up for one such unfortunate event. Only this time it involved one of his kids and one of his dogs. We all spent years shuffling dogs from the garage to the house, careful to not let their paths cross. Mitzi, the mother of these beasts, was dead now from a virus she picked up at the vet. Max was in the house by himself. The three dogs left were now eleven. They were getting slower and cared less about killing one another. Cindy and I were juniors in college—21 years old. In one bizarre moment, Cindy and I would slap each other hard and a dog would change our lives again.

Cindy and I never physically fought with each other. We really liked one another. This night though, we hit each other hard enough to knock each other out—and we weren't even fighting over some loser boyfriend. I came home late from babysitting. Cindy was sleeping and mom was in the kitchen. Lou was out having a beer with his friend Bob. (That's when Bob was still Lou's friend.). The house was quiet and dark. Max was sleeping in the living room. Without really thinking about the old adage, "Don't wake a sleeping dog." I did just that.

As I stooped to nudge his shoulder, Max whipped around and with no warning had me by the arm. After I wiggled free from that grip, he got me by the back of the thigh. Because of my high-pitched screams of terror at the thought of being killed by my own dog, mom came running in and put herself between Max and me. Max snapped out of his funk and stopped snarling and biting. More blood and tears followed. This time, an ambulance came. So did the police.

Cindy was sleeping and heard the commotion and ran downstairs and walked right into a scene from some slasher movie. I was crying and screaming uncontrollably. Cindy, being compassionate to my situation, did what any loving sister would do in a moment like that. She slapped me across the face to shut me up. I opened my eyes wide and thought, “What the fuck was that for?” I did shut up and collapsed on the floor so she and mom could assess my wounds. Being twins, Cindy would not be left out of this story. It would be a great one to tell friends over the years. As Cindy was looking down at me, she thought it was as good a time as any to faint. My mother knew nothing about life saving and proceeded to flip out. This was my moment and I had to somehow get up and take control. I told Mom to call 911 and call Mike (our oldest brother).

Cindy started to convulse a little and was not breathing. Terrific. I, left to my own defenses, had no choice but to show my sister the same kind of sensitivity and compassion she just showed me. I slapped the shit out of her. After all, she wasn’t breathing. It worked; no thanks necessary. Mike arrived simultaneously with the firemen. He looked down at Cindy, knowing what just happened and said, “What’s your problem?” Nice, Mike. He was more about sarcasm than compassion. When the hunky firemen walked in, they could have given a shit that I was almost eaten alive. They ran to the twin not breathing. I ended up walking to the ambulance, bleeding from ten bite wounds, while little sister got the full treatment.

At the hospital, Lou showed up and seemed genuinely concerned. He stayed with me and mom went with Cindy. I was relatively calm after just having the living daylights scared out of me. Meanwhile, Cindy was puking her guts up. The doctors bandaged me, told me I would be scarred for life and sent me packing. Cindy was hooked up to every machine known to man. They tested her for everything from epilepsy to anemia.

When dad and I got home, he changed his demeanor. He said all the right things at the hospital. His reaction to situations like these was usually to minimize the outcome of the event and he used whatever words he could to make sure he didn't look bad. In this case, he told me that Max was fine and that he really didn't mean it. He had to go back to the hospital to get mom and Cindy, so I was going to be alone. Alone with the beast in the kitchen. I saw the kitchen door ajar and, in a panic, told dad to hurry and close the door. Of course he screamed back and said, "You're fine. He's not going to hurt you." I hated him for even thinking it, let alone letting the words pass his lips. The dog should have been dead before morning, but he felt sorry for Max because everyone was mad at him.

The next day, the dog warden came to the house to take a report and see what Max did to me. My left arm and right leg were black and blue and I couldn't walk. In fact, I couldn't walk for weeks. In tears I recounted the events of the night. Lou chimed in to tell the warden that it was a "nip" and that I wasn't really attacked. He'd been nipped before, so this wasn't much more than that. What the fuck kind of disjointed logic was that? The good thing was that I was old enough to make my feelings known. I proceeded to correct his recollection of events, especially since he wasn't even there.

I was sitting there thinking what an asshole he was for trying to justify what happened so the animal warden wouldn't take his dog. He should have been more afraid of me never speaking to him again. Most fathers would have beaten, shot or poisoned the dog before morning. Not him. Max lived another year after that and managed to corner my mother twice, biting her in the process. Lou could have given a shit. Marie should have taken one of his guns and shot him instead. It must have occurred to her at least once over the years to do it.

The day Max called it quits, he decided to lie down in a small bathroom and stay there. While my father cried in his room, mourning the inevitable loss of yet another one of his precious pooches, Cindy and I had to somehow convince the vet to give us tranquilizers so we could move him. Here we were, 22 years old, and we were still taking care of his bullshit. Lou never came downstairs that afternoon until it was time to take Max to the local county veterinarian to have him put to sleep. We had to roll this unconscious dog onto a blanket and carry 80+ pounds of dead weight out of the house and down the stairs. Cindy and I almost dropped him twice. Our arms were quivering under the weight.

As we tried to help this poor animal die with some dignity, we kept thinking what an asshole our father was for putting this task on us. He stayed upstairs and hid from his responsibility which, frankly, should have been taken care of the day Max attacked me. A year after Max almost killed me and bit mom twice, all dad could manage was to show up with his car keys. As he was driving, Cindy and I shed our tears. We didn't feel sorry for Lou, just the dog, who flew to the floor when Dad slammed on the breaks. Jesus Christ, why did we let him come? We should have finished this job by ourselves. I could not stand Dad's crying and just wanted to push him out of our moving car. Is it ever OK to tell your father, "Shut the fuck up you big baby?"

That was the end of Max, the troublemaker and another one of Lou's babies. Ben and Sam could finally come inside for the remainder of their lives. Since I was married at this point, Cindy was the only one left to help Lou put down the other two when the time came.

By the time all of these dogs were dead, we were 23 or so. They had wreaked their havoc on the house. The honeysuckles and roses were gone. They'd eaten the bushes like wild animals. Their urine killed every beautiful flower we had. They pissed on everything. Their elephant-sized piles of crap left brown patches in the grass that would take years to repair. But those were his friends. He showed more compassion towards them when they were sick or injured than when any of us broke a bone or split our skulls. At least it seemed so.

It was several years before another dog would make its appearance. In 1994 or so, a Neapolitan Mastiff named Max (another Max) was the apple of his eye. For some reason, he liked to use a dog's name over again. He said that you could control a dog with more authority if the animal had a one-syllable name. Was this tested somewhere? Who knew this but him? This Max was a screwball and it served Lou right. He was unmanageable and silly. He wanted to bronco-bust his way through the house, which we encouraged just to watch Lou's blood pressure soar because he'd always lose control of the situation.

In one of Max's high-spirited moments, he took off like a jack-rabbit and ran from the dining room to the living room. It was enough room for him to go from 0 to 60. When he jumped on the couch, he flipped around in the air and slammed his bony hip into the wall. Until the day we sold the house, a basketball sized dent remained right above dad's couch. Of course, Cindy and I laughed our asses off and Lou started screaming. For Max, Lou's screaming encouraged his defiance even more.

There wasn't a toy known in the dog world that could entertain this animal. He had a 36-inch neck and shredded whatever you gave him. He reminded us of a giant gorilla who could pass the days with a truck tire and a bunch of bananas. Max's favorite thing to do was play with a 16-pound bowling ball or a cast-iron skillet. After all, the dog had a right to some fun. Over time, when Lou became puzzled at the dents on his car, he was quick to blame teenagers for the damage.

The guilty party finally made himself known to my father. Lou freaked out the day he saw Max flipping that 16-pound ball up onto the hood of his precious station wagon! Max was intrigued to see the ball roll off and thud back to earth. He was actually proud of himself but ran like hell when he heard Lou's thundering voice. Smart dog. Lou saw to it that Max lived out the remainder of his years with rubber balls and plush animals. He took the bowling ball and threw it away.

So what was the harm in letting him play in the water? Seems innocent enough but Lou, we could only imagine, could see the waste in that kind of fun. It simply ran up the water bill. However, as adults we began to exercise our insubordination and did what we wanted. We turned the hose on full blast into the dog's face. Watching Max chomp and bite at something he couldn't get his mouth on was simply funny. We got away with this for only a few minutes before he yelled at us to stop getting the dog wet. It was the middle of the summer and 85 fucking degrees, so what the hell was his point. We tried to help his dogs have fun, to live some kind of life that included more than sleeping under the kitchen table.

Max had to be put down years later for renal failure. There is only so much a 150-pound dog can stand. Usually it's less than eight years of hauling around so much beef before a poor dog just gives in and his hips give out and the organs start to fail.

The last dog my parents ever owned was a curly-haired Rottweiler named Luba. She was a stray some friends of ours found and Cindy promptly walked her over to my parents' house and introduced them to their new best friend. They welcomed her as they figured she would be cheaper than being burglarized in the middle of the night. My mother named her. The only one in a long line of big, hairy, shitting beasts. Luba was a sweet dog. She was completely devoted to her senior citizens and I doubt seriously if Luba would ever have taken a chomp out of anything, let alone Lou.

She stayed by their side and shared their meals. She was loyal and obedient and truly loved them. Cindy and I actually walked her right through the front doors at the hospital and told everyone she was a therapy dog just so she could see mom for the last time. The trick is to put a bandanna around the dog's neck and tell the front desk her papers are on file. Of course when you do this, it should be after hours so no one can check out your story.

On a sad day in 2013, our father called sobbing uncontrollably, saying that Luba was dead. Mind you, we were all at our oldest brother's funeral, who himself had died in his sleep only a few days earlier. Dad had become so combative over recent years that we knew an entire day with him in the car and a funeral two hours from home would be more than any of us could stand. He never really had a heartfelt relationship with his stepson and neither of them really liked each other. Taking our father to his funeral would have been hypocritical on our part at best.

At my brother's reception, I could see from across the room that Cindy was on the phone having a difficult conversation. I could hardly believe it when she said Dad was on the phone in shock trying to tell her that the last dog he would ever own just dropped dead in the driveway. We were two hours away and had no one to ask for help. As painful as it was, she called her son who was 18 at the time and said, "You're up. Get one of your rugby buddies to help because you have to get a 130-pound dog off the ground, into the car and to the vet in the next 30 minutes. As an added bonus, grandpa is going with you. Before you open your mouth, shut up and please deal with it."

The hard part was that yes, Luba was gone and flopping around like a dead harp seal as they tried to maneuver her into the back seat of his car. Cindy's son and his friend were as kind as possible. The hard part was that our father, his grandfather, was acting like one of his own kids had been slaughtered before his eyes. He was inconsolable. He was also not going to sit in the back seat with his own dog. He made the rugby player do it. When this kid asked, "What the hell is the matter with him?" Cindy's son said, "Shut the hell up and get in the car. She's not going to bite you now and be thankful we left all her piss and shit in the driveway. Sit down. Please. This is not going to get better." He further lamented that dad would most likely mumble something about suicide and a lack of a will to live.

Cindy, Greg, George and I left our brother's funeral prematurely so we could get back home. His blubbering on the phone only convinced us further that we were in for a long night. The irony was that the three of us would have to help him overcome his grief when he hardly said a word to us about our brother. I know we all tried to think of a reason to leave him alone but nothing reasonable or sane came to mind. We took a deep breath and walked into his house.

Lou was sitting at the kitchen table writing feverishly. None of us could imagine what he was writing. Of course it had to be about the dog, but what took up two sheets of paper? While Greg distracted him, I took a quick look at his chicken scratch. I could only make out words like poison, arrow, bullet, sudden death, heart breaking bitter tears and desolation. There were 1,000 words written on the dog's cremation invoice. I kept reading and said, "Seriously, what the fuck is he writing about?"

We asked him how he was doing, and I really thought he was in shock. He thought she might have been shot with an arrow or poisoned. He was talking about suicide and that the love of his life was dead and he was totally lost without her. As I looked further, he had started to write out the words to Whitney Houston's “I Will Always Love You” and “As Time Goes By” from *Casablanca*. We all felt sorry for him, but no one could sit there and watch this. Our brother was dead, our mother had died three years prior and I had just buried my own dog two weeks before this. I didn't care if he killed himself over his deceased dog. I left. Greg and Cindy were right behind me. We needed to have a drink and cry about our brother. The weight of my sorrow was sitting so heavy on my shoulders, I was ready to collapse.

So that was it. In his 90+ years he had a beautiful, sweet wife, five kids and 14 grandchildren but he wrote a love letter to his dog and was going to kill himself. Most likely it was because he was finally all alone. It was pitiful. He was pitiful. In the end, we survived all the mess, the dog fights and sorrow of putting a family pet to sleep. What he ultimately ruined for me and my sister for the rest of our lives was the enjoyment of running barefoot in the grass.

vacuum in squares

There are many tasks and chores that, on the surface, seem relatively simple to master. Common sense will usually get you through it. No instructions necessary. I tell my kids to dust the furniture by handing them a clean towel and furniture polish. If I want them to do the dishes, I tell them "Load this stuff and wash the pans." When I want them to clear snow from the driveway, I hand them each a shovel. We are not redesigning the space shuttle. Figure it out. I know my father's intent was to teach all of us to do a job "right" the first time. What Cindy and I learned from our father was to not screw around and do it his way the first time. That meant we got done with our chores and were free to go about our own business.

When Cindy and I were unlucky enough to have Lou watching us do housework (which was most of the time) we felt as much pressure as a new brain surgeon. He ran his business out of our home so he was always there. Which meant he would stop whatever he was doing just to catch you fucking things up. Unless, of course, he was taking a crap. For him, taking a crap could take 30 minutes, so if you timed it right, you could get a lot done while he was in the can. If we were smart, we would have slipped Ex-Lax into his brownies or cake and he would have lived in there and we would have been able to work unsupervised.

Because my brothers married young and got the hell out of there, we (Debbie, Cindy and I) were left to clean that whole place and take care of the yard. I am sure at one time that the 90-year-old, 100% wool carpet in our house was something to envy. It was meant to last a 100 fucking years but I could not stand it because it was such a bitch to clean. It was a deep maroon, rough and itchy as hell. I understand why the dogs loved to roll around on it. It probably felt as good to them as a bear grinding its hind end on a pine tree. The problem with the dogs and this carpet was that it was almost impossible to get the hair off. It was like flies on fly paper.

Five large, hairy dogs and a 30-year-old Electrolux canister vacuum created a huge problem. To solve this dilemma, Lou told Debbie who told us that if you sectioned the carpet off in squares and cleaned it that way, it would come cleaner. Don't just push the canister around any old way. Squares. In your mind you should divide the carpet into about four foot by four-foot squares and vacuum each square before you moved on to the next. Dad was totally serious. As we stood gritting our teeth and sighing under our breath, we did it. I don't know if "what the fuck" came to mind since we were only ten, but I can tell you we were thinking something.

What could we do? By the time we were old enough to take over the job from Debbie, Cindy and I had to crawl around on the floor and scoop up the dog hair into little piles first and then use the ol' Electrolux. The vacuum didn't have enough suck to handle the job so we had to pick up what we could with our hands first. The carpet was actually so gnarly, we got rug burns on our kneecaps. Cindy and I got good too at dividing up the job between the living room, the front hall and the dining room. We knew exactly where to draw the line. Our world was 50 frigging 50. Not one extra hair, turd, dish or blade of grass went one way or another. We split every job right down the middle.

That carpet stayed in their house until we were 40 years old and he still had that stupid vacuum cleaner. He insisted it still worked fine. Guaranteed, like some closet junkie, he kept that piece of shit to make a point and used the new one we bought him when we weren't looking.

My mother worked harder than all of us. She spent hours in the basement washing clothes and cleaning than anyone I ever knew, especially the other mothers who lived in our neighborhood. By the time Cindy and I knew better, it was too hard to watch her wash the kitchen floor on her hands and knees or stand in the basement for hours using a wringer washer. That's right. This was the 1970s, for Christ's sake. She washed our clothes in a wringer washer and hung them to dry until we were 25 years old, which made it 1987. Can you imagine? This thing had a giant red bar on the top so that in case you got something stuck, like your hair, you could release the wringer. It wasn't the money. It was because he thought it was good enough for her.

The worst part of washing and drying our clothes that way for us was that all our shirts had those little marks and bumps that stuck out on the shoulders from the clothing pins. It was a dead giveaway. And our friends knew there was a problem when one of them finally asked, "Why are all of your zippers broken?" When Cindy and I graduated from college in 1986, the first thing we did was buy her a new washer and dryer.

Mom kept at the laundry over the years, but the rest belonged to us. Saturday morning was the day to get it done. Lou purchased rental property by the time we were 11, so he would usually leave on Saturdays to go work at "the houses." Thank you, Jesus. We could clean how we pleased and listen to the radio. We vacuumed any way we pleased and jammed to Rick James.

By this time, washing the kitchen floor was tricky. We had to use the right amount of Mr. Clean and hot water and remember to change the rinse water frequently. The floor got so dirty from daily living and five dogs that the "right amount" of cleaner usually meant just pouring the ammonia right onto the floor. Screw the hot water. All we had to do was let it sit for a minute and not only could we wipe up the dirt, but the floor was slowly coming up with it. Over time, the rinse water was yellow, which was the color of the linoleum. Cindy and I envied anyone who could just mop their floors without turning it in to a major production and risking ammonia chloride poisoning.

We comprehend that from a child's perspective, doing chores always seems like torture. It's a rite of passage to have your children work around the house. We do it now as parents. On the flip side, we are our own kid's biggest fans. We tell them we love them often, praise their accomplishments and minimize their short comings. If Lou would have added some "warm fuzzies" to his parenting skills, Cindy and I might have been able to choke back the manner in which he forced us to do everything.

Yard work was the most unbearable chore of all. It was a huge process that started with picking up giant piles of dog shit and then pulling weeds. The weeds were those tall, light green blades of grass that had to be pulled out from the root. It wasn't until we all moved out that Lou discovered weed killer and gas-powered equipment. Until that moment, we were the eradicators of all that was unnatural in his landscape. Before weeds could be pulled and thus the grass cut, we had to clean up the shit first. Armed with big bags and our own shovels, we were determined to get it done as quickly as possible. Debbie participated in this hazing ritual for a few years but by the time Cindy and I were 14, she was gone and the job was ours. This job never went smoothly or quickly as we cried all the way through it.

Not only did Cindy and I fight over whose turn it was on the fast bike, we fought over who got the good shit shovel. Picking up dog shit was easier if you had the shovel with the pointy end.

We had to get the point of the shovel just right or we would leave crap on the lawn.

After the crap was cleaned up, we had to pull those weeds. They were like bad pennies. They never went away. Every week they were back in the same places and it seemed like they multiplied. Maybe they were fertilized by the crap. Figures. We weren't permitted to pull the weed from the top. We had to get it by the root which meant touching the grass, which meant most likely touching the dog shit that was just touching the grass a few minutes ago. No gloves. We went about this task commando style. This had to be another one of Lou's twisted pleasures. We never once saw him bend over and pull one fucking weed—ever. If he did, it was in secret.

So, we cleaned up the shit and pulled the weeds. Now we had to cut the grass. This was a huge yard for 12-year-old girls. Not just the back but the front too. The weapon of choice? A Scott's lawn mower. The push kind. Only, for extra fun, this thing was never in the garage out of the rain or out of range of pissing dogs. Lou left it outside against the garage so it could rust. Cindy and I pushed this thing for eight years. It was so rusty that we had to get a six to eight foot running start just so the blades would spin.

Of course, the hardest part wasn't necessarily the physical exertion necessary to push a rusty mower. It was his prying eyes. The first time he said to us, "one quarter up, three quarters back," we thought, "what the hell is he talking about and what difference does it make as long as the grass gets cut?" What he meant was that you needed to measure about 1/4 the width of the mower and push it over the uncut grass. When you came back the other direction, you would do the same thing only this time you would measure about 3/4 the width of the mower. To this day I don't believe Cindy or I can cut the grass without thinking of "1/4 up, 3/4 back." It makes me crazy.

It wasn't over yet. Lake Avenue property had to be suitably groomed. To finish the job, we scooted around the yard on our bony butts and trimmed the edge of the yard, around rocks, the pond and the trees with hand trimmers. I am talking about an acre of property that had to be trimmed out with nothing more than crappy kitchen scissors.

When we were old enough, which was about 12, he thought it was time for us to ride our bikes two miles down the road to his rental property. There were two yards that were bigger than the one we just finished. Cindy and I had just gotten new ten speeds. They were beautiful and we were proud to ride them. We just had no idea the price we would pay. Our price was to preen his rental property. Lou would throw the same rusted out, crappy mower in the back of his station wagon with the rake and trimmers and meet us at "the houses." He abandoned us for a few hours until he was sure we had ample time to finish this work. We bitched and moaned the entire time, convinced there wasn't a boy alive that had to do this much work.

We humped that mower over all three properties until we graduated from college. We lived in a neighborhood that had landscapers and housekeepers. Embarrassing us made no difference to Lou as we were seen cutting the rental property grass at 17 years old by the girls across the street who were being picked up for the Homecoming Dance. We wanted to die. Since we couldn't do that, Cindy and I just had to hide in the back yard until the limos left.

Cleaning any house and taking care of the property should, to some extent, be a family affair. All children should be required to toe the line. My problem was there was always so much to do and we were the only ones doing it.

Thinking back, there wasn't a task that we didn't do. We did a lot of the normal tasks like dusting, cleaning bathrooms and washing floors. We also cleaned the windows, inside and out. We were on ladders outside with buckets of ammonia water, squeegees and rags. We stirred concrete and tarred the garage roof. We shoveled mountains of snow and cleaned up tons of whatever the dogs left behind. Besides dog shit there was dog hair. We never figured out how to weave a sweater out of dog hair. If we had, we would have been rolling in dough. What were we thinking? St. Bernards have really nice hair.

The drive in our backyard was old and developed several deep cracks. One of our ill-fated tasks was to clean dog hair out of these fractures. The dog hair blew around the yard like tumble weeds. It settled in everything. This job was especially objectionable after a few weeks of rain and heat. To an outsider, this must have seemed unimaginable. "We can't come over and play right now. We have to pull dog hair out of the cracks." These long strands of matted hair looked like dread locks. Wet hair is gross to begin with but in those quantities, it's simply revolting. It became a sick little game to see who could pull out the longest strand without breaking it. Cindy and I would fill another one of the empty dog food bags with hair. It became clear why Lou saved these bags. They were free and they had a purpose. So, not only did we have to brush these dogs (constantly), but whatever was missed was scraped off the cement.

Whether it was because of him or in spite of him, Cindy and I maintain cleaned and well-organized homes. We still crawl around on our hands and knees wiping, scraping and picking. Although we don't have to use push mowers or use wringer washers, we still meticulously fold our laundry and cut the grass. Resentfully, we do it with his voice chattering in our heads about squares and inches. There isn't a task I perform today that doesn't get my post-traumatic stress going.

a mouth full of marbles

From the time Cindy and I were small, it was very difficult to carry on a conversation with Lou because we knew he was listening to how we were speaking instead of what we were saying. He claimed that we, especially women, do not speak properly. Not only do we not have proper diction, but the tone of our voices makes it difficult to hear. He had been hard of hearing for most of his adult life and at 92, he was considered clinically deaf. Everyone knew it except him.

For a man with fake knees, false teeth, glasses and practically a new heart, what was his problem with hearing aids? He walked around for years with no upper teeth. He should have been more worried about that lasting impression than whether or not you could see a microphone in his ear. I have heard about this phenomenon from other women about their husbands refusing to admit that they can't hear clearly. It's typical behavior. He turned his head sideways to catch every syllable or tried to read my lips and then responded with some stupid non-sequitur. He kept doing this even when his hearing aids looked back at him from their box every breakfast, lunch and dinner for at least two years.

Lou had hearing aids sitting on his dining room table well within plain sight but refused to wear them. Every time anyone tried to talk to him, he started his bullshit about us not speaking clearly or too fast, and I wanted to smash him in the face. More than once I slammed that box on the table and told him, "Put these fucking things in! I am not going to keep repeating myself and I cannot slow down my speech anymore. It is not me goddamn it—it's you!" To which he replied, "Stop yelling at me. I'm not deaf." Give me a break.

Over many years he had been under the impression that we said things we simply did not. He thought we could not communicate and that any issue he had with not hearing us clearly had was because we don't speak like men. This is because he always said we spoke like we had a mouth full of marbles. None of us can recall a moment in time when we weren't always being told "Stop talking like you have marbles in your mouth." Just for the record, we have never tried to speak with a mouth full of marbles and have never actually known anyone who could do it.

So, this is another area at which we strived to reach his level of perfection. We worked at never saying "um" or raising our voices at the end of a sentence, to which he would always remark, "Are you asking me or telling me?" His criticisms of our speaking styles as young adults were fair and proved invaluable later in life. Public speaking was part of all of our careers and our coworkers and superiors thought we excelled. However, even after we mastered many of the speaking skills he believed were critical to survive in sixth grade and subsequently in life, he continually reminded us that we spoke either too quickly, not slowly enough, slurred our speech or cluttered our conversations with meaningless slang. We always thought we were thoughtful, funny and entertaining. He simply thought we were lazy and inconsiderate.

Lou had stopped me from speaking a million times. I might have been mid-sentence and my sternum would tighten just to stop the flow of my words. Why? Because I was speaking too fast and he felt compelled to tell me to slow down. He did it to me, my mother, Cindy, his grand kids, a customer service rep at the phone company. Everyone. We spoke at 45 rpms and he wanted 33 rpms. All anyone ever wanted to do was have normal conversation. The funny part was that no one ever really gave a shit whether he was involved in the conversation anyway.

When he hit 90, he started telling me to stop using extra words. To this day, I have no idea what extra words I was using. Trust me, I never arbitrarily toss in extra "whats," "whys," and "wheres" during any conversation. He said, "It sounds like you're talking in an echo chamber. Stop using so many extra words. Slow down; it's not a race. I can't hear a word you are saying." Until the day he died, I continued to talk myself out of being self-conscious whenever I spoke in front of him. I also had to talk myself out of getting a hatchet from the kitchen and dismembering him on the spot.

Cindy was having coffee with Mom and Dad in March, 2008. She had not intended to speak with him about politics, religion or his rental properties. On this particular day, the subject was Cindy's son. She was trying to be cool and just tell him a feel-good story about her kid. The conversation started innocently enough but within minutes Lou stopped her cold. As usual, he had been trying to listen to what she was saying but because he could not hear, he had no choice but to turn it over on her.

Cindy was so pissed but sat there trying to choke back his criticism like a giant piece of grizzled meat. He had no comment about her son. He could only talk about her speaking style. He said, "Why do you feel the need to speak so quickly. We are not in a race here. You are inconsiderate of the recipient. You should listen to Charles Gibson speak and learn from him." Have you ever been told to speak like a newscaster when you were not pursuing this as a career? They read the fucking news from tele-prompters. Charlie Gibson is not trying to have conversation with his viewers. Cindy was now supposed to learn to speak like a 60-year-old man. Sexy. I want to hear Charlie at the dinner table. I hope for his sake he doesn't speak like that at a party. If he does, he better forget telling a joke.

Cindy could not take Lou's advice and started to cry at what she considered another injustice. Why couldn't he just shut his mouth. She could not finish her conversation and merely said, "Fuck this." She stood up, gave mom one of those "WTF" looks and walked out of the house. He didn't want her to leave mad and would spend the next two days trying to undo what he'd done—again.

He said to Mom a few times, shortly before she passed away, "Jesus Marie, it sounds like you are chewing your words. Speak up!" I sat in her room at the nursing home and heard him say it.

My dear, sweet, Mrs. Claus-like mother was taking so much medication and had most likely suffered some mild stroke along the way so she spoke like she was a little out of breath. She asked him what he meant and before he could answer, I launched my attack. "How dare you come in here and think just because you toss a bag of candy at her, you have any right to say anything at all! She doesn't care if you think she talks like she's got a mouth full of shit! She wasn't talking to you anyway! If you can't keep up, it's your problem, not everyone else's. Do not interrupt her again."

One evening was similar to many we had had over the years. My mother called Cindy to ask her husband to please come over and take a look at his car. You can roll your eyes all you want but when you live across the street from your parents/in-laws, they own you. You get to feed them, shovel their snow, cut their grass and pull their weeds. And on this night, someone had to fix the old man's car.

George dutifully went over and rang the doorbell. He stood

outside waiting for what seemed like an eternity and found himself listening to Alex Trebek through the door helping his contestants give their answers in the form of a question. Dad opened the door and George said, “So, I hear you need me to look at your car?”

“What?” my dad said, “Do I want to buy an electric guitar?”

“No!” George answered. “Your car! Do you need me to look at your car?!”

“I don’t need a guitar.”

George just said “ok” then said “fuck it” to himself and went back home. He was laughing so hard trying to tell Cindy what happened he almost hyperventilated. When they told me that story I laughed so hard I thought I broke a rib.

Many times I have had to explain this expression of talking like you had a mouth full of marbles to my kids or friends. I would tell them to imagine having marshmallows or a whole pack of gum in their mouth while trying to speak. I emphasized with my own children to use the English language properly. And they did. When it really mattered, they spoke exactly as they should have.

I have to admit that I am grateful that he made Cindy and me aware of the impression we would make by failing to communicate clearly. To the contrary, I must also admit how frustrating it was to speak to someone who refused to acknowledge that he had a hearing problem. I knew that by the time I was thirty years old I had mastered the ability to carry on a conversation. But until the very end of his life, he stopped us cold in our tracks during almost every conversation by telling us to stop yelling or slow down or stop mushing our words and so on. It all came down to the fact that my father refused to listen to anyone who did not properly enunciate their words. He said one time, “It's not woulda, coulda, shoulda. Say would have, could have, should have.” To this day, Cindy and I go a little crazy when we hear the very thing he forbade in us.

And so it went. He managed to get free hearing aids from the VA until he was 94 years old, and for years they were neatly packaged and left sitting on his dining room table. I am confident that was just an act of mockery meant to drive us nuts. When he was finally incarcerated in the assisted living facility, the doctors and nurses insisted he wear them. They were not going to scream and holler at him in an effort to have him hear simple instructions. He fought them every step of the way. They too finally acquiesced and left him alone. It was sad because by this time he was going blind from macular degeneration. But, if my father wanted to sit in a dark bubble out of spite until he died, it was his choice. Ironically though, when he was dying I have no doubt he heard my words loud and clear.

enough ain't enough

Lou had a way of justifying everything he did. Screwing anybody out of anything was sport to him. It did not matter if he could shoplift a handful of nails or con someone out of a few bucks. It was irrelevant if he did not need the nails or the money. It did not matter if he got caught. His game was to get something for nothing because that made him feel clever and somehow smarter than the next guy. He also wondered why everyone else didn't think the way he did. This is the difference between a person with a conscience and one without, which is why no one who knew him well could understand his motivations.

Sometimes luck fell right into his wrinkled lap and other times he had to actually dream up a scheme just because he was bored. Maybe fucking people over started when he was younger after he witnessed how easy it was for his mother Mary to pocket a mountain of dime store jewelry or candy. His mother had sticky fingers and made use of them on a daily basis. She had every color of costume jewelry known to man and dishes of hard candy. After her death, most of the jewelry she possessed was still affixed to the cardboard mountings. She did not steal because she truly desired blue rhinestone earrings. She stole them because she could.

Lou made sure he came out on top of every deal. None of us, including our mother, ever got the better of his bullshit deals. Whatever fraud he committed against his insurance company, his tenants, local department stores or his kids, it fed his ego and filled his wallet. When at all possible, he just shoved another wad of cash in his box so he could one day have it all to himself. That day came the moment our mother died. He was no longer under any obligation to share his money or his things. He could covet his stash in private. And at 90 plus years old he was still coveting his mother's rhinestones.

My parents' nest egg was the size of an ostrich egg. This was great except they never figured out when to start spending it even when it was painfully obvious to those around them that they were both "retired." They were well into their eighties and Lou still believed they had many more years to live. Our mother was very sick for the last few years of her life and although he paid for her medication and hospital stays, he did it begrudgingly. "Will there be any left for me?" he said.

The first time I recall him doing something corrupt was about 1970. We had just had a brand-new refrigerator delivered from Montgomery Ward. It was big and clean and shiny like a new car. It smelled like new rubber gaskets and fresh ice. Dad filled it from top to bottom with gallons of milk, fruit, meat and giant tubs of ice cream. By the way, Pick-n-Pay sold milk in clear plastic bags in the early '70s. This had to be the dumbest marketing tool invented. I cannot imagine how milk in a bag was shipped and stocked. It was a pain in the ass once you got it home because you had to put it in a pitcher without dumping the whole thing all over the floor. But I digress.

Always hiding in the back of his refrigerator was a fresh jar of pickled herring. It looked like billy goat puke in a jar and it smelled like Lake Erie in the spring. He ate it right out of the jar with a fork. It was utterly disgusting. Thank God he hid it in the back because if I had to look at that jar of headless fish floating in cream sauce I would have puked.

We didn't have our new department store fridge for more than a month when it took a shit. Cindy and I helped Lou haul all of the food to two different basement refrigerators before it spoiled. What a relief to have two other working refrigerators in the house because if pickled herring smells like an old diaper when it's fresh you can imagine what that stuff smells like after it warms up.

Lou promptly called the department store and insisted they come to look at it to see what was wrong. The handy men dressed in blue arrived ready for a quick fix. The repairman stood there with folded arms and puzzled looks. I literally saw a light bulb blazing above my father's head. Lou was convinced it was a "lemon" and wanted a refund instead. Not only that, he proceeded to give them a list of the food that had "spoiled." He promptly explained the entire family had been gone for days and no one realized our only refrigerator had stopped working. He continued to explain that it was necessary to throw all of the food into the trash so that his children were not accidentally exposed to food poisoning. None of us knew it, but apparently we were in for a treat of filet mignon, baby back ribs, designer ice cream, fresh squeezed orange juice and whole milk, cheese and eggs delivered from our very own milk man. That's only a partial list of what he expected to be reimbursed for.

His game this time was to get a little something extra for having been inconvenienced. Just for the record, his buying food with that price tag would never have happened since most of the time we were eating Wheat Chex with powdered milk for breakfast and some kind of stew for dinner.

Dad was in for a pleasant surprise. Somewhere the communication broke down and not only did the guys from Montgomery Ward come to get the broken fridge, they brought a new one to replace it. Free of charge. They moved it in, unpacked it, set it up and took the old one out. Montgomery Ward refunded him his money for the broken fridge, replaced it with a new one and sent him a check for the "rotten food." Of course there had been nothing in the refrigerator that couldn't be picked up at our local Fazio's. He toasted his brilliance with a highball made with Jim Dant Whiskey and Cindy and I got to haul all the food back upstairs from the basement.

A few years later he scored again. This time it was 2000 square feet of carpeting. Some minimum wage grunt made the mistake of misdelivering wall to wall carpet to his rental property three miles down the road. Instead of confirming the address and waiting for someone to let them in, they broke the back window, unlocked the door and left the carpet in one of Lou's empty apartments. He discovered this because, as usual, it was the weekend and he was going over there to work. He was mad as hell when he found the broken window but felt much better when he discovered that Santa Claus left him a useful present.

He called his friend Bruce and had him get his van over there to get rid of the carpet. I have no idea where he stashed it for seven years, but it disappeared. Just in time too since the carpet delivery guys called him to say they had made a mistake and left the carpet at the wrong address. Boy, were they right about that.

Lou told them the only way that could have happened is if they broke in. He kindly explained that he had already filed a police report and would press charges for breaking and entering if they admitted to breaking in and leaving the carpet where it didn't belong. He had them by the short hairs. They knew they would get fired for being stupid. They just needed to decide if they wanted a police record to go along with their unemployment checks. After a short amount of consideration, they said they must have the wrong guy and Lou never heard from them again. That carpet was proudly laid on the second floor of my parents' home and stayed there for 35 years.

My father finally graduated to the big leagues in the early eighties and purchased a brand-new Buick Park Avenue. It was maroon and had beautiful maroon velour interior. It had four doors and was a really slick ride. It had just enough chrome to make us fit right in with our Lake Avenue friends. However, he hillbillied it out because he couldn't get over using every car he had as a truck. He filled the trunk of this luxury sedan with tools of every kind and went to work at the rental properties. When he would get home Cindy and I unloaded the car so we could take it clubbing. We would head off to The Rampant Lion with his car and $20 and be gone until 2:00 am.

My parents had this strange routine of driving out of their way to save ten cents a pound on chicken. If it was on sale, it was worth the trip. They decided one late Saturday afternoon to go to a Kmart in a predominantly lower scale neighborhood. What he actually said in hindsight was "We shouldn't have gone to a neighborhood full of knuckle draggers." If this was the truth and the neighborhood was unsafe then he was going to have to justify his stupid behavior and pay it forward. To himself. He was going to steal from his insurance company to make it right.

I bet he felt really good when he came out of the store to find his Buick gone from sight. The brothers must have loved that thing because when the cops finally found it, the seats were low riding to their absolute maximum. The stereo was gone and the seats were cut up. They took it for a joy ride and then beat the shit out of it. It is ironic how pissed he was that shit-head little punks took something that didn't belong to them. Can you imagine the indignation he must have felt?

Of course he was going to get more out of this insurance claim than he had coming to him. He saw an opportunity and he took it. Lou spent weeks researching the current prices of stainless-steel Milwaukee power tools. He had a Sears catalog in front of him and wrote down every model number he could find. He said his brand-new glasses were in there too.

At the time, I lived in one of his apartments and my then-husband took a butter knife to open the door to the apartment below us. All of Lou's tools were placed neatly on the floor in front of us. So, he got a nice fat check to replace his car and a few grand for his precious tools. What I should have done was take his tools just to teach him a lesson. I never did. That was really stupid because it would have been funny as hell.

Life continued on like this for him forever. I am certain that he had as many opportunities before I was born as he did after to lie, cheat and steal. My parent's house on Lake Avenue had a Spanish tile roof. It was impervious to any normal catastrophe that waged war on a regular shingled roof. Short of a 400-year-old maple crashing into it, a Spanish tile roof was meant to last forever. I bet you didn't know that. The insurance adjuster didn't either.

My father had an insurance adjuster visit him one year to survey the "damage" done by a pack of angry squirrels. Apparently they were as big as house cats too. They had the nerve to build a nest at the top of a three -story home. Their nest was apparently so large that it diverted enough water to cause a major leak inside the house that ran down three stories. That was Lou's story. He had some toothless, tar-encrusted roofer give him an estimate for the damage and state that "squirrels" were the obvious culprits. Squirrels were as likely to make that kind of a mess as were a family of beavers building a dam.

Jesus Christ, I could not believe what I was hearing. I was embarrassed for him that he might actually say this out loud and expect someone to believe him. That "someone" would have to be a complete fucking idiot. At the time he was making this claim,

I shared the same insurance agent and my rates were going to go up because of his fraudulent bullshit! I almost ratted him out I was so pissed. I half expected Roger to call me and ask, "What the fuck is your father up to now?"

I kept my mouth shut just to see if he would actually get away with this. And thank God Roger never called me. Lou was eventually given a check for $10,000 for the damage. Again, he never "fixed" the roof because the roof wasn't the problem. He had leaky pipes throughout the house and really needed a plumber to fix his problems, not a roofer. His solution was to shut off the water to certain portions of the house and stick more money in his box.

The goal for him wasn't always to just shove money in a box. Sometimes it was about not paying for something that he was legitimately using. In the late '70s cable television was really a luxury. Anyone could still watch a television with an antenna and rabbit ears. The privileged in society had cable. I could not believe the day when I came home from high school and a giant television was sitting in the living room with a cable box on top of it. Was it true I could watch movies 24 hours a day?

Back then, the price for cable TV was about $10 a month. When I thought to myself, "Where is he getting the money for this?" I remembered how he got the money for everything else. So we watched HBO, Showtime and MTV for years without incident. Then, about three years later, our cable TV was gone. He stopped paying the bill because they raised the rates. However, the cable company was not going to stand for an unpaid balance and quickly told him to pay or he would end up in court. His argument was that he claimed he told the cable company he didn't want it anymore and it was because of their ineptitude that he was still receiving a signal.

He paid it in full because he could not provide enough

documentation to support his cause. Cindy and I were expected to abruptly go back to a lifetime of rabbit ears and local programming. It was a shock to him as well when as quickly as we had lost our cable, we had it back. Dad claimed he had no idea why we were watching MTV instead of Dynasty since he canceled our subscription. Just in case, though, he would do his best to cover up any evidence that we were getting cable television for free. Who knew how long this would last? So, he hung an old metal garbage can lid on the side of the house to cover up the cable wire's entrance into our home. Brilliant.

He believed that the guy on the pole could not possibly follow the wire from the pole which sat directly on the back of his property 70 feet away. Apparently, I over-estimated the intelligence level of a cable guy. Sometime much later in the future, the cable company figured out he was not a paying customer and cut the line. It only took them 15 years. By the time his line was cut, the cost of cable went from $10 a month up to $30 and he never paid a dime.

Lou kept conniving even into his nineties. If there was a way to get something for nothing, he tried his best. The weather in Cleveland can be occasionally brutal. We don't get snowfall measured in feet like Buffalo, tornadoes that regularly flatten neighborhoods or rainfall that floods entire cities. However, we get enough bad weather to cause some damage to our properties.

A fall night in 2010 was one of those weird evenings. A crazy front passed over northeast Ohio right at Lake Erie's edge late on a Friday night. When my husband and I looked the windows, we saw a wall of shit headed our way. The hail left behind was the size of golf balls that beat the shit out of cars and houses. The biggest damage was from falling trees and hail. Since eight out of ten residents in Cuyahoga County were calling their insurance agents, my father figured he had a shot. Something of his had to have been destroyed.

It took about a month for him to get his story together and get the nerve to report damage to his primary residence. According to him, his garage roof was destroyed. The water damage to the inside was significant as well. Not only was there a huge hole in the roof but his grandfather's wood working tools from the 1800s were destroyed as well. What is bullshit about this is that the hole in the roof and ensuing water damage had been there for years. As far as I knew, the tools in the garage were just old and had no sentimental value. His statement to the adjuster was that these tools were antiques and were priceless. My thought was, "what a way to store priceless, sentimental heirlooms; out in the open so they could rust beyond recognition." Once again, my father thought he could tack a few dollars on to his claim and no one would know the difference.

He methodically explained the damage to his property and personal items. In addition to the garage roof and the priceless, 100-year-old tools, he told the adjuster that the storm had taken away his front screen door just like Dorothy's in The Wizard of Oz. I know for a fact that the door was wooden and shot and he wanted a new one to replace it. When the adjuster asked him, "Well, where it is? Didn't you recover it?" My father's response was that it must have been carried away and someone must have put it in a burn pile.

He received some money for the garage but nothing else. Although that claim was barely legitimate, thank God the adjuster could recognize a scam artist when he saw one.

The most offensive to me was his behavior after our mother passed away. She died December 27, 2009. He started his scheming only a few weeks later. He attempted to get her assisted living facility to write off part of her charges. He spent two months staring at a $10,000 bill for mom's care and medication. He was also staring at her hospital bill which was nothing compared to the care she received at the end of her life. It wasn't that he was unwilling to pay. He just wasn't willing to pay for all of it.

Again, he thought he was being screwed. He had notes written on invoices and scrap sheets of paper with his thoughts and his own accounting. His notes made no sense. He spent hours on the phone trying to desperately convince the finance director at both the nursing home and the hospital that he was low on cash. He tried to convince them to refund him the cost of the medication she never finished. He tried to get them to not charge him for the last two weeks of December, 2009 because she was in the hospital and not using her room. At the very least they should not charge him for the utilities and upkeep for a room that was unoccupied for two weeks.

What he failed to understand was that while mom was flat on her back in the hospital with her life hanging in the balance, they were unable to rent her suite to anyone else. My sister and I, along with the finance director, tried over and over again to explain to him that her things were still there and that there was a slim chance she might make it back. He then realized the faster we got her stuff out of there, the less money he would have to pay. He saw over $100 disappearing before his eyes every day she lay dying in the hospital instead of the nursing home. I believe he was pissed because he was handcuffed. It was all in the fine print which he failed to read the day we checked her in.

We had her funeral services on December 29. Cindy made the funeral arrangements and wrote her notice for the newspaper. This was going to cost him another $3000. A few hundred for the death notice in the paper, a few hundred for her favorite flowers (day lilies and yellow roses), $400 for her solid cherry urn with brass name plate and the balance for her cremation and service. He was not happy with her death notice, especially because he said it was too long. Every line written on her behalf cost $10. She had five kids with spouses, 14 grandchildren, one great grandchild and a brother and sister-in-law.

He was cutting checks so fast his head was spinning. In the end, he took until mid-January to pay for her funeral and two months to pay the nursing home and hospital. Cindy and I managed to get the nursing home to shave off a few bucks for her medication and not charge him interest for not paying a nickel for her care until after she was dead. However, he had to pay the whole enchilada at once and stop harassing them about her expenses. This was the lesser of two evils since arguing with them was costing him $350 a month in interest.

In 2013 at the age of 94 I believed there was nothing else he could steal, unless you count my soul, my sister's soul and our time. We thought we could relax a little and just make sure that he was somehow surviving in his house all by himself but we were wrong. Since we had taken his car in 2012, he had to rely on rides from the neighbor or from us.

Since he had already been busted by me for trying to scam The Veteran's Administration out of disability checks, I thought I was ready for the next time he tried to pull a fast one. I never saw it coming. In the summer of 2013, Cindy saw a strange car pull in the drive. Lou came out the front door and got into the car. Cindy called me and said, "Where the hell is he going now?"

I said, "Forget that. What the hell is he up to?"

We scratched our heads until the next day when he gave himself up when Cindy asked him point blank, "Where did you go yesterday?"

He said, "I had an appointment and the VA picked me up."

Cindy reminded him that she was his ride to the VA and wanted to know who that was in the shiny silver Lexus. He said, "None of your fucking business. I had to go to a different office at

E. 70th and Euclid." That was all Cindy needed to know. She did not waste another second of her time with him, hung up and got on her computer to check what office was at that location. She figured out rather quickly that this was the office for homeless and at-risk veterans. This was another "what the fuck" moment that required our immediate attention.

It was not difficult to call the number and get his case worker's name. When Cindy spoke with her the first time, she was less than helpful and would not divulge any information regarding our father's inquiry. That was fine, for about five minutes until I called and asked for the program director. Cindy and I played "good cop, bad cop" all of the time. It was my turn to be Dirty Harry.

His caseworker promptly called me back and was slightly more helpful because I am certain the director of the program did not appreciate me interrupting her day. The reason for our inquiry was not to save him from them. It was quite the opposite. I allowed his "new friend" a minute or two to explain to me all the wonderful services that this office provided to its veterans before I told her I had a few questions. I asked her who picked him up and was this common practice. She stumbled around the question, but since it had nothing to do with what he wanted, she told me, "I did."

I could not help my sarcasm when I asked her, "Did he look homeless to you or at risk for homelessness when you pulled up to his big house with a landscaped lawn?"

She simply replied, "No he did not." The meeting should have stopped right there.

However, I continued down this road and asked her, "Do you think he is a candidate for vocational training at 94 years old?" Without allowing her to really answer, I asked her if she was aware that the main office has a file on him six inches thick.

I asked her if she was aware that two years prior to this day, he was diagnosed with frontal lobe dementia and is considered severely impaired by the VA's own shrink?

As I spoke, I could feel her slumping further down in her chair for having been conned by an old man. I told her she did not have to agree or disagree with me and thus would not be violating any privacy laws when I told her what I believed him to be after. He was trying to convince the VA that he might lose his home because he could not afford the upkeep on a paltry $637 a month in social security. He was looking for housing vouchers or a dollar amount equal to that and/or free services from contractors to work on his home. She was speechless when I added that he had meals delivered every day, a driver to take him where he wished to go and two pieces of rental property in addition to his residence. I asked her kindly to close this case and do not talk to him again.

When I informed him that Cindy and I had spoken to his caseworker and the program director he was furious. He had a game, trying to get something for nothing, but my game was to catch him doing it. Cindy and I got so much pleasure from beating him at his own game over the years that it became like a sport. So being able to tell him again that there was no benefit waiting for him, no money and no caseworker to listen to his problems he promptly told me, “You and your sister are nothing but miserable, nosy bitches. So what if I talk to them? I just want to see if I am entitled to anything.”

My response was short. I said, “You are not entitled to a goddamn thing! You own too much. These are 'needs-based' programs and you are not fucking needy!”

He slammed the door in my face that day. As I walked back to my car I wondered if I even gave a shit that my father really didn’t like me. I don't have an answer to that question. I don't think it's me per se. I think he hates all smart, attractive, assertive vaginas. It was only two months later that he discovered how smart Cindy's vagina was.

To be eligible for food stamps a person's assets cannot be valued at more than roughly $3,300. Even if you lived in your car, it better be a pile of junk or the government will not deem you needy enough for government cheese. The application to apply for food stamps, like all government-based program applications, is lengthy. After you fill out your name, address and social security number, you are asked about all of your assets. My father's willingness to skip this part was a conscious effort to lie. He figured if he didn't mention his assets, then he wasn't lying about anything. Lying by omission is still lying, a point that we were always bringing to his short-sighted attention.

He made the mistake of asking Cindy to make a copy of a six-page document. Cindy said she would but not in an effort to help him. She wanted to take a look at his latest scam. All she could think was, "Is he that fucking stupid to hand me an application for food stamps and think I might go along with this?" The application was never mailed.

When Cindy told him he lied on the application he said, "So what!?" He always said that as though this was a solid explanation for his schemes. He figured he would never go to jail. The worst that might happen to him was that he would simply be told "no."

I believe our father desperately wanted us, or anyone, to tell him he was clever and support his efforts to get something he wasn't entitled to. He was able to confuse us enough as children so that we didn't know enough to say anything about carpet, refrigerators, insurance claims, veteran's benefits and government cheese. These sinister acts are only a small fraction of what I believe to be a lifetime of cons and lies.

He kept it all. The refrigerator is still plugging along, the carpet is still upstairs, he still used phones that he had my brother steal, and whatever cash he managed to collect by defrauding retailers, insurance companies, his doctors or his family is collecting dust. The money was the only thing he never put to good use. In his mind he continued to live in the depression era and a smart person would not spend it on anything unnecessarily. Just like the Jews did in their fight against the Nazis, my father hid his possessions from everyone.

All the insurance company did was reward him for neglecting his property. His dentist and eye doctor didn't charge him for new teeth or glasses because he complained so much about the quality of work. He didn't care if that meant he had to find someone else to treat him the following year. He lived in the moment like most sociopaths and was only concerned with the task right before him.

He could confuse and annoy anybody so anyone he came in contact with would ultimately give him money, a rain check, a refund, food, services or simply forget to bill him just to get him to shut the fuck up and go away. As far as I know he never spent a dime of what he got on anything good or fun. He never shared his "good fortune" either. He kept whatever he could get his hands on so that he would never have to really work or ever worry that there might come a day when he would have to do without.

After he died, Cindy and I had so many possessions to re-home, sell or donate that it was mind boggling. There were two rental properties whose basements were full of God-knows-what and his own 5,000 square foot home which was completely full. It took us two years to touch every single thing he had accumulated over 94 years. We cried through much of our efforts to do the right thing with his books, trinkets, furniture, clothes and collectibles. I feel good that we succeeded in deciding what to keep and what to sell. We donated a semi truck full of items as well. There were no extravagant purchases with what they left behind. We paid college tuition and purchased a few musical instruments for our boys. My mother would be happy because she only ever said, “It will be yours one of these days. Enjoy yourselves and help your children.” She wanted to do those things for her own kids but sadly could not out-maneuver Scrooge. What Cindy and I had to endure is a lesson in that we remain fully committed to only leaving our sons money and jewelry and not fifty year old wedding presents and photographs of people they don't even know.

magic kingdom

If you are like most people, including me, you hate the hospital. You hate the smell and the person you have to share a room with. It's not because these are bad people, it's just because they are perfect strangers and you are literally exposed. You have to share a bathroom with this person and hope that when they walk to the john they are courteous enough to tie up their gown.

You have to listen to your roommate's conversations even when they are not talking to anyone but themselves at 3:00 am. You have to wait for food that you wouldn't feed a starving dog and you open your mouth for any pill the nurses want to shove in it. You know you are going to get jammed with needles and bothered at all hours of the day and night when all you want to do is sip ginger ale and watch television.

It is noisy at all hours of the day and night and there always seems to be some crazy person walking around who should be shackled on the sixth floor. If you ever hear security announcing a "code brown," be afraid. This means that some psychopath is on the loose. The whole experience just represents a huge cluster-fuck so who would really look forward to going to the hospital unless he or she really had to?

The reality is that the hospital is full of sick people waiting to go home and sick people waiting to die. It's very depressing. Each time I had to walk through the front door to visit my mother, I felt sick to my stomach. I had to get past the perverted greeter who could not resist making some comment about my breasts. Then it was the smell. And lastly I never knew what I was likely to find. Did mom have a new roommate? Was she better? Was she worse? Cindy and I always made a point of trying to cheer her up by saying, “You’ll be going home soon. The doctors think you’re much better.” I don’t think she gave a shit. Going home meant a multitude of unpleasant things. It was either too cold or too hot in my parents’ house. It was dusty. It was lonely. There was no cable television to watch and then there was the star of the show—Lou.

However, sometimes staying at home to throw up or cough up your lungs just isn’t possible. Sometimes you just have to go to the hospital. Don’t get me wrong. I love the nursing staff, the doctors, food service and the cleaning staff. We are a family that gets to know all of these people by name. Every time Mom was ordered into the hospital you could tell she was secretly happy. It always represented a huge pain in the ass to the rest of us but at this stage of the game, it was cheaper than any alternative we could come up with.

Every trip to the hospital for Marie was hugely inconvenient for the rest of us—especially Cindy and me. We tried to be patient with the practice of having to visit her daily, talk to her doctors and take care of dad. Taking care of dad meant holding his hand like he was a little baby and listening to him complain about how much it was going to cost. We had to keep the rest of the family posted on her condition with phone calls and emails. No one, including us, really became alarmed when she needed to go the hospital because it was pretty frequently towards the end of her life.

I would guess that her doctor started suggesting a nursing facility for her back in 2004 because she was regularly going to the hospital at least three times a year. Traipsing after her became routine for us. It cost us $5.00 a day for parking and $10.00 for coffee for her, us and the old man. For the record, he never offered up one dollar to buy us anything. He might have offered up a few bucks for parking if we were nice enough to drive him there and park in the garage so he didn't have to walk too far.

Typically, her admittance was through the emergency room. All she had to do was say she felt weak and dizzy and she usually moved to the front of the line ahead of dislocations, lacerations, eye infections and fevers. Cindy and I sat with her while the nurses hooked up a heart monitor and ran a central line for IV's. We would wait patiently for x-rays and blood tests knowing that she would be admitted and we'd start another round of running back and forth between kids, husbands, jobs and dogs. For her, just walking through the front door and getting into a hospital bed was more peaceful than listening to Lou's television blaring or his incessant bitching about his tenants, property taxes and the cost of medication. The nurses dressed her in a hospital gown, put socks on her feet and gave her a warm blanket. Dad usually stayed home because he only aggravated everyone. Since he could not hear very well, he was pretty much useless anyway.

It was sad that Mom never seemed to mind when her doctor would order her back to the hospital. She would pretend that it was a major annoyance but the truth was very different. She was cared for, sheltered and no one ever raised their voice to her. If anyone complained, she never heard one word. She was like a child in their care and was lovingly tucked into bed each night. This was something she was missing for many years. Although Lou would make her tea and check on her occasionally, he didn't pay attention to the important things.

When she was cold he would give her another sweater, not turn up the heat. When she was sweating, he would tell her to relax because it was all in her mind. To cool off at night, she would put wet wash cloths across her body and let a fan blow on her. He bitched every June when Cindy and I would tell him to put her air conditioner in her bedroom window. When she needed to eat regularly, we ordered her Meals on Wheels and he canceled them. Instead of ordering her cable so she could watch her favorite shows, he forced her to watch a television with rabbit ears on the top and the volume turned up full blast.

Through it all, Cindy and I fought with him and struggled with her inability to demand more for herself. The hospital was our mother's "magic kingdom." She could go there and get everything she wanted and during the last few years of her life, it was simply care and compassion. She had the entertainment she wanted and the attention she deserved. It was the one place where she was appreciated simply for being herself.

Cindy and I knew what kind of person she was but our feelings and emotions were always tainted and prejudiced because of how she and dad interacted. We hated that they were married and we made it our business to tell her that each and every day. We told her how to respond to him and were tenacious on the subject of how he should treat her. Frankly, we probably should have minded our own business and let them be married. My sister and I are "fixers" and we did our best to fix them, right down to telling her that all she had to do was to tell him to "fuck off" and he would straighten up and fly right. Her response was, "Really?"

The hospital was one place where no one knew her history. They didn't know that her mother had been married five times or that her younger brother died in WWII. No one knew that her parents were in vaudeville and she and her brothers spent their summers with the "carnies." They didn't know she was a widow at 32 with three young children to care for. They didn't know that she worked like a dog her entire life and had 14 grandchildren.

They didn't know she never learned to drive and couldn't ride a bike. They didn't know she dropped out of high school at 16 to help support her family or that she knew how to sew and knit. To them, she was just a person who deserved smiling faces, fresh towels and little soaps in her bathroom.

Her private Disney World was on the third floor of Lakewood Hospital. This is where her dreams came true. This was a good thing since the end of her life was approaching and she wanted the magic that only those dressed in white and carrying stethoscopes could provide. She was happy to be there even at the end of her life when I am certain she knew she was dying.

garage sale–7 years only

I rented one of my father's apartments with my first husband when I was 24 years old. We had just gotten married and we could not wait to live alone. The year was 1986. My salary as a college graduate was $14,500 per year for a 50-hour work week. My husband was still in school and worked part time until he was able to finish his college degree. Money was tight.

In an effort to ease some of our financial burden, my ex spent the year prior to our wedding finishing the three-bedroom apartment we would eventually rent from my father. He worked at a rate of $5 per hour and managed to earn us a year of free rent. That's 1,104 hours of work at minimum wage. My father was not cutting us one break. We would have to pay the same as anyone else. He charged us $460 per month. On top of that, we had to pay for gas and electricity too.

As with any deal my father concocted, there always seemed to be a math differential and he always thought he was getting screwed. I will never forget the argument my husband had with my father, who accused us both of screwing him on our "one year of free rent" deal. I should have paid more attention to one of Lou's non-stop diatribes that included this famous line, "There is no such thing as a free lunch." I was about to find out how true that was.

Our numbers did not jibe with his and my husband suddenly became the flavor of the month. Lou called him a "cock sucker" to his face and to my husband's credit he did not reciprocate too harshly. He just reminded my father how hard he had worked and that he thought we got the short end of the stick. The rent he was charging us was nothing short of extortion. That night we decided that we were getting out of there as quickly as possible.

As long as we were there, Lou could never stop telling us how to shower and wash our clothes. He told us which light switches to use so that he didn't have to pay for electricity we were using. Since he paid the water bill, he thought he could remind us every fucking day to turn the water off while we soaped ourselves. He instructed me to spy on our fellow tenants and call him when I saw extra cars in the driveway. I don't know why that mattered unless he thought more cars meant someone was using more water.

I knew that we would never get any peace as long as we stayed but we knew we had to stay for one year or my husband worked for him for nothing. We ended up staying for two years when we were finally able to buy our own house. Lou was pissed because he was losing a tenant instead of being happy for his daughter at buying her first home. His parting shot when we were taking out the last box was, "A lot of good this does me." Driving away, I looked at him standing on the front porch with his arms folded blowing smoke rings from his cigar.

On moving day he came to watch us take our things. He stood there coldly, watching my sisters help me take my possessions to a happier place. Everyone was excited about my first house except my own father. He walked through the apartment to make sure we didn't damage his property. I am sure he was looking for anything out of the ordinary just so he could get more money out of us.

There were no tenants below us on the first floor so we were very cold in our apartment. We weren't going to pay one more nickel than necessary in order to survive so we put plastic on the windows. He walked through our three-bedroom apartment that day ripping this shit off so hard that it pulled the finish off the bare wood. He made a mess of the windows with his temper tantrum. He screamed at all of us for ruining his hard work. We didn't leave so much as a scrap of food for the mice. We got the hell out of there and never looked back as he mumbled "good riddance."

My older sister Debbie and her husband went through the same thing when they lived there in the late seventies, except they rented a third floor apartment from him that had only one bedroom. They had cramped quarters so when they had their son, they knew it was time to move. Again, Dad wasn't happy because he would not only have to replace a tenant but find a new spy for the property. In fact, when it came time to move, they moved from one small apartment to a slightly bigger one just to get away from him. However, they couldn't get away from him fast enough before he asked to borrow $15,000 dollars. He told Debbie, "I need the money to pay the mortgage and property taxes or your little sisters are going to be homeless." Really nice. Now I have to ask "did she have a choice?" He got his interest-free loan and Cindy and I got to live in our Lake Avenue house another day.

None of the other kids were stupid enough to fall into his rental property trap. Cindy and her husband took refuge in his parents' rental property where dinner showed up regularly and they came home to clean laundry. However, they moved in together before they were married and because Dad walked on such a high moral ground, he couldn't resist making a comment about my sister's living arrangements. He said to me, "I don't care if your sister wants to leave so she can whore around." Mind you, she was 25 at the time. She didn't care if her father thought she was a whore. She was going to live in peace and quiet and the rent was cheaper. I was actually jealous because although I was married, I was foolish enough to rent from my father believing that he would treat me differently than he had my older sister when she lived under his watchful eyes just a few years before.

When he ran out of kids to rip off, he had to actually put out a legitimate "For Rent" sign. My father's tenants ranged from degreed professionals to crack dealers. If a person flashed a few bucks and told a good story, he handed them the keys. As time went by, he was more likely to offer a bartering deal to a guy digging through trash on his tree lawn because he thought he could get cheap labor. He never did background checks on anyone so he was extremely lucky if a tenant turned out to be a decent human being.

What always happened is what you might expect. His tenants were usually late with their rent or didn't pay at all, wrecked the place and left tons of their shit when they had to make a run for it in the middle of the night. They left cars, bikes, clothes, household goods, food, tree stumps and appliances. The problem wasn't that these tenants left their crap. That happens all of the time to landlords. The problem was that my father saw "value" in their shit so he rarely, if ever, got rid of it.

Cindy and I always asked him how he managed to be left standing with his dick in his hand when a tenant disappeared. We knew the truth was that he was a crummy landlord with high expectations and no regard for anyone's privacy. When tenants had enough of his demands and bullshit, they left. He then spent months chasing them down for unpaid rent or damage to his property. The longest he spent on one guy was seven years. The guy owed him $2,000 and he chased him to Florida and still couldn't get his money.

Lou's tenants, with the exception of his own children, always got the better of him. There was one guy who got the best deal of all. This prick managed to be in arrears to my parents for over $12,000 in back rent and all of his utilities were in my father's name. His bills came to my parents' house because his credit was so bad he couldn't get them turned on in his own name.

His name was Peter and my father thought he was a golden goose who would lay him solid gold eggs. Trust me, there was more going in this guy's ass than coming out so you could forget about gold eggs shooting out of his ass. Peter was something special to our father that I don't think any of us would ever fully understand. Part of me doesn't want to know. Peter must have had a great story because he offered nothing else. He was a leach and my father was too stupid to see it. He took advantage of our parents for almost 20 years.

Peter lived on the second floor in the west property. He was about 30 when he moved in with his gay friends and 50 when he was taken out in a body bag. He chain smoked and was a pack rat. He was openly gay and I was sure my father would find any reason to throw him out. Peter was tall and dark and fussy like only gay men can be. Peter called often to complain about his fellow tenant's noise or some mess and Lou always came to his rescue.

Peter had our father convinced that he had some online music business that was on the verge of taking off. My father did not know whether or not this was true because he knew nothing of the internet plus he thought Peter walked on water so whatever he said must be straight from the gospel. The worst part is that dad complained constantly to Cindy and me about his "Peter" problems. He would tell us he was a "whiny little fag" who needed too much attention and could never pay his rent. We could not stand the stories because the minute we gave him advice like, "Evict him and don't look back" he would shut us down.

Lou finally evicted him. I am sure it was after some lovers' quarrel those two had. You see, Cindy and I could never figure out why our father let Peter live there for so long and simultaneously continued to be such a drain emotionally and financially. They had to be lovers. That was it. In our own twisted minds our father had to be in love with this guy. He would never cut this "fag" a deal unless he was emotionally attached. It was easier to believe that our father was a homosexual than believe he was a nice guy trying to help someone out.

At any rate, no one gave a shit at this point because Peter was gone! We knew our father would lose a few bucks in unpaid rent but this bottom feeder was out of our lives. We were done talking about this guy—or so we thought. A few months went by and the conversation about "Peter" surfaced again. I couldn't believe what I was hearing. He let this asshole back in the apartment! His justification was that he would rather keep him close in case there was any money to be had. My father was going to be first in line.

This routine of breaking up and getting back together with my father went on for years. Dad would get pissed, throw him out and Peter would tell another story and get right back in. Peter died in 2003 from cancer and complications from AIDS. In typical fashion, Lou tried desperately to get Peter to sign papers leaving him whatever Peter had left. He had nothing more than outdated VHS tapes and CDs, cassettes, old cable-knit sweaters, and sweat-encrusted, smoke-stained furniture. If you added it all together it didn't amount to $1,000.

Lou was pissed, however, because Peter's brother Michael came to pick the bones first. Michael and his friend took whatever was worth more than $10 and left the rest to scavengers. There was no will that named our father as his beneficiary. Peter had nothing and if he did, his brother took it quickly. It made no sense to my mother or me or Cindy why dad would want any of his crap. There might have been a few movies or CDs that were worth a look-see but the rest needed to be donated to the Salvation Army.

Weeks and months evaporated before our eyes and his belongings still occupied a three-bedroom suite. During this time Lou carefully inventoried the clothes, kitchen items, music and miscellaneous knick-knacks. He carefully stacked Peter's pants in a box and marked the size. He hung his shirts on hangers and put all of his socks in a box. He paraded his kids and step kids through there to see if there was anything we wanted. I really think he wanted us to be proud of his recent score, ooh and ahh at all the cool shit and marvel at all the money waiting to be made. It was excruciating.

My nephew wanted a poker set to which dad said, "Keep your fucking hands off that." He tried to sell clothes to my brother-in-laws and give my husband used socks. It was a joke. Cindy and I took a few things out of spite. We walked out leaving the entire mess to dad who we figured would get rid of this dead guy's stuff in a few months.

In 2008, mom came home from the hospital recovering from a staph infection. It was the wintertime and as usual their house was chilly. 65 degrees was too cold for mom. She really needed 72 and a sweater. Cindy and I told her we were going to go out to get her a few new outfits for the house. New clothes always make a person feel better and we knew she needed cheering up. Dad was in one of his non-stop foul moods so we knew we would have to buy her what she wanted and worry about the money later.

When we told her what we planned mom said, "Your father already has a few things for me."

Cindy said, "Like what? I want to come and see." Cindy went across the street to look at what he had for her because she and I both knew there was no way he went out to buy her anything.

When Cindy asked where the clothes were, mom pointed to a chair in the corner of the dining room. Cindy marched right over there and without even touching them, she said, "Oh my God. He wants you to wear Peter's clothes?!" Mom didn't say a word. Six years after Peter died, he was still trying to use his stuff to their advantage. This guy's stuff was still in that apartment and the grotesque part, besides the obvious, was that our father would go there to look around like he was shopping at Walmart. Except in this case it was all free.

It is one thing for dad to try to pawn his tenant's used shit off on strangers. When he does it to family, it's quite another. The fact that Lou expected our mother to wear clothes that belonged to a 6'3" guy who died from AIDS and cancer and was a chain-smoking fool, made Cindy want to kill him with the first thing she could get her hands on. She marched into the kitchen and told him, "Mom doesn't have a problem wearing hand-me-downs, but they at least have to be from a woman and not your dead tenant! What is the matter with you? You're out of your fucking mind if you think I'm going to let that happen." The fact is, he was content wearing Peter's clothes and figured if they were good enough for him, they were good enough for her. We felt so sorry for her that we spent a few hundred dollars that afternoon.

We purchased outfits for her, coincidentally, just before she was admitted into an assisted living facility. She looked very pretty sitting in her new home wearing her gray sweater jogging suit and her red cotton pant suit. I can't imagine what she would have looked like wearing Peter's flannel shirt and Reebok sweatpants. I also cannot imagine what the nurses would have thought. In addition to the arms and legs being rolled up two feet, she would have stunk like a pile of wet ashes.

The time arrived where Cindy and I had to set up her private room at the assisted living facility. This meant taking a few things from their home to make her feel comfortable at her new home and buy what we didn't have. I mentioned to Dad that it would be nice if she had a small table and chairs for her visitors to sit with her and have coffee. I asked him if we could take the small dinette with matching red chairs that Peter left behind. Mind you, this set, which was worth about $150 was still sitting in the apartment that Peter died in six years prior.

Forget the fact that dad lost almost $40,000 in rent by storing his shit for so long but what was the big deal in asking him for something that no one was using? Peter wasn't going to sit at this table anymore. When I asked him if Cindy and I could move it for mom, he said, "Absolutely not." What he forgot was that we knew where his box of money was. With mom's permission, we took what we needed and went to a second-hand furniture store and bought her what we wanted. It wasn't until a month passed and she was settled in her assisted living facility that he asked us, "Why didn't you put Peter's table and chairs in her room instead of buying something new?" I put my head in my hands and shook my head. I was staring at a pair of scissors and felt myself wanting to rise up and finish him off. Maybe he thought I should ask him the same question 14 fucking times before he finally said "yes."

After Mom passed away Cindy and I knew we would have the task of donating her things to charity. On her death bed she said, "Make sure you give my things to a nice woman's shelter. Don't let him sell my stuff." We didn't realize that Dad would want us to come over there within a week of her dying and pack up her clothes. He had kept Peter's apartment intact for over seven years. It looked like a shrine, yet he couldn't wait to get mom's things out of the house she lived in for over 40 years.

As we sat there looking through her clothes, every outfit reminded Cindy and me of a birthday or Christmas or a day at the park. We cried as we shoved her things in plastic bags. He sat there with his critical eye and nasty expression and wondered what we could get if we sold it all. I reminded him of her last two requests, in case he had conveniently forgotten. “Mom said two things before she died. First, donate my things to a woman's shelter. Second, bury me with my first husband. Now, leave us alone. Seriously. Don't make me get ugly. I'm sad and you're pissing me off.”

It never mattered what mom’s opinion was of my father’s relationship with Peter. She never openly questioned why Lou treated him with such respect and deserved his protection above all else. I would have been furious at his justification for Peter’s inability to pay his rent because it simply meant the rest of the family would have to tow the line. The hot spot was that Lou was charitable towards Peter while the rest of us, including his wife, were subjected frequently to the “I don’t have enough money” lecture. Had Peter paid his rent, our mother would never have had to worry about what the end of her life was going to cost. If Lou had donated Peter’s things to charity the second he died, Lou would have pocketed an extra $50,000 by renting out his apartment.

After seven years he still had not parted with Peter's possessions. My father left his junk in that apartment and never made any real effort to dispose of it and move on. Our mother's clothes were gone 48 hours after she died. In fact, every single apartment he had available for rent was empty. This was mind jarring and like everything else Cindy and I had to take care of, we knew we would have to lie and sneak around to get anything done. Peter's shit was going to disappear along with every old appliance, bundles of lathe, linoleum, paneling, clothes, household goods. Everything.

For seven years Cindy and I had to watch him try to play

"store." Every time he called about Peter's stuff, I thought I would go insane. "No, I do not" was the stock answer when he asked if we wanted or needed boxers, socks, pants that were 34x36, XXL sweaters, red dishes and 25-year-old VHS tapes. He literally tried every consignment shop and resale store within a ten-mile radius of his house and everyone said "no thanks." Peter was a chain smoker and all of his stuff smelled like swamp water. Peter's stuff disappeared as well as every piece of garbage left behind in two houses over a 30-year time frame.

The idea was that we would take Lou's car and therefore he would have no idea what we were doing at his rental properties. It worked for awhile until one day he showed up with his neighbor whom he had asked for a ride. He pulled in the driveway and almost ran into the back of a 30-yard dumpster. Cindy and I along with our sons and their friends had filled it beyond its capacity. All of the garbage and junk he had collected in one house over 30 years was overflowing. Peter's shit was sitting on the top. He looked like a rabid animal. His eyes were wild, his fists were clenched and he was starting to foam at the mouth. Our father's days of playing "store" were over. I wanted to run. Cindy and I felt good about what we were doing while we simultaneously wanted to barf.

He spent the next two hours screaming like a hyena and swinging his cane yelling, "Goddamn you two!" over and over. He asked, "Where is the shopping cart? Where is all the lathe? Where is the old toilet?"

All we kept saying was, "It's gone. All that shit is under four tons of the rest of the garbage from these crap holes." We kindly asked his neighbor to get him out of there before he had a heart attack or killed one of us. We also said, "Don't torture yourself by bringing him back here again."

We continued to plow over him for two years while we got

another dumpster for the other house and just kept tossing shit from every window until we filled it. In the end we threw out eight tons of garbage and 13 appliances. Cindy and I crawled around and put a face lift on six suites. Our hands look liked we had been dragging them through gravel. He never said thank you. He just stuck his hand out for the rent. He never saw a dime of rent from that moment forward.

Looking back, the task might have been daunting for a mere mortal but for us it was easy. Most of his tenants were scumbags so all Cindy and I said was, "Chuck it." I hated the thought of keeping other people's junk. Trust me, if it was worth something they would have taken it with them when they stuck you in the ass for half a month's rent when they split in the middle of the night.

the wild pair

Have you ever stood in front of a mirror and wondered if you were dressed alright? If you have a brain you have. Checking yourself out before you leave the house so the rest of us can look at you is nothing short of a public service. Bulges, wrinkles, sags, stains, tears and ugly shoes are unacceptable. In fact, no woman should be seen in public in sweatpants or Crocs.

My mother had impeccable taste. I remember her looking like Lauren Bacall in *How to Marry a Millionaire*, with her hair perfectly done, her cocktail dress hanging over her curves, her shoes always matching her purse and smelling of Youth Dew by Estee Lauder. She looked beautiful in her fur and long white gloves when she'd leave with my father to have drinks and dinner. They might dance a little too. To this day, I always dress with her style in mind and it never fails me. "The idea," our mother said, "is to always dress to impress."

I can remember my father polishing his wing tips with flair that only time served in the military could provide. He could get lost just shining his shoes. He looked like Rock Hudson when he left the house to take my mother on a date. Both of my parents looked marvelous together.

He carried a crowbar under the front seat of his car, bragged about his arsenal and trained all of his dogs to hate black people. (For the record, I don't know how he did that, except to say, if you were black you should not step on our property.) He cussed out every driver who crossed his path and sometimes shaved with a straight razor. This is how we thought everyone lived. I thought my father was a bad-ass.

When Cindy and I were young, around ten or so, my mother was on one of her shopping excursions with her Aunt Frances. They frequently took evening bus trips downtown to shop at Higbee's and Halle's. This was fine since it usually meant Mom would bring home bags of new clothes even if we couldn't wear them until next year. The bad part was that this left us alone with Dad. A typical night alone meant we were in the kitchen doing homework or coloring quietly waiting until our savior's return. Cindy and I hated it when she left. It was like the breath left our body and we could only breathe upon her return. It was more like a sigh of relief when she walked through the front door.

We usually stayed in the kitchen while they shopped because Lou kept the house dark. We never really knew where he was and really didn't care. We watched the clock. Our older sister was usually out with her friends or in her own bedroom. Hiding in a dark house while Cindy and I stayed in the kitchen went on for years until we were old enough to leave the house with our friends and stay out until all hours of the night. By then, we could not have cared less what he did alone in the dark. Frankly, I didn't really want to know.

Dad was very open about wearing panty hose during the colder months. The first time I can recall seeing these on his legs Cindy and I were probably nine or ten. He used to tell us that they kept his legs warm and helped with his circulation. He had to think of something because he caught the "what the fuck" look I was giving him at the tender age of ten. Can you imagine a guy six feet tall and weighing 220 pounds feeling warm and cozy in his nylons? Now listen to me. This is total bullshit. They make support hose for varicose veins but there isn't a pair of nylons that do jack shit to keep your legs warm.

I found his justification for wearing panty hose very creepy but suppressed it because I thought, "Who gives a shit as long as he never wears them to one of our basketball games." The truth was that Cindy and I did give a shit. He shifted between doing yard work and the silky-smooth feeling he got from his L'eggs. I think Cindy and I knew something was screwy but just could not put it all together. Besides, we had better things to do and the truth was too scary.

Our parents stopped sleeping in the same room in the late '70s after his mother died. A spare bedroom was open and mom claimed it for herself. Even when they did sleep in the same room, they slept in separate beds. She couldn't wait to be away from his tossing and turning and his shit sitting everywhere; stacks of books, boxes of shoes, shirts, socks and jars of change.

His room was always messy and she preferred all of her things neatly in place. But, mixed in neatly with his Florsheim shoes were boxes from The Wild Pair. In the '70s, this was a pretty cool shoe store—for women! I might have been tempted to look in these boxes but never did because we were taught to respect each other's privacy. Lou always told us, "Mind your own fucking business."

When we were in our 20s and in college, Cindy and I came and went pretty frequently. We had part-time jobs, college course work and a social life, which meant Mom and Dad never really knew when we would show up. Now, if I had a habit that I didn't want anyone to know about I would be sure about the schedules of the rest of the family before I got busted with my skirt up.

I don't know where I was on this particular day, but Cindy showed up at home at the wrong time. She had just finished a class at school and didn't have any other place to be. A nap probably sounded pretty good and she was on her way upstairs to take advantage of a little free time. When she came through the back door and then through the kitchen to the foyer, she just happened to catch sight of a pair of bright red "come fuck me pumps," attached to a set of hairy, thick ankles disappearing up our front stairs. Her nap just turned into a nightmare. I would have cried myself to sleep.

Cindy never said a word to me or to Mom and certainly didn't bring it up over dinner. Dad didn't say a word either and reappeared moments later as though nothing had happened. Unless there was someone else hiding in the house or he had a boyfriend, then that had to have been him wearing those shoes. She quickly put that sight out of her memory as best she could. She would deal with it much later when we would all find out the truth.

She told me about it years later. We talked over and over again about him wearing stockings and this "red shoe" incident and tried to figure out when and especially why he started to dress like his mother. We never came up with a reasonable explanation. We never had the nerve to ask him or Mom how long this had been going on. It would have been easier to just ask, but it made us both really uncomfortable just to think about it let alone let those words pass our lips.

Many years later when we were in our forties and had kids and houses of our own the subject of shoes and panty hose came up. When Mom's health had seriously hampered her ability to keep her house clean, it became my and Cindy's mission to do it for her. We managed to inject ourselves into their lives and their filthy house at least twice a year to embark on some serious back-breaking work. It had more to do with not being able to stand the dust and clutter than really helping them. Whatever our reasons, old habits die hard and our parents benefited. I don't know why Cindy and I would ever willingly go back there to clean. We hated it the first thousand times and it was worse now than when I was a kid.

On the day of reckoning, Lou was in the hospital with some illness, most likely bronchitis. Marie was home alone, which meant Cindy and I could work our magic without his interference. Lou's bedroom was especially a mess. The dust was an inch thick and there were books, jars of quarters and shoe boxes stacked four feet high. Shoes boxes, you say? Did these boxes that said "The Wild Pair" contain old photos or rolled coins? Cindy and I always wondered what was contained in these plain brown boxes with black writing. Fuck his privacy.

Cindy and I were both sick of the charade. We suspected something for many years and today we were going to get our answer. These boxes were hiding in plain sight. Cindy took one box downstairs that contained a smart patent leather number with an ankle strap and a fucking four-inch heel. I couldn't walk in these things if I tried. They were a size 10. Our mother wore a size seven if she was lucky. So, whose shoes were these?

"Mom, who do these fucking shoes belong to?" Cindy asked. By Mom's reaction, you might have thought Cindy asked what day of the week it was or what was for dinner. Mom simply replied, "Well, those are your father's." That was it. I thought I heard Cindy's jaw hit the floor. The door was open and she and I were walking in. Except on the other side I was sure there was no floor and we would fall to our death. With a deep breath, and trying to keep herself calm, Cindy wanted to know the how, what, where, when and especially the why. I stood there with feelings that ranged from disappointment to rage.

Mom tried to explain to us that it was harmless. She said that his mother had always wanted a daughter and ended up with a single child—a son. His mother Mary let his hair grow long and occasionally dressed him in girls' clothes. His father died when he was seven from a burst appendix and this left him without good role models. His mother was a little eccentric and a classic kleptomaniac. He knew she pinched items from every dime store she could. She had more rhinestone-encrusted jewelry than the queen of England. He didn't have a father guiding him but a string of uncles that he claimed picked on him. He needed a father's love just like we did. Ironic, wasn't it?

Was all of this enough to cause him to cross those tracks? I can barely speak the word "transvestite." It makes me sick when I associate that word with him. Not because he had this harmless habit but because it now made everything he did and said especially hypocritical. I am not so misinformed that I cannot comprehend that this behavior borders on a type of mental illness. Neither am I cruel enough to think that all men who choose this activity are sick, maladjusted perverts. But it was the simple fact that it was my father who, with such a secret to hide put us in front of his highly tuned lens daily. Now I know why he was always so hard on everyone. He was so afraid that he would be perceived as weak, unmanly and out of control. He was afraid of himself, his mother, his kids, his friends and his wife. He was afraid we would find out.

So he would try to overpower us not with knowledge but with the simple fact that he was our father. He pounded his fists or screamed or simply walked out of a room and left poor Mom standing there with this sad, shocked look on her face. Even while he faced the end of his life, he communicated in bellows, temper tantrums and threats. I sat in front of him one hundred times during the last five years of his life with the word "transvestite" sitting on the tip of my tongue. Every time he criticized me or screamed at me I swear I was ready. However, I choked back the temptation of telling him we all knew about his secret. It seemed too cruel.

Our mother Marie helped him shop for matching outfits at May Company or Halle's. Can you imagine that scene? They're both flipping through racks looking for just the right blouse to match a "must have" skirt. Every time I try to imagine this scene I am immediately redirected to thoughts of Norman Bates. I cannot escape it. Marie said it was harmless. This was how she justified it. "He never wore this stuff out in public."

So fucking what? That made it better? I imagined him sitting in his green Naugahyde chair, crossing his legs perfectly fashioned, sipping a martini and doing what? Watching television!? What the hell was Mom doing? She said she sat with him and let him do his thing. What was his "thing" exactly? Did he ever get up to walk into the kitchen for a refill? Did they ever have sex while he was all dressed up with no place to go? How could you not laugh your ass off. He must have looked like George C. Scott in a dress.

His habit might also explain how he thought he could get away with telling us how to walk in high heels. Christ, he actually knew something about it. I remember him having Cindy and me walk across the living room over and over again in wooden platform heels when we were about 16. He drove us 25 miles to Beachwood Mall to buy shoes that he fully intended to tell us how to walk in. I bet he was dying to say, "Listen a goddamn minute. Don't walk so duck-footed. And remember to lengthen your leg with each step. Do not keep your knees bent. And for Christ's sake, if you can't handle the height of the heel then don't wear them at all."

Wanting to dress like Rosemary Clooney might explain why we never had a curfew in high school and why he preferred to stay home and drink. And as long as his underage daughters were out getting drunk at high-school parties he was free. He could do his "thing" with the curtains drawn while downing one martini after another. He must have despised his need to wear high heels and a skirt so much that it required a fifth of Beefeaters to get through it. I don't wonder anymore why he was always so nasty and bitter. He hated who his mother wanted him to be and what he had eventually become.

Sometimes I wish the dogs would have talked. No. I take that back. Just thinking about what my father did is creepy enough. No one ever wants to know about their parents' sex life or any of the other kinky shit they did behind closed doors. I swear if my mother ever told me they had sex while he was dressed like that I would have eaten a whole box of rat poison.

It wasn't until my kids and Cindy's kids got much older that I let the cat out of the bag. I was a little shocked that they weren't completely mortified at the news but in hindsight, they didn't really know their grandfather that well so I was confident that all of them could easily reconcile what we were telling them. Our boys had the attitude that as long as he didn't wear this shit in front of our friends while we were growing up then who cared. Wow. Our kids really aren't judgmental and are totally well-adjusted. I was proud of them as they never poked fun at my father.

At first, Cindy and I were horrified at the thought of our father dressing up like Maude and we were very angry. We found him to be completely judgmental of the actions of every single person he knew. He never hesitated to point out what he considered was a flaw be it emotional or physical. He put all of us under a microscope so that he could pick away at our self confidence and character. Yet, here was this huge thing that was odd for our time and he pandered it off by saying, "so what."

As the years have passed, Cindy and I have eased off of our feelings of betrayal. At this point in our lives, knowing that our father enjoyed wearing women's clothes isn't that earth shattering. After all, he didn't hurt anyone and there was no point in making a big deal out of something that by today's standards is no big deal at all. I really don't care what people do in their private lives. The unresolved conflict for me is that I know in my heart that had my father been a nicer man I really wouldn't have minded his attraction to five-inch stripper shoes and wrap dresses.

reservation for one

As mom got older she seemed to experience greater physical pain with each passing year. You could hear her coming down the stairs from the time she was 50 because her knees would grind so much from the arthritis that was taking over her body. Over time, she used a dump truck full of Aspercreme and Ben-gay to ward off her pain. To this day, I can't smell that shit without thinking of her. The truth is that I have a tube of each in my nightstand. Each time I feel the need to frost my shoulders with this stuff I ask my husband if he minds the smell. I don't think it's sexy and I wonder if my kids will be thinking I am the same train wreck my mother was at 55. Grinding, wincing, muscle spasms, headaches, naps and painkillers. I can smell the nursing home already.

By the time Cindy and I were 30 years old, mom confessed to taking in excess of 20 acetaminophen a day for pain. It's a wonder her kidneys did not shut down much sooner. Add to that a house that was ice-cold during the winter months, had no air conditioning in the summer and was loaded with dust and you've got a prescription for major illness. Oh, and she had to live with him.

By 1992, Marie was diagnosed with COPD, type II diabetes, high cholesterol and arthritis in every joint in her body. By the year 2000 she had two stents put in and a pacemaker for her failing heart. Since Cindy and I were young adults, our goal was to ease our mother's suffering. We hated to see her in distress. To that end, we tried desperately for over 15 years to convince Lou to get out of that huge house and make living easier for Marie. Condo living or a nice ranch would have suited her perfectly. Moving from his house on Lake Avenue was simply seen as a step down in societal ranks. He would not consider it.

After several attempts to appeal to his sense of reason, the conversation always ended quickly with his last words being, "shut up about it" or "get off my fucking back." By 2002 or so, this left us no choice but to make him clean up the home they insisted on dying in. We offered to pull out the old carpet, tile the kitchen floor and paint or wallpaper the bedrooms that had bare plaster walls for at least ten years. Cindy and I had "people" and assured him we could get this done in less than a week's time.

Lou was the human stop-gap. No one I ever knew could shove it into reverse quicker. I have never known a human being who could more quickly halt forward progress. This applied to everything, not just spring cleaning. He could not make a decision about anything. He always had to think about whatever it was that required the ability to pull the trigger. He used to refer to this as "contemplating my navel." So, that is exactly what he did. He spent hours and days contemplating the state of his belly button while the world continued to function around him.

One day my husband and Cindy's husband attempted to help him clean out the garage, which they did spectacularly. There was a big pile of crap ready to be moved to the tree lawn. Garbage day was less than 18 hours away. Hell, in Lakewood, nothing lasted on your tree lawn longer than an hour any way. This was especially true if you lived on Lake Avenue as they did. The trick in our case was to get it out there. When the sun went down, people literally drove up and down that four-mile stretch in our city waiting to see some golden nugget abandoned on the tree lawn. It could have been rolled up carpet padding or a box of dirt but because it came from a Lake Avenue home, it was a treasure. The dumpster divers pounced on it like wild cats on a field mouse.

Lou had a three-car garage that he couldn't park a car in. What's sad is that over the years he let a Buick Electra 225 from 1968 and a Pink Buick (from probably 1956 or so) completely rust out in the driveway because he couldn't part with mountains of useless shit that he carefully stored in the garage. The dogs were eventually climbing on the black Buick like mountain goats. The mice had a permanent home. The only reason it was ever towed out of their backyard was because Cindy was getting married (in 1988) and was having her wedding shower at their home. She frankly told him, "Get that thing the hell out of here."

As the thought of losing his "stuff" on garage clean-out day forever loomed, he slammed on the brakes and made the boys put it all back. Seeing all of his things piled in the driveway was making him break out in hives. He was more content surrounding himself by marine grade plywood that dogs had pissed on, rusted iron from the Granada Theater, broken ladders and one coffin than having a garage he could park in. One can imagine then how difficult it was to help them improve their living quarters. My mother never asked for or insisted on a higher standard of living for herself and he never volunteered it.

It seemed as though every year since 1998 Marie was hospitalized with pneumonia or bronchitis at the very least. Her house was either too cold or too hot and always dusty. It was very likely that "the house" was a sick house and thus exacerbated her illnesses. It usually took a trip to a hospital to get her well. By 2002, the linoleum on their kitchen floor was missing in many places and there was no paint on the walls. He had taken the cabinet doors off with the intention of refinishing them. At the very least, she deserved to have her kitchen put back together.

While she was getting well this time, we insisted he clean up the mess he started in the kitchen 20 years prior.

Lou had purchased 8" ceramic tiles and grout that he intended to put in the kitchen. However, he spent so many years and so much time contemplating not only his navel but everyone else's that the grout hardened like concrete. You couldn't even pick up the bags because they were so heavy. Cindy's husband had a "tile guy" that would lay the tile in time for Marie's return. Lou had already painted the walls and ceiling in the kitchen, so we were ready to bring in "our guy."

These tiles were nothing special. They were mottled colors of beige, tan and brown. Lou decided that these tiles had to be laid in a certain pattern because of the arrows on the back. He thought that the dark brown lines on the front of the tile should connect from piece to piece. He opened every box and laid them on the living room floor and painstakingly figured out "the pattern." This took days and no matter what we said to convince him he was wasting his time, he would yell, "Goddamn it. Shut up!"

He was so proud of himself he could not wait to show the "tile guy" what he'd figured out. The "tile guy" humored him and basically ignored whatever pattern Lou thought there was and laid the tiles himself. Lou watched him the entire time trying to catch him making a mistake. Of course, it never happened and Marie got her new floor. It only took 15 years from the time he bought the tiles to the time the floor was laid.

It was about 1998 and mom was hospitalized longer than normal this time so we took the opportunity to try to get more work done. Cindy and I were on a roll. We decided that bare plaster walls were too fucking ugly to look at anymore. We only looked at them occasionally when we went upstairs to see how cold it was. Poor Mom had to look at that mess daily. It was time to hang wallpaper in the bedrooms, especially hers. This, of course, was going to be nothing short of a miracle. If there was a chance she was going to die at home it wasn't going to be in a room that looked like a bomb shelter.

Somehow Cindy and I convinced Lou it was the right thing to do and we would be done in a few days. Only this time it was going to require more workers than just Cindy and me. It was time to call in reinforcements. Mike had smartened up long ago and moved far enough away so that he could not be "guilted" into menial labor, even if it did benefit his mother. Debbie, understandably, could not be around this nightmare. They would cheer Cindy, Greg and me on from the sidelines, enjoying our tales of horror at once again having to "perform" in front of him liked trained circus animals. Greg and his wife were always willing to pitch in to work as long as Cindy and I handled all of the pleading and arguing beforehand. They had a deal.

There was a huge hole in Mom's bedroom wall that Greg was going to have to patch. While he did that, I started to paper. I was no professional but knew enough to get the job done to pass Dad's inspection since I am certain he never hung one sheet. Our sister-in-law and Cindy were the "go get it gals," changing water and cleaning up behind us. The trick was to get Lou to do anything other than watch us. Fat friggin' chance. We couldn't even get him to leave to buy us lunch.

We were sacrificing tons of our time and you should have seen the look on his face. He looked like a caged animal. He looked pissed and disgusted. We were helping him and he could not have cared less. We thought about trying to get him drunk so maybe he would sleep through it. He was wise to us since we got him drunk before to do what we wanted so he stuck to drinking his lemonade. The best part though was that he knew nothing about wall papering so he could say absolutely nothing.

The wallpaper Cindy and I chose was meant to stay with the

character of the house. We knew that my mother loved flowers and would be thrilled with the choice we made for her room. The paper had a tea-stained background with giant poppies. They were burnt orange and we had the perfect fabric so that we could make her curtains, valances and matching pillows. We rearranged her furniture and set up a new TV.

We were very proud of the work we'd done in such a short period of time. We wall papered and decorated three bedrooms over the period of five days. Her room was especially breathtaking and we knew she would cry when she saw it.

He, of course, stood over us the entire time grumbling and reminding us that we made her room look like a whore house.

As Greg and I feverishly tried to finish, my sister-n-law and Cindy found themselves trying to complete a different mission. Even though the home was huge, there was not enough room for multiple walkers, bed pans and those elevated potty seats. Every closet we opened contained one of these things! One bed pan, we're sure, was my grandmother's, who died in 1978. They collected other things, like thread-bare blankets and sheets, suppositories and old television sets. They still had the clothes and possessions of Marie's dead aunt and shit from one of his dead tenants.

That was it. We had seen enough. When Lou had his back turned, Cindy and our sister-n-law shoved all this useless crap into 30-gallon garbage bags. Cindy quickly ran each full bag downstairs and threw it into the front bushes. Cindy's husband then ran across the street and grabbed the bag and threw it in his pick-up truck. By the time Cindy and Beth were done, they must have filled ten bags. I am a relatively nosy neighbor and if I had seen this, I would have called the police. It must have looked like we were stealing from him in broad daylight.

If Lou had seen any of this, he would have personally

inspected each bag and then put it all back where we found it. We were laughing uncontrollably at actually having pulled off this caper. He never suspected a thing. However, we would be forced later to lie miserably when he'd ask us if we knew where his 15-year-old suppositories were. We were certain that if and when the time came that either one of them needed a bed pan, they would be using one at a nursing home.

When Marie was finally discharged from the hospital, we were completely finished with our task. Cindy, Greg and I had redecorated three of her bedrooms. We were forbidden to go in Lou's room. If we got within breathing distance, he would yell at us to keep the hell out. So his room would stay dark and lifeless. Lou played along with the surprise and didn't shoot his face off to her on the way home from the hospital. Cindy, Beth, Greg and I were waiting in mom's bedroom with the door closed. She had new bedding, window treatments, fresh flowers and a red velvet chair by her bed.

When she opened the door, we yelled surprise, which almost gave her another heart attack. Maybe hiding from her was a bad idea. At any rate, she quickly sat on her bed and started to cry. She said, "This is the nicest thing anyone has ever done for me." Can you imagine that being the nicest thing in 78 years? She thanked us profusely for she knew what we had to endure to get that work done. She couldn't wait to go to sleep and wake up in a room that didn't look like the inside of a plywood coffin.

She liked the other rooms too because we reintroduced some color into her life. Lou wanted to paint all the walls either institutional white or cream. This would have been fine but the walls were cracked everywhere and to repair them would have taken longer than my patience could withstand. So Cindy and I proceeded to pick colors our mother would like and confidently ignored Lou's repeated protests. This was going to happen even if it was over his dead body.

She loved to look at her new rooms as she passed them on her way to the bathroom. However, Lou had this habit of shutting the bedroom doors. This was fine in the winter as they could not afford to heat all of the extra rooms. But in the spring and summer? Cindy and I walked through that house opening windows and doors to let the fresh air in and he would yell at us in his usual fashion and quickly shut them. What was his aversion to sunlight and fresh air? You would think he was Dracula for god's sake, preferring the acrid smell that accumulates in the absence of a warm sun and breezy spring air.

In 2003, Marie was hospitalized again for her usual bout of bronchitis. However, this time for extra excitement she was being treated for a mild heart attack. This would result in two heart procedures and loads of antibiotics. She bought herself a two-week stay at Club ICU.

Cindy and I did our customary begging and pleading for Lou to at least let us take out the old carpet. The wool carpet was original to the house, built in 1920. You could not allow yourself to think of all the dirt, dog hair, piss, shit and vomit that had been on that carpet. It was impossible to professionally clean as it would disintegrate the moment a drop of water touched it. Removing this ratty old shit would cut down on the dust so that she could breathe better. Damn it, she deserved it. The thought of ripping out this carpet though had the same effect on him as any other change.

You should have seen the hysterical fit he had when we asked him to put an air conditioner in her bedroom. Lou pushed all of her trinkets and photos onto the floor, bitching the entire time. He barked, "The house cools off at night." Or "Your mother isn't complaining." Or this priceless remark, "Being hot and sweating is all in your head." Right about then I was thinking about a bullet in his. It was the middle of July and you could cut the humidity with a knife. If Cindy and I hadn't demanded he take care of this, Marie would have endured it. As it was, she slept with a cool washcloth across her chest and a fan blowing on her. What's pathetic is that we had to have this knock-down, drag-out fight with him every fucking June for ten years.

Come to think of it, nothing really changed since Cindy and I were kids. Lou insisted that one exhaust fan in his bedroom window caused enough of a breeze to blow around the outside of the house and into our bedroom windows. We thought he was crazy. We were sweating our asses off every night and one fan for 3,500 square feet was unacceptable. It never occurred to us as children to want air conditioning. That would have never happened anyway. However, would one fan per person have been too much to ask?

Greg was determined to figure out how to get his own air in the attic where he had to sleep. In 1960 when he was in seventh grade, Greg engineered a regular wind-up clock to make his own fan run on a timer. He took the guts out of the clock so the alarm would not go off and replaced the springs with a pulley from an erector set. He tied a string around the toggle switch on the fan and then to the pulley. Greg had his fan for two hours every night and Lou never knew a thing.

In 2003, Cindy decided to play hard ball and flat out refused to let mom go home if he would not comply with our demands. He was going to let us pull out this putrid floor covering, or else. Cindy would have her live across the street with her until he complied. This threat turned out badly for Cindy. Lou let her stay at Cindy's for six weeks. He was not going to be told what to do and when to do it.

What was so appalling was that while mom enjoyed hot showers, home cooked meals and peace and quiet, he showed up daily for coffee in the morning and dinner in the afternoon. This also meant a martini or two made with top shelf booze. It was difficult to envision and must have been hard for Cindy. Difficult not because she wasn't happy to do what was right for our mother, but difficult because he refused to help and had the unmitigated crust to show up daily to visit his wife. Seriously, who the fuck did he think he was?

It had been two weeks already and there was no sign of Marie going back home. It didn't even matter now that we never got the carpet yanked. Cindy wanted her house back. Marie and Lou were turning her home into a bed and breakfast. Cindy spent her time cooking and serving with a smile. This would have been acceptable except they had a perfectly good house across the street. It had running water and heat. Lou needed to take his wife home.

One particularly lovely afternoon, Cindy's in-laws came for a visit. They were lovely people, unassuming and quiet. From his dining room window, it didn't take Lou long to see Cindy's father-in-law and our mother enjoying a beverage on Cindy's front porch. He was coming. Seeing that, Cindy automatically made his martini (gin, vermouth and two olives) and stood there waiting. It never took long for tempers to flare, especially when patience was wearing thin.

As we got older, we were less inclined to believe any of what he said and found many of his thought sequences and stories simply illogical. It should have been easy to turn our backs on a pointless argument, but it was not in our nature to back down. We had opinions too. We argued logic with someone who was illogical and reason with someone unreasonable. He never conceded his opinion and neither did we. Or if we did, it was to appease my mother, who openly disapproved of our discussions and looked depressed whenever we engaged in conversation. She was a peacekeeper. Therefore, conceding for the sake of peace was maddening. She rarely stood up to Lou to voice her own opinion and instead resigned herself to quiet mumblings for him to just shut up.

This day was no different. Arguments occurred each time Lou said something ridiculous or offensive, which was often. Tempers exploded almost immediately. On this day, it was not clear how the argument started. Cindy caught the edge of some comment and that was it. Anyone else in the vicinity was an innocent bystander who hopefully knew enough to get out of the way.

This time Cindy backed him into some unrecoverable corner. He had no place to run so he proceeded to end the argument in typical fashion by raising his voice and telling her to "get out of here." It dawned on her that they were all on her porch and he was drinking her gin. It's not in her character to be outwardly rude but given the position Cindy was in, he left her no choice. My mother taught us tolerance and forgiveness and knew that Cindy had been pushed too far. She told him to leave and take his wife with him this time. She hated to say it.

As was usually the case with a bad ending, Cindy called me and wanted to know what to do. She said that Mom's expiration date had arrived. We needed to get her back home. First we needed to get Lou out of the house. Remember, we had carpet to get rid of. So, as luck would have it (or maybe there was a full moon and the powers that be knew we were up to something sinister), Lou announced the following day that he wasn't feeling well. He was going to call the doctor.

Cindy had a very good relationship with our parents' physician. She quickly called his office and told the nurse that the doctor needed to find something (anything) wrong with him. We needed him in the hospital for at least two days. We personally felt that the carpet was so old and nasty that it should have been able to walk out of their house by itself. We could not wait any longer for it to develop legs, so we helped it along.

When Lou returned from the doctor, he looked completely rejected. As Cindy, mom and I sat looking at him with the best concerned look we could muster, he proceeded to tell us that his doctor thought he might have bronchitis and should go to the hospital for x-rays. We put on our best "I can't believe it!" faces and played the game. That doctor was good. We assured him that he was most likely fine and that all he needed was some antibiotics and he would be sent home. He was pissed at the thought of having to waste his time and we agreed with him of course. (When you think of it, here's a guy who's 82 at the time and did absolutely nothing all day. Unless you count sorting screws in the basement or watching *The Price is Right*, he had plenty of time to get checked out.).

Since it was Friday, we convinced him he should hurry to get to the ER before dinner time. After all, Friday evening was a time for drunks and he might be there all night if he didn't get a move on. He agreed. Cindy was compassionate enough to drive him there as we all know no one wants to sit in an ER alone. What bitches we were. We were like the *Witches of Eastwick*. All three of us knew he was getting set up but simply did not give a shit. Even if no one admitted him, we would at least get three or four hours of peace and quiet. The stars were about to align.

It was time to assemble to troops. No one had any idea if Lou would buy himself an extended stay or not so we could waste no time. I got on the phone and called husbands, brothers-in-law, sons and nephews. Marie, of course, was a nervous wreck as she thought we would all pay a terrible price tag for our disobedience. She was in on it so if it got bad enough, she was going under the bus with us. He told us, "Do not touch a goddamn thing while I'm gone." Right.

We listened well enough as children but as we aged, we learned to take matters into our own hands. This translated into, "ignore the old man and do what we wanted." We told him we had more important things to do than clean up his messes and that he had nothing to worry about.

Before Cindy headed off to the ER, she made a point of telling Mom that she would have to make up some lie to get Cindy out of the ER and back to help. Apparently, we are a family with a talent for lying. We've known this for some time so constructing a story that Lou could choke back was no problem. Within minutes of arriving at the ER, Cindy got a phone call from Mom, explaining that "Louis had fallen and hit his head pretty hard." Although there was no blood, Mom thought Cindy should come home and tend to her injured child. That was it. Lou could not argue with the "story" which meant Cindy could leave with no guilt. Lou was a grown-up and her baby needed her.

We were appalled at the condition of the carpet. It disintegrated each time we pulled it away from the carpet tacks. My oldest nephew brought his pick-up truck, which took no time to fill. By the time we were done, we filled the bed of his truck with so much carpet that it was low-riding to within six inches of the ground. We were laughing, sweating and drinking the entire time. Cindy and I knew that no matter who helped, it would be our heads on the chopping block.

That was fine since we were done being afraid of his big mouth and his empty threats. What would his argument really be? "You are ungrateful, sneaky bitches. How dare you come to my house and clean up my filth so your mother and I can live in a cleaner environment? I wanted to pay someone to pull that shit infested, threadbare rag out and you had the nerve to do it for free? What kind of horrible children are you?" You see, it would not matter what he said. The job needed to be done. That

80-year-old carpet was in a local dump and he could not get it back. End of story.

The next morning Lou called from the hospital to tell us that he actually had pneumonia. He would be gone at least a week. There was a God! As it turned out, Lou was hospitalized for 14 days. We had plenty of time to ransack their entire house and throw out all that was moldy, moth-eaten, freezer-burned or otherwise unfit for human consumption. We started with the refrigerator and their pantry in the basement. I know it's a generational thing, but who the hell needs a pantry that is eight feet wide and six feet tall? They even had a refrigerator in the basement too that held extra gallons of milk, yogurt and produce.

When we were young kids the worst part of grocery day, besides hauling it inside, was deciding what stayed upstairs and what went downstairs. We had several layers deep of canned vegetables, soups, peanut butter, cereal, muffin mixes, pickled vegetables, gravy and condiments. Even with three kids living at home at the time, it seemed like a lot of food. You can imagine my horror this day when I discovered almost as much food stored for two senior citizens as they used to keep for a family of seven.

The funny part was that many of the contents of the boxed dry goods had been eaten from the bottom. Mom said she thought they had a few mice but what she didn't understand was that where there was one, there are a hundred. Apparently they were well-fed.

It didn't take us long to play the "what the hell can this be and how old is this" game. Put your bets down people, we had a Vegas-style game happening. So, I would sit jars from the basement or packages from the freezer on the counter and start taking bets. There was one jar of pickled vegetables that looked like small body parts in formaldehyde. Maybe it was one of his dead dogs. Maybe one of the hungry mice fell in this one and was killed instantly. Were my parents actually thinking of eating this? The oldest food item we found had an expiration date of 15 years prior.

My parents grew up in a time when food had a shelf-life of forever. I was certain that my parents would not die from old age but something much more sinister. They wouldn't even die from a stroke, a fall down the stairs or carbon monoxide poisoning. The coroner's autopsy (if they even bothered with doing one on someone over 80) would surely identify the cause of death as food poisoning.

We broke out 30-gallon garbage bags and tossed almost everything. When they got back home, they would no longer have to go downstairs for dinner. Everything they needed would remain on one floor. If the rodents were going to snack, by God, it wasn't going to be easy. They would have to make it upstairs and under the nose of a 120-pound Rottweiler. Unfortunately, it was not long after we purged their cabinets that Lou discovered Costco, Aldi and Big Lots. We were doomed. Now they would purchase even larger containers of olives, spices, cereal and cleaning supplies.

I knew that the shock of what we had all done might send him into a tailspin from which no one might recover. In two weeks, we pulled out the carpet, padding and tacks from the downstairs. We pulled the carpet off of the stairs and replaced it with a runner. We wallpapered the back hall and painted the kitchen cabinets. We threw out so much old food that the EPA could have labeled their home a bio hazard. We weren't sure if Lou would be pissed or not at our efforts, so we took the coward's way out and sent George to the hospital to tell him before he came home.

Cindy and I knew Mom could appreciate a surprise, but Lou could not. As George confessed our sins, Lou had a look of amusement on his face instead of his usual look of an enraged bull with steam shooting out his nostrils. Lou in turn confessed that he knew we were up to something and wanted the details. Overall, this story had a happy ending. He was generally pleased with our efforts. Mom thought it looked fabulous although I doubt seriously if she really wanted to go back home.

However, in typical Lou fashion he pointed out our shortcomings over the next several months. He simply could not bring himself to just say "thank you" and shut the fuck up. He said we scratched the floor and the wallpaper looked crooked. We left nails in the floor and to save his life, he could not figure out why he was missing large quantities of food. I said the mice carried it off. On-the-other hand, our mother was tickled at the sight of clean cabinets and shining hardwood floors. We tossed or donated everything she was forbidden to put her hands on over the years even if it had belonged to someone in her family. For that, she seem relieved. He was a hoarder of anything he could get for free. I don't think he ever really figured out how much rotten food and "stuff" left the house in just one afternoon.

Today when I look through my cabinets, I am proud that I have a manageable supply of dry goods. I buy what we can eat in a few weeks and regardless of what I hear on the news about nuclear war, riots or global warming I do not keep fifty pound bags of rice, cases of water or a truck load of canned meat in my basement. And when the local food bank is looking for donations, I happily fill a bag.

the great escape

2009 started out in typical fashion. In past years, Mom was frequently plagued with bronchitis or pneumonia, low blood pressure, high heart rate or low oxygen levels and this was always to the point of needing hospitalization. There was always some infection attacking her body. February 2009 was no different. This time it was a staph infection to the bone from a wound on her foot. The wound was from poor circulation due to her diabetes.

Great. This was a new one and she would require IV antibiotics. One of the possible side effects from IV antibiotics is C-Dif (Clostridium Difficile). This is nasty. You might think that lime green is a really pretty color until you see it shooting out of your ass for a week. She had it before, she could get it again. It was also very contagious so any prudent person would stay the hell away from anyone locked up in the "infectious diseases" unit. Not us. Mom would call us asking for just about anything under the sun and we would risk our lives to take it to her. She never asked Dad because frankly, she could not stand his presence.

Her doctors spent a year and a half trying to heal this wound so they did not have to start amputating her toes, which would lead to her foot, then her leg. They would have to keep chopping off body parts until she was nothing but a stump. She wore an orthopedic boot, and literally stopped wearing shoes because they were irritating her skin. The wound that would not heal would be the beginning of the end. Little did she know that the problem with her foot would be her last great escape from living in a house that was too big, too cold, too hot, too dirty, too noisy and too stressful. It would also be her way out from living with a man who controlled all of these things.

Cindy had every intention of having 2009 (or at least the first half of it) be all about her. She planned to have the world tip off of its axis in her general direction for at least six months. She thought she had tip-toed through our parents' healthcare land mines and scheduled something she desperately needed and was all about her. Boy was she wrong. She had back surgery scheduled for February after trying to rehab a bulging disc and two broken facets. She needed a spinal fusion or every move she made would continue to be excruciating. The surgery was complicated and would require titanium and coral to repair the damage. There would now be a way for people to tell the difference between us as her ass crack was now going to be six inches longer than mine.

When Cindy came out of her anesthesia, I broke the news to her that mom was up on the third floor. All she could do was roll her eyes, for she knew this would mean she would take a back seat to whatever was going on with mom. The world tipped back to the south side of Lake Avenue instead of the North.

I now became the "go get it gal" for mom and Cindy. For five days I ran between the first floor and third floor of the hospital taking coffee, panty liners, socks, nail files and slippers to my two favorite gals. Have you ever given thought to how many panty liners one woman can go through in an entire year? They should sell them by the pallet instead of a box of 48.

For a second I had Cindy in a wheelchair and decided that we were all going to visit together. I was going to make my visit to the hospital as time efficient as possible, damn it. But, as we thought more about it, that idea became a medical no-no. Cindy was recovering with a six-inch incision and Mom was being treated with an open staph infection. Fuck. We had to keep them apart, so I resumed my walk between floors and I did it with a smile on my face.

Every trip to the hospital cost dad at least $750 plus the cost of medications. He made sure she spent as much time as possible there so he could get every nickel's worth. This included her physical therapy and Dad always had an opinion about her rehabilitation.

He would always tell us, "Your mother just needs to move more." He's lost his damn mind. Has he taken a good look at her? Does he ever listen to the doctors? She can't walk up a flight of stairs without bringing on angina. However, he ignored whatever they said and insisted that she just needed to pick up some two-pound weights and swing her arms around. Now seriously, what fucking good would that do? Leave her therapy to the experts.

Her trip to the hospital this particular February was relatively short in comparison to previous years. Only five weeks this time. She made it back home, but it seemed like the starch had been drained from her sails. She was now walking with a walker full-time and we became more concerned that she was bound to fall in their home because of tripping hazards and stairs. We worried she would fall and break her neck on one of the six large chairs in the living room and throw rugs laid out on every square inch of bare floor. We tried to tell him that we weren't getting rid of this stuff. We were just going to relocate it somewhere else in the house. We would move something and he would move it right back. Mom stayed silent, of course, because falling and killing herself would be less painful than arguing with him about her own safety.

Cindy, Greg and I were becoming equally more pissed with each trip mom made to the hospital over the years because it seemed to us that the very house we grew up in was the very reason she kept getting sick or hurt. So, in typical knock-down, drag-out fashion we insisted again and again that Lou allow us to make accommodations for her on the first floor. We suggested the idea over and over again and offered to do the work. It made no difference as he would never willingly bend.

We confronted him one Saturday morning with a new attitude. Kill or be killed. Greg, my husband and I were going to steam roll him and make a room for her that mattered. We didn't give a shit any longer. She was still in the hospital; however, we knew she would be coming home soon. My parents did what they could to make sure she stayed in the hospital as long as possible. They treated it like a nursing home, but Social Services was wise to their routine. I think the thought of going home just made her even sicker, so it always took weeks of care and therapy to get her curb side and into his care again. She was considered a "frequent flier" and was not going to be allowed to stay one second longer than her health insurance provided for. We understood that she wanted to stay because she was well taken care of and the alternative was "him" and a hot, dirty house. He wanted her to stay because it was cheap and he knew a nursing home was too expensive for his taste.

So, as we tried to do the best we could to make their first floor more like a one-room efficiency, he kept referring to us as "you fucking people." We were intruding and didn't understand that he would do things his own way in his own good goddamn time. Well that was not good enough any longer.

Cindy's husband showed up, asked us what we were doing and proceeded to open the doors to his outer office because the three of us sat there trying to be kind, politically correct and persuasive. We were wasting our time and we knew it. This was where we were going to make her comfortable or we were going to do our best to get her out of that hell hole. Period. Lou was not going to give us permission to move his crap out of the one room we wanted so we were going to have to do this by force.

Cindy could not join us in dismantling his downstairs because she could not even pick up a gallon of milk since her surgery. She got a free pass this time. We plowed through him and started moving shit. We moved it to the basement, garage, and when he wasn't looking, to the back of my husband's pick-up truck. The fact that we had to do this under his constant supervision was bullshit. He had a four-foot-high pile of tree-lawn crap in an eight by ten-foot usable space and he was acting like a fucking baby the entire time. He simply could not allow himself to keep his eye on the ball.

There were old kitchen cabinets (from someone else's house), a 100-pound red cast iron sink, and boxes of crap that I could not imagine needing for any reason. We didn't care if he kept this shit, we just insisted it could not be kept there. So, World War III had begun. He kicked stuff across the room, swore like a longshoreman and in typical fashion was as useless as any human being could be. He was not the kind of person you want with you in an emergency because by the time he did things his way, you would be dead. It took us all day to empty the room and take measurements for carpeting, blinds and baseboard heating. He kept saying it was all impossible and that mom could just go upstairs to her room when she got home and stay there. Like Norman Bates' mother. Absolutely not.

So, for three days straight we ignored him as best we could and screamed at him when we couldn't. The thought of burying a butcher knife deep into his chest came into mind more than once. Cindy's job was to bring us coffee or alcohol. Or alcohol in our coffee; we really didn't care. Other than that, she could only watch us from across the street.

The one thing he insisted on doing during this project was to mop the floor. Any one of us could have done it but he insisted so George, Greg, Steve and I stood there watching him mop the tile floor so we could lay the carpet. I had the most experience as not only did I work for McDonald's for 11 years, but I graduated from Hamburger University in Oakbrook, Illinois. I passed with honors. They teach you how to do everything as quickly and efficiently as humanly possible so there is no way I could watch this without snarling my upper lip. I hated watching him.

You have to know that our father could wear clothing long past its usefulness. The outfit he was wearing this particular day was at least 15 years old and it showed. He started slopping water all over the floor instead of just dry mopping it. He was just making a bigger mess so we stood there drinking our coffee and waiting. He ended up dumping the entire bucket of water. As he said "son-of-a-bitch," his pants landed around his ankles. He had no boxers on. It was our lucky day. We all got to see him bend over and, with what was left of his ball sack, yank up his drawers.

I felt sorry for him. He just didn't know when to call it quits and always seemed to want to prove he was still a capable man. No one really laughed out loud, but Dad knew he made a fool of himself. In the end, we assigned new places for his crap and managed to make Mom a really nice little space. He hated that we took items from inside the house to make a new room just for her. The boys ran new electrical so that she had baseboard heating and power for her new television. We laid carpet and cleaned everything. He fucking hated it because he had nothing to do with it. Like in the past, we had a surprise for her when she finally came home that he could not take credit for.

She came home after being gone for five weeks and loved her new space. She sat on her bed and looked out her own porch doors. Like what we did with her upstairs bedroom, he hated the layout, her curtains and bedding, all of which we provided. He tried to insist that we hang a set of draperies that were vinyl backed. They had yellowed over the years and were simply awful. Cindy and I thought that this would be the room she died in so it would be over our dead bodies that he forced us to put anything in there that wasn't pleasing to the eye. This included him. We made sure that there was just enough room for her and the dog.

I found a nice antique bookshelf in the basement that was completely empty. I stopped asking his permission to move things and took it upon myself to clean it and carry it upstairs piece by piece. He was furious that I wanted to use this in her new room and literally screamed at me not to touch it. I stood right in front of him and said, "Get out of my face. This is as much hers as it is yours and you aren't using it for a goddamn thing. I am moving it upstairs so get out of my way!" I knew to expect this when I started moving it but still had another "what the fuck" moment. Like other things Cindy and I moved, this was in an obscure corner of the basement and he hadn't laid one finger on it in 40 years. Fuck him—it was going upstairs if I had to push him out of the way to do it. I would have rather pushed him down the stairs instead of just out of the way, but we were already in the basement.

In addition to decorating her new room, we put in an intercom system so she could call for help, plugged in new portable phones because he still had the old rotary phones, scheduled Meals-on-Wheels and arranged for in-home nursing care. Lou was furious. He didn't see the need for any of it, but we did. In fact, her social service advocate recommended a number of things. "Done," we said.

The meals lasted three weeks, as did the nursing care. The meals, which abided by her diabetic restrictions, cost about $3 per meal and were delivered daily at 11:00 am. Neither one of them liked the taste so he canceled them and insisted he could do better. He also refused to allow visiting nurses to come a few days a week to help her bathe and arrange her medication. They were also going to do light housekeeping for both of them at a rate of $17 per hour. He said, "bullshit to that!" She would get only what their insurance company would pay for.

She was on her own again. He was not going to pay for any of this. I swore I wouldn't feed either one of them. They could starve as far as I was concerned. I wasn't going to bathe her, clip her toenails or wipe her ass. He said he could it, so let him try. He would have to call me begging.

Over the course of 2009, we saw her health slowly declining and we were not able to make either one of them understand that what Mom needed could not be taken care of at home any longer. Not unless, of course, Cindy and I were going to dedicate our lives to caring for her. This idea was palatable except for the fact that we would have had to do it in front of him. No fucking way. I know how I felt when he watched me do the dishes so there was no way I could handle him watching me care for "his wife." And that's how he ended every argument. He would proclaim, "She's my wife." Then you take care of her and don't call us with your bullshit.

Even helping her a little bit was impossible because he interfered constantly. He followed us upstairs to supervise us bathing her and setting out her medication. He told us how hot to make the water and reminded us to turn off the water while we soaped her down and then turn it back on to rinse her. He wanted to know what we were doing in the refrigerator when we came over to fix her lunch or dinner. I felt like telling him I was in there cutting the grass. What the hell did he think we wanted in there?

I swear to God, I don't think he has any idea how close he came to dying each and every time he opened his mouth.

He bothered the nurses with his ideas of physical therapy. He interrupted every conversation with his nonsense about how well he was taking care of her. He always questioned her doctor's protocol with regard to her care. However, he always left out the part where he didn't provide air conditioning for her in the summer or would leave her alone for hours at a time without a prepared meal or a way to reach him. She would call us and ask, "Do you know where your father is? I haven't eaten in five hours."

"At the bottom of a gorge?" I would say with a hint of gleeful anticipation.

She was getting to the point where she was becoming infirm and he still wanted her lifting weights. I shit you not. We knew we were entering a new level of care for her and we were scared. He thought it was the same as always. He didn't see her slowly dying. We did. Tough decisions were going to have to be made this year and Cindy and I were not looking forward to any of it. We already had a knock-down, drag-out fight over making a room for her on the first floor. We were now going to have to convince him somehow that she needed 24-hour nursing care.

Marie, it seemed, turned into a giant experiment. The doctors were pumping her full of drugs to regulate every part of her body. What worked on one problem exacerbated another. Give her steroids for her lungs and her sugar went through the roof. Give her pain meds and it affected her liver and kidneys. She was standing on the edge of a cliff. Each illness combined with her ongoing problems threatened to tip her off the edge. Our job, with the doctor's help, was to pull her back. So with little complaining, we continued our pattern of phone calls and emails and trips with coffee. What else could we do?

She seemed to be fine during her last few months at home and even managed to get out with Cindy and me to watch us bowl. She made it to the end of May before she required another trip to the hospital. This time her potassium skyrocketed and no one really knew why except that her kidneys were failing and it was starting to show. This time she spent over two months in the hospital and we were more apprehensive about this visit than previous visits. For extra fun, Dad somehow got double pneumonia and he bought himself an extended stay at the same hospital at the same time. This was unbelievable. Mom seemed more ill than the last time and at 90, he could die from pneumonia.

At one point, we told Mom that there was a chance they would put them in the same room because they were married. She looked panicked so I told her that when they asked her how she felt about that, she should say, “It’s not ‘no,’ it’s ‘fuck no.’” Don’t mess around with the delivery. Say it just like that. Good girl did it, to which they laughed. The nurses completely understood and kept him away from her.

During all of this, Cindy and I paced frantically because we knew they both had a death sentence looming over them and could check out at any moment. I could not believe either one of them any longer when they said they had their paperwork in order. I wasn’t interested in either one of them dying before we had control of their estate. It was just bad business.

Now enter their lawyer, Scott. We had no power of attorney in place for their health care, no DNRs and no will. In the midst of trying to get them healed and out of there, we also had to make them understand that they were gravely ill and could die and they needed to provide us with a way to make decisions on their behalf. Mom was willing but Dad thought we just wanted an excuse to prematurely cut off his oxygen. At this point, none of us needed an excuse.

To us, it made no difference what he thought. This needed to happen in spite of him. We were not going to be left with a nightmare in paperwork and three houses full of shit. We would be 55 before we would be done sorting through all of it. So Cindy and I ended up introducing them to their new lawyer (because his other lawyer was dead) and sitting with them for hours over a period of weeks to help them figure out their estate. In the end, we got the power of attorneys and DNRs signed. They never had a will drafted.

They both ended up coming home again to continue to recuperate from their illnesses. It took over two months for Mom to heal enough to be released and three weeks for Dad. Except this time, we were sent home with a BP monitor and cuff to check Mom's blood pressure a few times per day and what seemed like a mountain of medication. She was taking almost 20 pills per day so we made certain we sat with her every Sunday so she could have what she needed for the upcoming week. We talked again of Meals on Wheels but Mom and Dad insisted that they tasted like shit. They preferred Cindy's cooking of course but said they would manage and cook for themselves. It seemed like we never caught a break.

We noticed over the next several weeks that Mom seemed less able to have even a three-minute conversation on the phone so we knew that she could not prepare a meal for herself. In between getting our kids to baseball games, football practice and swimming we monitored her health the best way we knew how. We became more and more frustrated at her condition each time we entered their front door. Her existence had become to wait until Dad fed her. Period. In fact, she had to wait for anyone to help her do anything.

He still had not ordered cable for her over the past six months so she could watch her new television. So, when she was awake, she sat at the dining room table and stared into space. Cindy and I thought she was dying. Literally. Her complexion was gray, her hair was uncombed and she looked very unhappy. Her pajamas were dirty and the house started to smell. We suggested again that she consider assisted living and if they could not agree to that, then assisted living should come to them. All she could say was, “I don’t care.” Or, “Why can’t he just drop dead.”

My thought was, “Yes, that would be helpful but until then, you better learn to speak up.” She needed a full-time nurse but we were already exhausted from arguing and could not find the right words to convince either one of them to do anything other than what they were already doing. A big, fat, friggin’ goose egg. Zippity do da. Zilch. Nada. Squat. Fuckle. Jack. Nothing.

Cindy and I called Greg often and talked openly with him about what we should do but we never seemed to arrive at a proactive plan that would satisfy Dad. We had great ideas but were helpless to put any of them into play. All we ever did was react to the situations Mom and Dad created for themselves. Scrambling to punt with two seconds on the clock.

September 2009 proved to be a pivotal month in our mother’s health and subsequently her care. Our kids were back in school and Cindy and I were taking a much-needed walk. It was 10:00 am. We walked frequently as a way to handle the stress of the previous few months and figure out if there was any way we could help Mom more. We usually just talked ourselves out. If you know us, then you know how difficult that is. The problem was that there was a nasty, 220-pound obstacle in our way.

As I was getting ready to leave Cindy’s house (which was directly across the street from Mom and Dad’s) we both heard an ambulance. We looked at each other and said, “What are the odds that that thing is coming this way?” We both stood staring out the front window with our arms folded and waited. No shit. That thing stopped right in front of their house. We ran out the front door and across the street.

We followed the paramedics right through the front door and

we expected to find someone dead. Considering what the next four months would bring, that really wasn't a bad alternative. Dropping dead I think is always a better option than some long, drawn-out death watch. We walked in to find Mom lying on the floor in her first-floor room, flat on her back. She smelled like a toilet. Dad was standing over her stammering about what had happened. She just kept saying she couldn't get to the bathroom and urinated on herself twice. Dad was talking about when he went to bed the night before and that the dog didn't wake him up. The fireman stood there as confused as we were. I told Dad to be quiet and let Mom talk. I think he was afraid she would embarrass him. Too late for that.

I finally asked her how long she had been lying there. 11 hours! He was mortified, not for her but for the fact that he was somehow responsible for it. He should have been more embarrassed by not wearing any shirt. As he was talking his man boobs moved in sync with his arms. I felt like I was going to vomit.

Mom said Dad went upstairs to bed at around 11:00 pm. It was then that she decided to make one last trek to the bathroom alone. That was her first mistake. Remember, we put an intercom system in for her so all she needed to do was hit one button and ask him for help. The fact that she didn't was her second mistake and that choice changed the rest of her life. She lost her balance and fell backwards and hit the corner of the doorway and then hit the floor. For the next eleven hours she called for him and there was no response. She could not reach a phone or the intercom, so she laid there helpless like a turtle on its back. What a bitch of a position to be in. Their dog, a 120-pound Rottweiler walked by her and sniffed her a few times and then went back upstairs to bed.

She said she didn't want to go to the hospital and Dad was

inclined to agree. I couldn't believe what I was hearing. If we allowed that to happen then we were sure to get a phone call three hours from then with Dad telling us he changed his mind. Fuck that. She was going while her ride was waiting patiently. Cindy and I insisted and told the paramedics we would get a "yes" from her and then get her ready. Cindy took one of the guys outside to explain the situation (meaning how dangerous it was for her to live there and how many times she's taken a trip via ambulance in the last 12 months), and I told the other guy to get the stretcher.

Dad was looking lost as Cindy and I took complete charge of this situation. Mom was soaking wet with urine and I wanted to wipe her down and change her clothes before they left with her. Dad asked if I was coming to the hospital with them and I said, "Go get dressed. You are going alone to explain how the hell this happened. If I go, I swear to God I will throw you under the bus." With that he walked upstairs and did what he was told.

I cleaned up Mom and the boys took her away. I wonder now if Mom took a good look at her surroundings because that would be the last night she would ever spend in her home. I told Mom that Dad would be following the ambulance and she asked if Cindy and I would be there too. I was so fed up with this bullshit routine that I wanted to scream. I had to take my son to a photo shoot and get home before my third-grader got off the bus. My answer was, "I will later if I have to. Dad will handle it for now." They never ever asked where Debbie, Greg, or Mike were in an emergency. They only ever asked for Cindy or me. This was becoming a huge burden but we both tried to maintain our compassion and continued to help them both.

A few hours passed and Dad called Cindy to proclaim that "she's coming home." Cindy called me and yelled so loud you could hear her in the next county.

"My ass!" she said and with that Cindy flew to the hospital to straighten this out. Cindy marched into the ER and demanded to see the head of social services, her physician and the ER doc. While Cindy was gathering her medical arsenal she heard Dad raising his voice to Mom and made sure the nurses heard every word. What was shocking was that Dad was telling Mom why she was there. The answer was—her hemorrhoids. He was insisting somehow that these pesky protrusions were the source of her dizziness. Not the failing kidneys, not the CHF, not the diabetes, not the fact that she's 85 fucking years old and taking a dump truck full of medication. Hemorrhoids. And, while she was there this time, he wanted something done about them.

Cindy walked in the room and told Dad to shut the hell up because everyone could hear his nonsense. After that, Cindy said she wanted to see Mom walk unassisted because she was wheeled in on a stretcher and there was no way she could get back in that house without help. She was staying until she was completely checked out and that was the end of it. Cindy promptly told the nurses that it was already two o'clock and that Mom had not eaten and at any moment that in-and-of-itself was going to be a medical emergency. She asked the nurses for lunch saying, "Can you make it a twofer? Dad hasn't eaten either."

Because of Cindy's 22-minute rampage, Dad went home alone again to ponder how this kept happening. He probably wanted to shit his pants when he saw Cindy burst through the ER doors and demand appropriate action. Mom was probably relieved that Cindy had come to her rescue and got Dad out of there. Cindy and I were pushed to the front of the line again. The only thing that was going to happen this time was that we were going to do more than just keep cleaning up their messes. Shit was about to change.

Her doctor contacted adult protective services to interview

them both and Mom finally declared that she didn't feel safe at home anymore. She simply said, "I am afraid to be at home." Thank God! Dad wanted to explode. She was betraying him right before his eyes. He could not convince anyone any longer that he was capable of caring for her. She had fallen too many times over the past few years and lying on the floor this time for eleven hours was cruel and inexcusable. It was mostly his fault. Yes, she should have asked for more help, but she didn't. And now she finally opened her mouth to speak.

Cindy and I had been screaming from the roof tops that her home life was dangerous and with Mom's help, we were finally being heard. A 90-year-old man is disabled just by being 90. Add to that his refusal to wear his hearing aids and his ship was sunk for good. When you keep saying, "What?" all the fucking time and you insist that doctors speak slower or repeat themselves, they damn well know you have a disability. I wish one time he would have told them they had marbles in their mouth.

Her doctor spent hours coordinating with social and adult protective services to finally get her to a safe place. This had the potential to cost thousands of dollars. For many years we tried to convince Dad that he needed to transfer his assets so that he would be under much less of a financial burden when the time came that one or both of them needed nursing care. Everything we had predicted over the years had come true and this was no exception. We told Mom that we would make good decisions for her with her doctor's help and not to worry about the money. He didn't want to spend $17 an hour for a nurse. He was now going to spend $135 a day, seven days a week.

After this recent fall, she never stopped trembling. She was afraid to go home, and who could blame her? While we were trying to make arrangements for care at a nursing facility, he was telling her they had no money and could not afford it. What a bastard. She was too weak to argue and may have completely forgotten that they had plenty of money. As usual Cindy and I had to calm her down and kick the shit out of him. All we ever told him was to "Shut up! Leave her alone and do the right fucking thing this time." This was all wishful thinking as he never shut up and he never voluntarily did the right thing. We had to tell her doc to find a nice place for her to spend what we considered was the last few months of her life. We knew it was not going to be years.

Everyone ignored him the best they could. They avoided giving him too much information and tried not to talk to him. However, the nursing staff and the Social Services Director at her assisted living facility were becoming agitated each time he would visit because he had her in tears. He was finally told to stay away from her. Although she was nervous, mostly because Dad was still being a complete fucking asshole about the whole thing, she was looking forward to peace and quiet. Can you imagine being forced to leave a house you spent 45 years in because your spouse won't help you with basic human care and keep his fucking mouth shut for five minutes?

Unfortunately, Dad was going to have to pay the bill and sign some of the paperwork associated with welcoming a new resident. We had to tell him how much Mom's new life was going to cost and what she was going to get for her money. He didn't want to pay $50 a month for cable, Meals on Wheels or a nurse for 20 hours per week. It was almost funny to watch the look on his face when we told him that she was going to cost him over $3000 per month. She would have a nurse and aides on call 24 hours per day, three meals per day, snacks, blood work and showers three times per week, and a weekly happy hour.

He said if she could stare at the walls there, she could do it at home. He didn't see that they were really doing all that much for her other than being babysitters on call. We tried to get her less expensive "babysitters" but he said "no." We now know what kind of babysitter he turned out to be.

He flipped out in front of everyone, including Mom and said, "I don't know where I am going to get the money for this!" He talked about her like she wasn't even in the room.

Our response was simple. "Pull it out of the bank, the box or your ass! Sell your rental properties. You are not going to deny her this little bit of comfort and happiness so you can hoard every nickel you've taken from her over the years to keep for yourself!"

He said this all in front of Mom, who sat there with a sad little look on her face contemplating letting him off the hook. We told her to sign the paperwork because half of their estate was hers. How could she not understand this? We put the pen in her hand. They were going to have to sign on the dotted line somewhere because she was not permitted to go home again. This place was as good as any and he was out of time. We put so much information about local nursing facilities in front of him over the years so that they could take their time to decide where she might go if she needed another place to live.

Perfect. She was on her way to new digs. We were happy to pack her bags and move her along. And Dad had to swallow all of it. He could bitch about it, but he had to pay the bill. He was told she could go back home when he made the appropriate accommodations given her physical condition. He never did and she never went back home. He contemplated putting a $15,000 shower/tub unit in but the way he made decisions, she would be dead before he decided which one and where it should go. In the meantime, Bradley Bay would be her new home.

By the time we had the arrangements made we literally had two days to move her into her little apartment. We told Dad we were coming over to take some of her furniture out of the house and set her up in her "new home." I asked about a table and set of chairs that his beloved Peter left in one of his apartments six years prior. He said absolutely not. So, we went and spent money unnecessarily because he was not going to make this easy on us. We knew where his box of cash was so we took $500 and bought what she needed. Fuck him some more.

He did not help us one bit. His contribution again was to sulk and be pissy. Greg, Cindy and I moved her in and added our personal touch so she would be happy with her new home. Again, he hated her being anywhere where he could not control her. Tough shit. She loved her room and especially her lift chair. That was a sweet ride. It turned out that what he loved was the free meals he was getting several times a week when he would go for lunch or dinner. He was going to get as much out of that place as possible. I am sure he didn't mind the free cable either.

Mom finally had her freedom but she couldn't figure out how to keep him out of there. He always brought his doom and gloom and occasionally he would toss a bag of candy at her. He would stay for hours, lamenting over their terrible financial state. He told her he was going to have to sell their possessions or that once he paid her bills he couldn't afford to eat. We all heard that bullshit a million times, especially when we were kids. Talk about a mind fuck. She was so out of juice, she actually believed him.

Cindy called the bank pretending to be her and found out exactly how much money she had. She wrote it down and showed it to Mom and told her two things. "One, don't worry about the money. You can have whatever you want. Two, tell him to shut the hell up. Tell him how much money you have and if he keeps his shit up, you want a divorce. That way you will get your 50% and not have to ask him for one more fucking nickel."

I then said, "If you can't do those two things then you have two choices left. One, you can listen to his bullshit until the moment you die or two, you can figure out a way to kill him so you can have peace and quiet and all the money."

Mom loved her new home. She made new friends and enjoyed the entertainment they provided and the weekly happy hour. She got her nails done and played games with her "inmates." On Thanksgiving, she didn't want to leave and have dinner at home because she was looking forward to having dinner with her friends. We told her Dad was coming to eat with her and she was not happy. He was going to be her problem for the afternoon, not ours. I happened to see him there that morning and he had nothing to say. He shuffled in her room and tossed a one-pound bag of peanut M&M's at her. Nice. I opened the bag and started eating them just to piss him off.

I fixed Mom's hair and did her makeup for her. The makeup covered up her black eyes from another fall she just had. This time she fell at the nursing facility. Mom did not ring at four o'clock in the morning for help to the bathroom. She tipped over and took the full weight of her fall right to the middle of her face. The nicest way to describe my mother's shape is that she looked like an egg on stilts. She had these thin, beautiful legs holding up 193 pounds. It's pure physics. Once the midsection goes over the knees and the head goes over the midsection there's no stopping the momentum. She was black and blue from her nose to the top of her forehead so I thought a little makeup would be nice for her holiday dinner. She looked really pretty and he didn't say a goddamn word to her.

She was taken for a CT scan just to be sure but she didn't do any permanent damage. She spent a few days back in her room and was right back in circulation. Thankfully she didn't break anything. We all took a deep breath and thought we would be relieved from any further incidents involving Mom for at least a few months. Disappointingly, only a week went by before we received another phone call that something was wrong with her again. Did she fall? No. Was she having a heart attack? No. The nurse told us her oxygen level dropped below 90% and she was throwing up. She was being transferred to the hospital immediately for tests. The date was about December 8. We all thought this next visit would be short lived and she would be back living the good life in no time at all. This time, we were wrong.

Any thoughts Cindy and I had at this stage of her life were worrisome. We both knew that there would be an awful moment when no one, not even God, could fix her. My husband was a fireman and paramedic and I know now that he most likely understood on a clinical level what was going on but was kind enough not to tell me simply that she was dying. So when the nurse called, Cindy and I said goodbye to our sons and ran out the door to help quarterback her care once again. My sons were too little to understand my grief and panic so I spared them any details other than to say that their grandma wasn't feeling well and that I had to be with her. I know how they react when I'm sick with a cold, thinking the absolute worst so even though they were under twelve years old at the time, they understood that I loved my mother like they loved me. And like my own mother, I told them not to worry and that I would be home to tuck them into bed.

tomorrow you're dead

When does it happen that the child becomes the parent? Is it when your parents can no longer pay their bills, wipe themselves or remember what day it is? Or, is it sooner, like when you realize that your parents have rarely made good decisions and have survived on little smarts and a lot of luck? If the second is true, then I think my sister Cindy and I were in our middle teens when the "we are going to have to supervise our parents" brick hit us square in the face.

We realized early on that our parents had a dysfunctional relationship. Our father would dictate "how it's going to be" and Mom sat there and took it. She occasionally tried to offer her opinion on something like doing maintenance on the rentals or paying a bill but was quickly silenced. Lou couldn't help but remind Marie in a roundabout way that she only had a tenth-grade education and didn't know what she was talking about. Nice guy. She just could not fight with a man who had an endless diatribe of his life experiences and who never seemed to run out of hot air.

Somehow, our father managed to amass a decent nest egg by the time he was 90. He bragged to us and perfect strangers for years about all his cool, priceless shit that he wanted to sell. He spoke of selling his mother's Hummel's to pay for a car, put food on the table or pay Mom's hospital bills the year she died. His mother died in 1978 so you can imagine how many times we heard he needed to sell her things to pay a bill. He finally sold all of her costume jewelry in 2007 with no particular goal in mind. Cindy and I were lucky enough to take a few pieces before he let a costume place take the entire lot for $200.

So he and my mother learned to live with less so that their steel box could have more. I am dumbfounded at how he was able to accumulate this kind of wealth without a steady income stream. He became relatively savvy with the ins and outs of tax preparations, living a life of frugality and was blessed with a truckload of luck. Oh, and the ability to con. It is funny how I want to block out all of the moments that my father took things that didn't belong to him.

Cindy and I had always told him, "I want to be as broke as you when I'm 90." She and I did some crude math and came to the conclusion that, barring any catastrophe, he and mom could live to be 120. The shame is that he saved it to their own detriment. Perhaps it's the generation, always telling oneself you can do without or live with less. He had a 4,500 square foot home he said he could not afford to heat yet kept living there anyway.

Our parents never took vacations, went out to eat or lavished themselves or anyone with anything. One of our biggest arguments was in trying to convince him to spend $50 a month on cable so our mother could enjoy some television when she came home from one of her two-month stays at Club Med. (Our definition for the hospital since her stay there was like Shangri-La compared to living at home.) Cindy and I bought her a brand-new television she never got to watch in her own home because he said, "she doesn't need it."

The time came for Cindy and me, our family's self-appointed officials, to have a very difficult conversation with our parents. There was a way to approach our father that required finesse so that in his mind, he didn't smell a rat. My mother, on the other hand, needed to be punched right in the face with information. She did not get subtlety, innuendos, implications or insinuations. Come to think of it, he didn't get it either. The more direct, the better.

Cindy and I needed to ask our parents if they had a will, DNRs, power of attorney, etc. This conversation, like so many others we had tried to have, was going to be rough. It would also be one for the record books. It was 2009 and our mother was not well and Dad was 89, about to turn 90. So again, we figured the best way to have this talk was to just have it. We asked exactly what we wanted to know. "Do you both have your shit together??" Our father's response was, "What do you two want?" The gloves were off.

We showed them articles about estates left to probate. We told them how hard it would be to pay any of their bills if they simultaneously became infirm. We told them how much a nursing home would cost if one or both of them had to be moved to one. His response was, "I'll eat a goddamn bullet first." That's fine with me but I tried to explain that he might not be in a position to pull the trigger if he had a stroke and couldn't use his hands. And, as much as we would have liked to help him along by putting a pillow over his face, we weren't risking prison for him.

Mom sat there with a blank look on her face because she didn't know how to answer any of the questions put before her. Of course she knew the answer to our question was "no," but she looked to him for the answer anyway. So, the result was the same as always. Cindy and I would leave their home having wasted hours of our time trying to convince them that they were not ready to die. At least not until we had signed and notarized paperwork that said they could check out.

Given the fact that he screamed at us to mind our own business we knew, of course, that the answer to our inquiry was a big, fat no. "No" to all of it. No lawyer, no paperwork. Nothing. He said he knew what he was doing, he had been around the block a few times, he wasn't born yesterday, blah, blah, blah. In his mind he was sure he was going to take it with him. If that wasn't possible then he was going to figure out how to control it from the grave. We were approaching the end of a fifteen-year debate. Our father wrongfully assumed right away we were angling for his money and property when all we wanted to do was protect it from the IRS and probate lawyers.

Cindy and I contemptuously continued to print articles from the internet to explain what can happen to your estate if it goes into probate. We explained what would happen if they did not have a DNR on file with the hospital. We explained what would happen if they did not give someone power of attorney over their healthcare and bank accounts. Christ. All he ever said was, "I know, I know. Now get off my back." In the midst of trying to convince them to get their paperwork in order, we also tried to convince them that they should move to a smaller house. Condo livin' was the way to go. This was ludicrous in his mind. "Where would we live?" he asked. Any place they wanted as long as they lived on one floor and had no grass to cut.

The decision to move, however, required them to lighten their load. We said, with our help, we could take it one floor at a time. We would start with the garage, then the basement, etc. He blew his stack because we intimated that most of the stuff he had in the garage was garbage. Excuse me. One time, we had the garage cleaned and organized with a giant pile left over for the tree lawn scavengers. He made the guys put it all back. Nothing we said ever worked. He never budged an inch. Over the years we had a few yard sales at our own homes. We encouraged him to bring some things to try to let us sell them. He only ever brought shit. We never sold one thing he contributed yet he would take it back home with him and store it for another day.

When both Mom and Dad ended up in the hospital at the same time in the summer of 2009, Cindy and I had to spring into action. Whether he liked it or not, we brought a lawyer right to their bedsides. We had meetings with them in their hospital gowns, toting oxygen tanks and coffee. By this point, we had enough of his fucking around, his promises and his irresponsible behavior. Scott was now their lawyer and we were going to get something accomplished. Before we introduced Scott to our parents, we informed him point blank that this would be the hardest money he ever earned. Not only would it be near impossible to drag this horse to water, but you'd have to drown him to make him drink. I was all for drowning him if necessary.

In the past, we tried to candy-coat their eventual demise. No one likes to talk about the reality of dying, but the fact remains that he was 90 and she was 84 and sick as a dog. What was also very true is that when we made this introduction they were both in the hospital. He had double pneumonia and she was just really sick with whatever.

I decided that we would not be subtle with him anymore. Our parents were going to get it this time with both barrels. Scott did his best to make allies out of both of them. Our mother was receptive but very nervous of Dad's reaction to what he considered was a surprise attack.

Scott explained, as we had many times in the past, why it was so important to have your paperwork in order and to make yourself invisible at this age. He tried to explain that they should own as little as possible. The best way was to "gift it" to his children. You should have seen the look on his face. Complete and utter horror. I think he said, "Fuck that idea."

Dad was confused about this strategy. He was under the misconception that we expected him to have nothing. That was true, but only on paper. He kept saying, "What are we going to live on? How am I supposed to pay the bills?" Of course Scott's job was to make them understand that his goal was to help them protect everything they had left so they could live comfortably with no worries. He also wanted to make sure that no one other than family got what was left.

I promised I would not get upset during this meeting and launch into one of my famous tirades. The kind where I stand up and shout, "What the fuck? Are you stupid? Do you not understand plain English? I'm going to jump out of a window if I listen to one more second of this!" I was sitting there thinking I had aliens for parents. Cindy kept looking at me, shaking her head at me to remain silent. I just couldn't do it anymore. We had been sitting in this room for over an hour, I ran out of coffee, I had to pee and we were no closer to an understanding.

I stopped Scott and I said, "I am going to say something as simply as possible." I looked straight at my parents and said with complete authority, "The scenario we are trying to explain here is simple. Tomorrow you are both dead. No one is really getting anything until then. However, we need certain things in writing or your family is screwed. If you don't have DNRs, the hospital or nursing home will keep you alive until your money runs out. If we don't have power of attorney over your bank accounts, we can't pay any bills. The courts will lock up the house and perform an inventory on your estate without us present and half your shit (the good shit), including your cash, will disappear. When we're done trying to settle your estate, there won't be anything left because you think you know what you're doing. Well, you don't and regardless of what you think, you cannot take it with you. You are living in fantasy land and we are here to burst your bubble."

To which he said, "I'd rather fucking burn it than give it to you."

When it came to talking about their will, Lou thought that what Mom wanted to leave each child after her death had to be given to them while they were alive. This is why we had to go to such great lengths to explain to them that no one would get a thing until they were dead. Both of them had to be dead before anybody got anything. I said again, "You are dead. Do you understand?" I got no response. He clearly did not get what any of us were saying. Mom understood and in her own way tried to explain it to him. I told her "Good luck." Three college-educated people, one of whom had a law degree, could not find the words to get him to grasp simple math and logic.

Scott, Cindy and I left the room to get a refill and take a break. We left mom and dad in there to talk, stare at one another or kill each other. When we all returned I was hoping she would be smashing his head in with her oxygen tank. We walked back in the room and she looked exhausted and he looked like he was ready to kill someone. I wish I could tell you that he came to his senses and made all of the proper arrangements. I wish I could tell you that he died from his pneumonia and therefore mom had control of everything. Sorry. He walked out of there after five weeks and came home again. We would fight another day.

We did manage to make some headway and got them to both sign their DNRs and assign us power of attorney over their health care and bank accounts. As far getting either of them to agree on a division of their assets, we might as well have been having the Middle East Peace talks. At that point it looked like Jimmy Carter could not mediate this nightmare.

Our debate regarding their estate went into its seventeenth year. The only gift anyone had gotten since ambushing him in the hospital was $20 each for Christmas in 2010 for the youngest grand kids. It cost him $120 and that was after Cindy made him do it. He could barely let go of the cash as he made each kid stand in front of him like it was a bread line and they were starving to death. He was such a prick about it that we regretted making him do something nice. We never asked again.

Perhaps that one moment made my sons realize how unimportant a few dollars really matters to them when they have the chance to brighten another person's day. Especially if you have it to give. I have witnessed both my boys on multiple occasions buy lunch or a movie ticket for a friend and never ask for gas money. They know it's important to help others and get an immense amount of joy out of giving a gift.

Cindy and I throw so much money back and forth between us that we have lost count who owes who how much. For the two of us, we want to travel this life together and will share all that we have until the end. And when the time comes, she and I will give away all our money and stuff to our children and trust them to pay for our little two-bedroom condo and the driver that will take us wherever we wish to go.

waiting for God

January 1, 2010. It was the beginning of a brand-new year. Our mother Marie had a difficult year in 2009, wrought with pain, illness and disappointment. In the past, she rallied from every illness and trip to the hospital. She somehow managed to get strong enough through medication and therapy to find her way back home again and again.

I often wondered why Mom stayed married to Lou. He was a person who turned every decision, large or small, into an agonizing process. And it wasn't just that he was unable to make a decision. He was mean about not making one. So, for years Cindy and I did our best to side-step any and all subjects which required him to pull the trigger. However, there were times where it was impossible to keep our big mouths shut. I can only describe the feeling as the one you had as a kid in school where you finally had the answer to some question and you thought you might spontaneously combust if you weren't the one called on to give it.

Over the years, Marie learned to speak more infrequently to her own defense. She would sadly mumble under her breath, "I wish he would drop dead." I could never make her understand that it was easier to turn up the fucking heat than wish him dead. Although, in her defense, I think she was going for a more permanent solution. Her wish never came true and if she said anything about anything, he would brow beat her into submission on every occasion. It became evident that he treated her like one of his dogs. In fact, he did that to all of us. He would give us a dark look or growl at us to shut up and leave him alone. And we did it. That's how it was.

Cindy and I always took him on. Fighting with him was simply sport. It was so easy to contradict him that we did so often. We knew that when he would scream at us to "get off my back," this just meant that he was dead wrong about whatever he was trying to shove down our throats. Marie never got the hang of it and just learned to suffer in silence. Cindy and I encouraged her to use two simple words, "Fuck" and "off," and use them together and as often as she could. Maybe it would shock him enough to leave her alone. I don't think she ever told him to "fuck off."

And because she rarely if ever spoke up, that left us holding the bag. It was a bag full of catch phrases we used frequently. "What are you talking about? Have you lost your mind? Don't talk to me like that. Don't talk to Mom like that. Grow up. Get a lawyer. Don't call me! Nobody cares. You are not broke! Do you hear yourself? Wait until this all blows up in your face."

It was this way until the end. Marie would never get any peace until she died or until he died, which was preferable to her. When people take that vow, "till death do us part" they usually mean they are dedicated to one another until one or the other passes away. Marie would only be free from her pain and suffering when she died because she could not leave him any other way. She said she could not desert him because she felt sorry for him and no one else would ever love him. We told her we didn't think he deserved to be loved but that didn't matter to her. She had to wait for God to decide.

God came calling during the holidays of 2009. In fact, he knocked on her door a few times that year just to be ignored and told "no solicitors." She used up eight of her nine lives already and 2009 was not looking good. She went into the hospital for the fourth and final time in December with double pneumonia and a crap load of other issues and illnesses. Her doctors were pumping her full of enough diuretics, antibiotics and painkillers to fill a semi. They were trying to get the fluid out of her but nothing was working. As a result, her kidneys finally failed.

Cindy and I got a call on December 18 while we were just starting a 24-hour visit to a local water park. This was an early Christmas present for our boys and a much-needed break from hospitals, doctors and Dad's never-ending bitching. We had been there for 45 minutes when our phones started ringing.

The first call was from the kidney doctor who told us in his nice Indian accent, "Your mother has days to live." I watched Cindy's face as she took that call and knew immediately that our 24 hours of eye-burning chlorine, bad food and other people's noisy brats had been ruined. We contemplated leaving but knew "days" meant at least four or five and she might not get critical in 24 hours. At least we hoped not. Besides, we left our sister and Dad in charge. Jesus, what were we thinking?

Between water slides and margaritas we made and took phone calls. We laughed a few times and cried a lot. Cindy and I called our family members and gave Dad the bad news. We also told him to be quiet and don't tell her anything until we returned the following afternoon. Lou could be about as subtle as a pile of crap in a punch bowl. In hindsight, I think he was relieved we let him off the hook. We were so afraid he would say something like, "Well, it's been a good run kid but there is nothing they can do for you."

When we went to see Mom the next evening, we left Lou at home. Honestly, he was in complete denial about her impending doom. Marie looked at us with a childlike expression as we tried to explain what was happening to her body and how hard it was working to fight off this infection. We had to tell her somehow that everything the doctors had been trying for the last ten days was not working.

Some moron mentioned “dialysis” to her so we had to explain to her that that was not an option for someone with her problems. Cindy and I looked into her eyes and knew that she didn’t understand a lot of what we were saying so we told her “maybe dialysis will work once the doctors clear up the pneumonia.” On the flip side of all of this, Dad was not wrapping his brain around the fact that she would most likely be dead by Christmas. He felt like having a different conversation with her because reality was too painful for him. He would rather act stupid instead of being brave.

He could never not talk about his money problems. It was ridiculous because he didn't really have any at that point in his life. However, while she was literally lying on her death bed, he was running his mouth about how much her assisted living, the attorney and the medication was costing. He actually told her, “I can make a few payments but I don’t know for how long. And, if I do that, I don’t know if I’ll be able to eat. It’s a good thing Cindy is feeding me.” Why, at this point, couldn't she tell him to either drop dead right there or get the fuck out of her room and let her die in peace?

Cindy sat with her while I escorted Dad out into the hallway to chew him a new asshole. The words spilled out of me so fast it was like a freight train out of control. I did not want to have this conversation one more fucking time and I was out of patience. Cindy and I were sick of insisting he behave, especially now that she was dying.

I wanted my mother’s death to be like the final scene from *Love Story*. Jenny makes a last request of Oliver. She says, “I want you to be merry. You’ll be merry, okay?” She dies in his arms, with him weeping at her bedside. Then in the last moment of the movie Oliver says, “Love means never having to say you’re sorry.” Is that really too much to ask?

This was the typical shit Mom and Dad dumped on me and Cindy daily. I think, however, we dumped it on ourselves because we wanted her life to end one way and we knew this might not happen. She would call and cry about something he said or did that was totally mean and he would get bitched out by one of us. What a way to operate. At this moment, with her trying to decide how much more she could fight to save herself, he was worse than the Grim Reaper. Over the next few days we tried to limit her exposure to him. We were sure that his voice was not the last thing she wanted to hear. His constant, self-serving complaining might drown out the sound of the angels singing.

The last few days of her life were very scary. We just didn’t want her to die, yet we were hoping that she would pass quickly and not suffer. There were many moments where we were brave and did not cry. We fed her Cornflakes and ice cream. We gave her Captain Morgan’s and Diet Coke. We filed her nails and cleaned up her vomit. We brushed her teeth (while they were in our hands) and combed her hair.

When we had to cry, we went into the hallway. We paced and sobbed or sat on the floor with our face in our hands. Not once did our father comfort us. He didn’t put a hand on our shoulders or give us a hug. He didn’t say one thing to ease our pain. Cindy, Greg and I sat on the floor outside her room, Greg in the middle, holding our hands. Dad was looking for that out of us. He wanted us to convince him that Mom had forgiven him for being such an asshole. When the time came, we all sat with her alone, while she was somewhat conscious, to say what we wanted to say. Dad was the last one to have this moment with his wife.

He stood in the hallway and cried. He had to go in and have a private conversation with her and literally asked me, “What should I say?"

My tears immediately dried up and Cindy and I took turns telling him what to do—again. I said, "Tell her what a good wife and mother she was or that she was a good friend. Tell her why you loved her."

Cindy then said, "We don't care if you have to lie. But do not go in there and make this about you in some last-ditch effort to ease your conscience. No one gives a shit how guilty you feel." With that bit of advice, he went into her room. We were nervous because no one knew what he was likely to say. We had to trust him. Oh my God, why did we do that?

After about ten minutes, Dad came out of her room looking confused and sick to his stomach. He motioned us over and told us she was having angina and the nurses weren't responding to her call button. She was in a great deal of pain. What the fuck did he say to her to bring it on? Dollars to donuts he tried to get her to forgive him for being such an asshole his whole life and she resented it. She would rather have her heart explode than tell him what she really thought. We tried to get him to do the right thing and it backfired.

Mom was asking for a priest. Cindy, Greg and I stood over her bed crying like babies. She was dying and we were terrified. She didn't look scared at all. She was in so much pain she was probably wishing one of us would put a pillow over her face.

Our oldest brother Mike managed to get a ride from his ex-wife after Cindy insisted he show up. She was going to die and his attitude was essentially, "What am I going to do about it? I don't even have enough money for a bus ride." Sixty-three years old and that's the best he could do?

Cindy explained how dire her condition was and that her kidneys weren't functioning. Cindy said, "It will be over soon, so you had better get your ass into Lakewood."

Debbie too had not come in yet to see her. Cindy had been trying to call her for two days. At the height of her angina attack Cindy cleaned up her tears, looked at me calmly and said, "Go to Debbie's fucking house and put her in the car. Do not take no for an answer." With that, I grabbed my keys and walked out of the hospital and drove two measly blocks to Debbie's house. I tried not to think that Mom might die before I got back.

I banged on Debbie's door and waited. Her oldest son answered the door looking surprised. He said, "What's the matter?" The poor kid at 27 years old did not know what was coming. He just kicked a hornet's nest.

I said, "Where is your mother? We have been calling for two days! Doesn't anyone answer the fucking telephone?" He told me she was in bed. I ordered him to get her downstairs and outside in front of me.

When she came out, she was in her pajamas and her hair was a wreck. She calmly said, "What's wrong?"

I said, "Mom is dying, Deb! Where the hell have you been? She needs to see you now." She proceeded to tell me how hard it was to see her like that. I said, "Tough shit. It's hard for all of us, but you are the only one she hasn't seen and she may not live through the night. Get some shoes on, get in this car because I am your goddamn ride." She didn't say a word to me.

Debbie managed to get a few words in and hold her hand for a little while before Greg's pastor arrived. He made it by eight o'clock that night. He sat with her too and read a passage from the Bible and administered last rites. Even after a few doses of nitro and morphine she was still in an incredible amount of pain. It was only after we got Greg to take Debbie and Dad home and Cindy and I sat alone with her did she calm down and go to sleep.

That was the last day any of us would have any real kind of conversation with her. After that day she took a serious turn for the worse and her life ended within hours. Someone was with her all of the time to make sure she was getting her morphine. Each time the nurses gave it to her, they thought it would be enough to stop her breathing and she would die peacefully. If you have never heard the "death rattle," thank your lucky stars. It sounds like a coffee percolator and it is truly unnerving. My poor sweet mother had congestive heart failure so the fluid in her lungs caused a constant, awful rattle with every breath she struggled to take. I listened to that for days and even though the doctors would suction her lungs, her breathing was labored.

She saw two more priests before she finally died. Even though they said "hours" it took three days. Dad spent two full nights with her but by the third night we told him to go home. At 90 years old I don't think he could take any more. Greg stayed with her on her last night. He read to her from the Bible and held her hand. At some point he had fallen asleep in a corner chair in her room and said he was jolted awake by the lack of noise. He realized that the awful rattling in her lungs had stopped. However, the fact that she was quiet meant she was gone forever.

Greg called Cindy and me and we went to the hospital to stand by her bedside for the last time. I could not believe I was looking at her—dead. It was surreal. Her mouth made a perfect ring. Greg said he tried to close her mouth but it would not budge. Her false teeth were a little askew so I pushed them back into her mouth. Funny, I had this feeling she would clamp her jaws shut at that moment. It made the hair on my neck stand up. It's like coming up your basement stairs thinking someone is chasing you when you really know it is just your imagination. My mother was not going to bite my fingers.

Dad sat on the bed across from her thinking of God knows what. Cindy and I went to her and took off her wedding ring. As Cindy and I each held one of her hands, we straightened out her fingers and laid them by her side. She was still warm. Dad was watching us the entire time and actually looked resentful. I really can't describe the look on his face. Maybe having no look is really a look.

As I was unbending her fingers he said, "I guess rigor and mortis haven't shown up yet." In all my life I was actually speechless. He then went on to say, "I can't wait to see what the ghouls are going to do to her." For a second, I had no idea what he meant. Who says shit like that at a time like this?

I only said, "The ghouls are coming for you." I think what he meant was that he wondered what the mortician would make her look like for her funeral. Did he forget she was being cremated?

I think Cindy, Greg and I might have told Dad we were sorry. Sorry that she died, sorry that he was alone now, sorry for him because he had to live with his conscience. I said it because it seemed like the right thing to say. I didn't mean it. I felt sorry for her and for us. I believe he slowly killed her. He did it by keeping the house too cold in the winter, or too hot in the summer. He did it by making her work full time with arthritis until she was 65. He did it by yelling at her and her children. He did it by telling her all of the time they had no money. He did it by being an asshole to her and everyone they knew. Every word that came out of his mouth was another nail in her coffin.

He never said a word to Greg, Cindy or me. He never said a word to her brother who came from Washington or any of Mom's grandchildren. He never offered any kind words to Mike or Debbie either or thanked her nurses for their phenomenal care. He didn't offer any condolences whatsoever. He was going to have his own pity party and it made no difference how we felt about the woman who knitted our hats and scarves, warmed our socks in the oven and handmade our Barbie's clothes. She cleaned up our vomit, changed our diapers and helped us every step of the way through school. She lied for all her children to keep us from getting in trouble. Life would never be the same because no one can fill that kind of void.

We left the hospital. We left her body there. I watched my father shuffle down the hall and tried to feel pity for him. I wondered if I would ever feel love for someone who was so self-centered. No one said a word in the elevator. Cindy offered up coffee at her house to which we all said "yes." What else was there to do at that moment?

When I walked out into the night, it was snowing lightly and all I could think was that the snowflakes were little bits of her flying free. She was at peace. She was free from his grip and her pain. On December 27, God called one of his angels home.

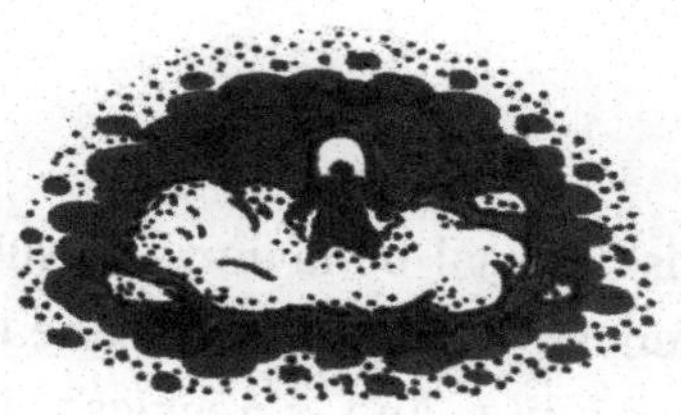

the shit storm

The definition of a "sociopath" as plagiarized from some source from the internet is this:

Antisocial Personality Disorder is also known as psychopathy or sociopathy. Individuals with this disorder have little regard for the feeling and welfare of others. As a clinical diagnosis it is usually limited to those over age 18. Antisocial Personality Disorder is chronic, beginning in adolescence and continuing throughout adulthood. There are ten general symptoms:

1. not learning from experience
2. no sense of responsibility
3. inability to form meaningful relationships
4. inability to control impulses
5. lack of moral sense
6. chronically antisocial behavior
7. no change in behavior after punishment
8. emotional immaturity
9. lack of guilt
10. self-centeredness

People with this disorder may exhibit criminal behavior. They may not work. If they do work, they are frequently absent or may quit suddenly. They do not consider other people's wishes, welfare or rights. They can be manipulative and may lie to gain personal pleasure or profit. They may default on loans, fail to provide child support, or fail to care for their dependents adequately. High risk sexual behavior and substance abuse are common. Impulsiveness, failure to plan ahead, aggressiveness, irritability, irresponsibility, and a reckless disregard for their own safety and the safety of others are traits of the antisocial personality. Socioeconomic status, gender, and genetic factors play a role. Males are more likely to be antisocial than females. Those from lower socioeconomic groups are more susceptible. A family history of the disorder puts one at higher risk.

There are many theories about the cause of Antisocial Personality Disorder including experiencing neglectful parenting as a child, low levels of certain neurotransmitters in the brain, and belief that antisocial behavior is justified because of difficult circumstances. Psychotherapy, group therapy, and family therapy are common treatments. The effects of medical treatment are inconclusive. Unfortunately, most people with Antisocial Personality Disorder reject treatment. Therefore, recovery rates are low.

Well, that's just terrific. None of us ever had a chance. Whether our father Louis was born with this mental disorder or developed it over the course of his earlier years is really irrelevant to me. I've known for most of my life there was something wrong with his thinking. As a friend of mine once said, "His behavioral justification is nothing more than his own pretzel logic." What she meant was that he justified what he said and did with a series of confusing lies and behavior. His thoughts were not the result of clear thinking, but twisted, rambling fragments specifically lacking coherence.

Cindy and I, along with many others who may or may not have been able to clinically define our father's mental illness, have known for a long time that something was rotten in Denmark. We scratched our heads for forty years trying to figure out what might be the root cause of his primary malfunctions. I know we commented on multiple occasions, "What the fuck is with him? Why does he talk like that? What is he trying to get away with now?" Even if he was never diagnosed with a personality disorder we knew he was always a few pickles short of a sandwich.

If you look closely at the definition and then recall many details of the stories you have already read, then it is not really difficult to put the pieces of the puzzle together. Our father grew up without a father of his own and was raised by a mother who did not like him very much. I am confident that his own mother's contempt for her child was the catalyst that started the car that would eventually run off into a ditch. Forget the depression, the wars and his troubled teens. His mother wanted a "Louise" not a "Louis" and he never recovered.

He did as little as possible to earn a living, often surviving off of the generosity of others like his mother, aunt and eventually his wife and kids. This was, of course, after he gave countless speeches littered with "I am in a bind. I don't know how this happened. We will be on the street if you don't help. I don't know how we will eat. Your mother will have to get a job. We will have to get rid of the dogs because we can't afford to feed them." What were Cindy and I going to do? We were only ten or so when he started complaining that "life wasn't fair." I had an idea. How about you get a fucking job and leave the rest of us alone.

Lou took every opportunity to lie, cheat and steal his way through life if he thought there might be a payout at the end. He did it sometimes simply for the satisfaction of getting something for nothing. He had his kids and wife participate in his charades and schemes under the guise that "he deserved it" more than the next guy.

Winning is everything to a sociopath so as long as my father perceived that he somehow got the best of a situation, that was absolutely perfect. Our father lacked morals, compassion, work ethics, maturity and a sense of right and wrong. I cannot believe that I had a parent who was so clinically depraved, such a degenerate, yet somehow I continue to function in society and raise my children to become the exact opposite of everything he stood for.

In the definition it states that an individual may participate in risky sexual behavior. That is somewhat nondescript. However, I am sure one could assume that dressing like a woman and parading around your own home in a skirt and five-inch stripper shoes classifies as "risky." I think the definition should qualify further the use of the word "risky" to include, "creepy, sick, disturbing and maladjusted."

So with the help of the internet, WebMD, The Mayo Clinic, and Google, Cindy and I were able to diagnose his psychoses and have it confirmed by his doctors. It took 92 years to have him labeled. All of my life I had been looking for any word to describe his personality, besides telling everyone for forty years he was a morally bankrupt prick. The problem was that now that I had this diagnosis, I also had to choke on the word "dementia." Think about it for a minute. My sister and I were dealing with a 92-year-old sociopath with frontal lobe dementia, hearing loss and macular degeneration. I swear to God there was no peace with this guy.

In 2011 at the age of 92 he was still mowing his own lawn and driving himself wherever he wished to go. Cindy and I did not care where he drove as long as it was within a five-mile radius of his home. He prepared most of his own meals and paid his own bills. However, we were seeing a decline in his abilities since Mom passed away and were unwilling to allow his behavior to go unchecked any longer.

Like my mother, he had an army of top medical professionals caring for him right in his own backyard. However, sometime over the past 18 months since our mother died, the care they provided was no longer good enough. He wanted to use the services of the Veterans Administration. Since he was a veteran of two wars, he was certainly entitled to some of what they had to offer. The problem was that the VA is 15 miles from his house and he wanted to go there three days a week.

His desire to visit the VA was also partly due to the string of bullshit stories he told to all of the physicians he had been seeing in his own city. They all did their best to accommodate him, listen to his never-ending tales of woe and tried to repair his worn-out body. Most of the time, they listened to him breathe and said, "You're fine. Go home." He never got pain pills or a whole lot of sympathy since they all knew he still lived in his house, was still able to drive, mow his own lawn, feed himself and wipe his own ass. I know some people who can't do that at 50.

Like getting something for nothing, he just wanted more lotions, pills, inhalers and suppositories to shove in a box. Free shit was his motivation. All he really needed was a good anti-anxiety med, a sleeping pill and a time out in the naughty chair.

In June, 2011 the only thing wrong with him was that he was 92. He refused to understand why nothing in his body worked like it used to. All he complained about was his back, shoulder, hip and his dry fucking skin. After he received the explanation of benefits for all of the free services and medication the VA provided, he drove his wrinkled ass back there with a stack of paper wanting someone in billing to explain what was written in plain English. Once they blew him off, he wandered into social services and continued on this path until he wasted a half a day.

He then came home to tell Cindy that "they" wanted to see him, yet no one would help him once he got there. He did his best to be intimidating and belligerent. Even at 92 and counting, his predatory stare was unnerving. He used that to get attention when his words had failed him.

Cindy and I warned him many times about asking for treatments, care or medication he did not really need. “Go down there and waste all the time you want but do not be a pest, do not try to rip them off and stay off of their radar screen.” Was that advice so hard to follow? Yes. Sociopaths will not and cannot take advice from anyone. They continue down their path of destruction until they get what they are after, get caught or die. By now, I think anyone reading this knows what my preference was.

I told him not to ask about a Veteran’s pension because the VA would want all of his information, including account balances, assets and property values. Did he listen? No. He promptly filled out the application, which I was able to view online so I knew exactly on what sections he bent the truth. He eventually started receiving monthly checks after he “forgot” to list rental income.

The VA believed he was destitute given that he “forgot” to include several thousand dollars of additional income he was capable of earning. It was irrelevant that he was a poor businessman who refused to put tenants in his property. I warned him he would be committing a fraud the second he cashed those checks and it would not take the VA very long to catch on. Coincidentally he let two checks sit on his dining room table for three months.

Having thought better about opening his mouth and shoving his foot in it, he told me, “I regretfully informed the VA I had made a mistake and will be sending the checks back.” Keep in mind he thought nothing wrong with what I considered to be stealing from a government agency.

He would have kept that money and risked jail time except he knew I meant it when I said, “I will turn you in. Period.” I tried my own predatory stare and it must have worked.

That one event seemed a small victory for me as I could not live with the fact that he was so willing to steal from an organization that provided benefits for all veterans from WWI to the present. I kept having to remind myself, however, that sociopaths simply don't give a damn about anyone but themselves. But I was in a position to fight back against his unswerving will to pull another con. I told him I would call them and "rat him out" if he did not stop. He knew I meant it. I didn't care by this point if he went to jail. That would be fine with me. He wanted whatever the VA offered because he thought he could get away with lying on another application; not because he needed or deserved the money. Little did I know that as the months passed, he was only bullshitting me with his sudden attack of conscience.

By the middle of 2011 he managed to stack up eleven pension checks. He did not cash them but felt good that he conned the VA out of a few grand. He got an immense amount of satisfaction just knowing they were sitting in plain view so he could look at them every day. Why did I think he would be truthful with me and subsequently do the right thing? I frequently forgot what my father was and what motivated him. Of course, like all sociopaths, he could not understand why everyone else didn't operate in a fundamental black hole. What was wrong with beating the system over and over again?

He tried the same stunt with the Social Security Administration. Where did it say anywhere that just because you were 92 you were entitled to disability income? In Lou's world it meant exactly that. Again, he lied his ass off and put whatever information on the application would benefit him the most. He asked every conceivable needs-based organization for support. At 93 he applied for food stamps and assistance from the VA to prevent impending homelessness. At that point he had the VA, SSA and the IRS snooping around. The only thing missing was a giant bull's eye on his forehead and his social security number plastered on a giant billboard overlooking the highway.

By the middle of June 2011, the VA had listened to enough of his complaining. He had macular degeneration in one eye which made him blind, yet he expected the doctors to somehow fix 92-year-old eyeballs. He complained his shoulder was bad yet continued to lift ten-pound weights—the wrong way—and cut his own grass. He complained he couldn't sleep but neglected to tell him that he drank too much alcohol or digested a super-sized root beer float before bed. He yelled at them to speak up but never told them he had hearing aids that the VA gave him that he refused to wear.

After his 92nd birthday party, Cindy and I had enough. In typical fashion he started one of his famous fights right after dinner that continued for 90 minutes until we escorted him across the street to his own house. This discussion had to do with our shitty attitudes, and we were about to get berated in front of our husbands and kids.

Just the week prior he called Cindy in a panic from the VA asking us to come and get him. He said, "They lied to me and put those goddamn drops in my eyes and now I can't see to drive." Somehow, he managed though to drive about a quarter mile to an empty parking lot, borrow a phone from someone in a mini-van and give my sister his location.

During his birthday celebration he could not wait to voice his displeasure with our attitudes when we finally showed up to get him. "I didn't appreciate you two yelling at me in public." Really? We didn't appreciate wasting a half a day driving through one of the many depressed Cleveland neighborhoods looking for an old man wandering around like Mr. Magoo.

Game on. He could not wait to start another one of his famous fights and I was all in. He could have cared less that six of his grandchildren were within earshot. Cindy and I tried to get straight answers out of him about why he was going to the VA so much and what he really wanted as far as medical treatment. Forget it. He slammed his fists on the table and told all of us to "drop it."

In the end, this was his true characteristic behavior. He started a conversation that he knew would get everyone edgy then refused to engage in a normal conversation and answer a single question clearly and succinctly. He backed himself into a corner because he was unable to keep his lies straight and then snarled and foamed at the mouth like a rabid dog. What he tried to do was drag us into a rat trap and then got pissed when we refused to take a leap from a 50-foot high dive into six inches of water.

The following Monday morning Cindy and I got our answers. Cindy simply called the VA and spoke to his case manager Michelle. Of course she was shocked to find he had two daughters trying to coordinate his care. She never knew we existed. His emergency contact was Mom, who was dead and as far as they knew, he was really taking care of himself. Cindy and Michelle spent well over an hour comparing stories.

Michelle explained that she told him more than once that he only needed to visit with the doctors about once every six months. He told us he was just doing what he was told. She said he showed up frequently with no appointment and a stack of paper, walking from one department to another seeking assistance. She also said that the psychologist he wanted to see was aware that he was trying to manipulate her as well. He thought he was being clever by toying with her.

And so, The Shit Storm began. With the information we provided, the VA's experience with him and his big mouth, his world was about to implode. He asked for an MRI because he was dizzy and thought the problem was in his ears. They performed the MRI to check for brain function because he would not shut up about listing as he walked. He was completely unaware of what was ready to fall right on top of his head.

Michelle kindly invited his daughters to sit through his psychiatric evaluation. I thought I might charge tickets to this event as his behavior would cover the gambit of emotions. This would be Oscar-worthy stuff. The drive with our father to the VA seemed endless. I was so busy having our inevitable three-way conversation/argument in my head I didn't even think about being carsick.

He was so afraid he could not control what Cindy and I were going to say during the follow up to his mental evaluation that he kept saying over and over again, "Don't offer any details. Don't give her any information." Jesus, I knew he was serious, but Cindy and I really would not have to say anything because it only ever took all of five minutes for him to throw himself in front of the train. We just sat there patiently and waited for him to fall on the tracks.

I could not size up his doctor. I was unable to ascertain if she had the chops to take him on or we were all just on another endless "kiss his ass because he is just an old man" journey. She was middle-aged or younger but with the uni-brow, I could not estimate her age. She had piercing eyes that revealed years of experience dealing with all kinds of mental illness. Her pedicure was pretty and her feet and hands were in great shape so based on that I would say she was about 35. He unkindly said, "She is uglier than a bulldog sitting on a mud fence."

I read her badge quickly as I shook her hand and saw that she had a PhD. Her professional designation meant she knew a lot more than Cindy and I could ever have learned from the internet. Her office was unimpressive which was really irrelevant to her abilities as a doctor. I had a tiny office once and I know I was smart and had my shit together.

As I surveyed my surroundings, I did not see one picture of kids, pets or other family members. There was just her name on the door printed in big black letters on a sheet of paper. This told me she was all business. Fine with me as she was facing a tough nut to crack and I wasn't in the mood to witness anyone tread lightly with him. I felt better, though, the minute she started to speak. My diarrhea was going away.

The doctor started to explain to our father why we were all gathered together. She respectfully communicated with him directly. She looked him in the eye and he glared at Cindy and me with contempt and we had not spoken one word yet. So far, so good, as we were secretly hoping he would show his true colors. She took out the results of his mental evaluation and simultaneously pulled up the results of his MRI on her computer. All I heard were the words "severely impaired" and I shot a look at Cindy that said, "Holy shit! He is going to smash her in the face with his cane!"

She was patiently and gently trying to explain to him that he was suffering from a cross between Alzheimer's Disease and dementia. His ability to follow a conversation and change subject matters was diminished. His ability for reasoning and rationalization were also diminished. She continued with her findings until he could take no more. He asked, "Am I permitted to disagree with the test results?

She said, "Yes. But our findings are supported by the results of your MRI." She explained he had "dead spots" in his brain from a lack of oxygen that would never get better. At this moment Cindy and I thought he would go from a manipulative sociopath to a full-fledged serial killer. The look on his face was deadly.

It was a little sad to watch his expression. He looked defeated for a few minutes and then found his voice again—along with his indignation. As he balled up his fist, he announced he did not agree with the questions on the test or what his results showed. He made a grand gesture that he was capable of a lot that the test did not show. All three of us waited to hear what that was.

The doctor kindly kept bringing him back to the issues, which were not very complicated. First, she wanted him to use a pill organizer. He said, "I won't do it. I am capable of taking the right medication every day." I felt my stomach churning again. After ten minutes, she gave up the notion he would ever cooperate on the importance of keeping his medications straight. Frankly, Cindy and I did not care if he overdosed or under-dosed on his meds. We volunteered to help but he didn't want us anywhere near his stash of class II narcotics.

We quickly moved on to the next subject. She suggested he was not eating enough because he had lost a few pounds. She said, "Sir, you have lost a few pounds. Are you eating ok?"

He blustered, "I am on a controlled diet. I want to lose weight."

Cindy's chin dropped and I rolled my eyes.

She said, "Who is restricting your diet?"

He screamed, "I eat fine. I cook for myself every day!"

This is where Cindy jumped into the conversation. She explained she lived directly across the street and literally walked dinner over to him three or four times a week. We informed her that he cooked eggs and made oatmeal for himself. Good enough for me. I don't think I really cared if he was eating Alpo from a can. He hated the food I brought to him from a gourmet grocery store so let him eat whatever the hell he wanted.

At this point she asked if he turned the stove on. He said, "Of course I do! How the hell else am I supposed to cook?"

She asked him if he ever left the burners lit and he said, "Absolutely not."

She looked at me and I nodded, "yes" and that's when things got a little nasty. I reminded him, for his own good, that he left the gas burners lit on more than one occasion and left a pan burning on the stove.

He said, "You're crazy."

She suggested he literally turn the gas off to the stove and start using the microwave. We could tell his head was spinning as she talked about buying frozen dinners and boiling water in a microwave. She also suggested going to the local senior center for a few meals every week since they were good and inexpensive.

Cindy and I sat there shaking our heads as if to say, "There is no fucking way you will drag him in there for anything, let alone a hot lunch. He would rather eat cold ravioli right out of the can."

She looked at us and said, "What, no good?"

We said in tandem, "Go ahead and ask him."

You could see she was running out of patience and time and in her head said, "fuck it" and moved on to her next concern.

She started her next conversation by asking, "Sir, how are you doing paying your bills?"

He commented, "I am not stupid. I spent a few years working at a leading accounting firm, so I know how to write a check." Of course, that's not what she was intimating so she looked at Cindy and me. The answer was that he paid his bills just fine. He did it on time and as far as we could tell, never overpaid or agreed to send money to some guy in Africa who told him he had to pay a small fee to collect an inheritance from some long-lost relative who left him millions of dollars.

Cindy and I squirmed in our seats trying to figure out some way we could inform her he was still trying to operate his rental units and continued to live in his rather large home. At this moment, Cindy stood up and said, "Excuse me. I have to make a phone call to my son." I thought it was odd timing since we were just getting to a good part.

I continued the conversation with his doctor and started to tell her about his rentals. Just as I uttered the words, "There are four of six units empty," Cindy came back in the room.

As she handed the doctor a folded-up sheet of paper she said, "The girls at the front desk asked me to give you this message." Holy shit! Cindy went out into the waiting area, wrote on a slip of paper "ask him about the other property he owns that he is trying to manage." The doctor looked at it and without skipping a beat managed to work it right into the conversation. It really was beautiful to watch. Did I mention we come from a family of skilled liars?

She said, "Tell me, do you own other property besides the house you live in?" Dad looked puzzled as though he was thinking whether or not he should continue lying or own this one.

He decided on the latter. "Yes."

The doctor flat out asked, "Tell me sir, how are you able to take care of these properties? Do you have a company or family who assist you?" Again, she was suggesting he was incapable, which only fueled the fire. Here we go again. He is mad now.

"No, goddamn it! Do you people think I am a cripple? I have been doing my own work for forty years!"

She said, "You mean to tell me that you are driving to these properties, climbing ladders and fixing things?"

He said, "Well, how the hell else will it get done!" At this point, Cindy and I had slid so far down in our seats our asses were hanging in the wind.

We all left her office with her telling Cindy and me she felt sorry for both of us but thought we deserved a pat on the back for trying to keep him from killing himself and everyone else around him. She told him she thought he was mean and wished us good luck. I am confident she hoped she might never see him again.

As we walked down the hall my stomach started to rumble which only meant my insides were liquefying and I should look forward to being carsick on the way home.

Dad sat in the car silently until he could gather his thoughts. It wasn't at all that I believed he was searching for the right sentimentalities to thank us for our time and compassion. He was thinking of a way to voice his displeasure and not come off sounding like a total prick.

He started his incoming lecture with "I don't appreciate you two divulging my personal information." After that, I never heard another word. I sat staring out the back window wishing somehow Cindy and I would survive a head-on collision. Since this was unlikely and not realistic, I began thinking what Cindy and I would do, now that we had a professional tell us that our father's brain was shrinking and his demeanor would only get worse.

He managed to give himself up to the last person at the VA who at least acted like she cared what happened to him. This relationship would never work however, because he did not reciprocate the kindnesses they bestowed on him. The only thing they asked of him was to "be careful." The only thing he ever asked for, besides free shit, was for everyone to mind their own business.

Six months after this meeting he was still driving and insisting he could run his rental property business. He spent more time trying to figure out who he could sue for my mother's death. His last contention was that she died from acetaminophen poisoning and was hanging his hopes on one of the hundred attorneys advertising on late-night television.

Although the shrink promised, she never contacted the BMV to get his driver's license revoked. Ninety-two-and-a-half years old and his own doctor didn't do a thing to have him declared incompetent. His doctor just chuckled at how long our father managed to live as he said, “I can’t have him declared just for being an asshole. He is not entirely crazy yet.” Everyone talked a great game about what we should do about him, but it was really just lip service. The doctors said what they needed to say to get us to leave. Cindy and I had been living with an insane person our entire lives and all we ultimately received was a pat on the back. The world is loaded with sociopaths who live among decent people.

In the end, despite all of our objections and a mountain of medical findings to support them, our father moved through the rest of his life unencumbered, infecting everyone with his bullshit. I had hope that a self-created shit storm of epic proportions would one day rain down on his stupid head and that we would have his doctors leading the way to his final incarceration. I thought that the day Cindy and I took our virgin road trip to the VA would result in the beginning of the end. I looked forward to the day that he eventually talked himself into a magician’s trick bag and could not get out. We desperately wanted validation from the professionals in the form of some kind of legal action.

What did we get? Nothing. No straight jacket, no shackles, no drugs, no advice and no escort to the front door. The shrink just kicked a sleeping bear and sent us out of her office with a pat on the head. If there was going to be a storm, it would be left up to us to bring it. Cindy and I would be the ones who would have to figure out how to restrict his driving and out-maneuver his repeated requests for government assistance.

He had the money, the brains and the resources to spend the last years of his life with dignity. He had an army of doctors and a family that really cared. He had 14 grandchildren who would do anything for him if he showed them a little attention. He lived his life in spite of all that he had and all that he had learned and openly and frequently remarked, “What’s the point of going on? I will just take care of it the old-fashioned way.”

How many times can a person hear that before he/she says, “Well, what the fuck are you waiting for?”

I was the delusional one who thought that he would stop being mentally ill. What was it about me that I continued to hope that one day my father would treat me differently than he had for 50 years? Cindy and I begged him to listen to reason and explained what he was doing was wrong. He hoped that he would voluntarily give up driving and start being a good patient.

In the end, I was hoping that my father would mellow but that just never happened. He was a troublemaker and a bully at heart. Cindy and I had to either accept that he was getting worse and steer clear of him altogether or decide we would do whatever it took to keep him off the road and away from the VA. We coaxed him to take medication that would help him feel better and promised to drive him wherever he needed to go.

He never recovered from our trip to the VA because he knew what Cindy and I were hoping to accomplish. The shit storm was coming, and it would arrive in the shape of his 50-year-old twin daughters.

a banana in the oven

People do strange things as they age. And whatever their strange proclivities are, old people become very defensive about what they do and why they do it. In my father's case he might have used the same plastic sandwich bag over and over again. He had drawers full of clean underwear, t-shirts and socks but insisted on wearing the same threadbare clothes daily even if he had an appointment with the doctor.

My poor mother wrote page after page in a journal about what she did or how she felt and what she ate. When she died, I read a few of her journals and when I couldn't take it anymore, I threw 50 books in the garbage. She once told me she was throwing old food from the fridge into the toilet and flushing it instead of tossing it into the garbage. I couldn't imagine why she would do that unless my father somehow convinced her it was a more efficient way to dispose of a pot of old chili.

My father was very insistent about where he and my mother shopped for food. I can recall many years ago when my mother would make her grocery list and she had no less than three, sometimes four or five different lists for different stores. She sat for hours every Thursday evening with coupons and circulars so that she and Lou could hit at least two grocery stores and a few drug stores. This was a great distraction for him since he really did not want to work and our mother did not drive. So he would sit in the car while she went in and out of stores matching her coupons to their weekly deals.

As a child I could not imagine how horrible it would have been to be dragged around all day so I could save ten cents on a gallon of milk. I remember them driving to a city about 30 miles from their home so they could buy chicken at twenty-nine cents per pound. I realize that that generation moved a lot slower than we do today and seemed to have far less chaotic lives than parents of this generation. Even so, their quest for deals on food seemed ridiculous to me even as a small child.

Fast forward to Walmart Supercenters, Costco and Aldi and my father had a new purpose in life. I felt somewhat sorry for him after our mother died since he had no one to pal around with or eat with but still insisted on buying enough food to survive a nuclear holocaust. At 90-plus years old he still insisted on going to Costco. He tried to tell Cindy and me that he needed to walk around 150,000 square feet and buy mega tons of whatever was on sale.

When he died, we uncovered enough furniture polish, batteries and jars of peanut butter to last us a decade. A year after his death, I was still using up his sandwich bags and I pack two lunches a day.

On a weekly basis, he would call me or Cindy and say, "I need to hit Costco. When are you going next?" After taking him there one time, I dodged that bullet week after week. He dragged me around there for two hours and he bought batteries, nuts, orange juice and a 50-pound bag of dog food. I wanted to know where the real food was. He always said he had no food, but he never bought anything to eat. Cindy always said, "Where's the meat?" This meant that Cindy would continue to cook his meals and I would drive him around so all he could come home with was two boxes of chocolate, plastic bags, toilet cleaner and a pack of 30 rainbow-colored Sharpies.

His excursions were simply because he was bored out of his mind, but he would ruin every outing by starting fights with both of us. Neither Cindy nor I could stand being in the car with him. We were in close proximity to a ticking time bomb. While driving in the car with him, we were compelled to either keep our mouths shut and simply listen to his never-ending "you two are going to pay for what you've done to me" threats or start World War III in a confined space. We always went for WWIII with guns drawn.

At 93 years old, he was moving slower and becoming more and more unsteady. The difficult part in managing him was his size—at 185 pounds—and his awful attitude. We tried to convince him to give us a short list of things to buy since between me and Cindy we were at a grocery store four times a week. He was having no part of it, so we continued to try to be nice while simultaneously being tortured on a weekly basis.

This particular day in 2013 he was especially agitated because he wasn't feeling well and had just been to see his doctor. His doctor suspected he had pneumonia but would call me shortly with the results of his X-rays. All I could think was if there is a God, make him sick enough for a stay in the hospital so Cindy and I could get a break.

In my head, I was down on my knees praying for a little miracle. In reality, I was helping him shop. I'd walk slower than at a snail's pace. I'd watch him stare at ten different kinds of jelly wondering which one to buy. I knew he already had five 64-ounce jars at home already. Really, why should I give a shit if he bought another one? But it was a very painful five minutes of my life I would never get back. In fact, I had so many painful five minutes with him that by this point in my life all I wanted to do was scream at him and say, "Grab any fucking jar and let's go. You'll never eat it anyway."

In the store, he seemed more interested in getting big

cardboard boxes, to the point where he was emptying the store's produce onto the floor. Mind you, he already had a hundred empty boxes at home in his basement, so I promptly stopped him. To which he said, “Mind your own fucking business. I'll take what I want.”

I was losing my mind. I was sure of it.

By this point in our little shopping trip he had somehow managed to grab an empty cart. If you are unaware of how Aldi functions, you put a quarter in the coin slot on the cart to get a cart for shopping. When you're done, you put the cart back and you get your quarter. Checking out with him was a cluster fuck anyway but now we had an empty cart too. I thought he was using it to hang on to but quickly realized he was taking this cart outside so he could get the quarter. He was getting a free quarter and I was ready to beat him to death right there with a bunch of green bananas he had in his cart.

When we got in the car my phone was ringing. It was his doctor and I was praying he was on the verge of death and needed the hospital right away. My prayer was answered. His doctor told me he had pneumonia and needed to be admitted to the hospital immediately. Ha! I gave my father the “bad” news and he was pissed but agreeable.

However, the minute I said we were going right from the store he threw one of his famous fist-pounding, foot-stomping temper tantrums. He kept screaming at me that he needed to go home. I kept asking, “What for?” He would not answer me and I was not backing down. I told him I would bring him his personal items later, but the hospital wanted him sooner than later as they had a room waiting. He said he had to take care of something important before he went to the hospital. I said, “Like what?”

He was furious I was challenging him and even once tried to open the door and throw himself out of the car while I was doing

35 mph. I finally screamed, "What is your fucking problem?! Tell me right now what is going on at the house. If you don't, I will have you locked up in the psyche ward. Understand?!"

He settled down and said, "I left a banana in the oven."

I thought I'd lost my mind as well as my ability to hear. "What's in the oven?" I ask. He repeated it again and I said, "Jesus Christ. What is a banana doing in the oven? Is the oven on? Is it only one banana? Is the skin on it?" He said he had frozen it and was trying to thaw it so he could put it on his cereal.

I said, "That's it!? You're ready to kill me and throw yourself out of a moving vehicle because of one stinking banana? This ranks as one of the all-time dumbest fights I have ever had in my life."

That was it for me. After that day, I arranged for a driver at $15 an hour to take him wherever he wanted to go and for as long as he wanted. We hired a nice woman named Grace to take him to the doctor or the grocery store. We paid her to follow him around the store and help him unload his groceries. And for as patient and sweet as she was, she commented a few times about his sometimes odd or mean demeanor. We just told her to ignore him as he was just old and let him buy whatever he wanted.

I wasn't going to be held captive in an enclosed space one more time. I didn't care what it cost. He actually pleaded for me and Cindy to reconsider and I said no. It was too stressful for me, for Cindy and for him. Every time he laid eyes on his daughters, he became enraged because of all the horrible things he said we were doing to him. He threatened us with bodily harm and/or legal action. His paranoia was in high gear and there wasn't a whole lot to do at this point but avoid contact as much as possible. Whoever was patient and brave enough could have the job. I didn't care if he starved.

My father never understood that his decision to put a frozen, ugly brown banana in the oven was ultimately the reason he never got in my car again. This is why Cindy and I tell our own sons that we will eventually be very happy with a big car with a big back seat and a bar. They can hire us a driver and I promise it won't be because I ever put whole pieces of fruit in my oven.

kentucky bride

Lying by omission: my father was famous for this. By not openly talking about something or sharing key information he figured he was exempt from being known as a pathological liar. My father had a set of twin cousins whom he rarely spoke with. I met them once or twice and found them to be hilarious in their characterizations—especially when it came to my father and the rest of their German clan. Forty or so years passed since my sister and I had spoken to either of them. I personally had hardly given them a second thought in my years through school, work, marriages and child rearing.

After my mother died, I thought it would be appropriate to let the distant relatives know that Lou's wife had passed away. Cindy took it upon herself to volunteer for this task and picked up the phone and dialed the last known number for our second cousin. Even at 82, our cousin was energetic and chatty, littering the conversation with questions mostly having to do with how everyone was coping. She was also very sorry to hear that mom was dead. She seemed a little surprised that our mother, whom I think she believed was too meek to be married to Lou, actually survived 50 long years of marital agony. There was never anyone who had spoken so matter-of-factly about my father. We never lived near a living soul who knew him at all, so no one whoever spoke about him. We never heard any stories. That was, until his Texas cousin accidentally threw him under the bus.

It is very hard not to vomit all my stories on people. So when our second cousin asked, "How are you handling your mother's death and is your father still a nasty prick?" she had no idea she just opened the flood gates.

Cindy was not kind when she explained our latest dealings, specifically with his dementia coupled with an unbelievable and selfish demand of our time. She simply said, "He is the same as always, just a thousand times worse."

The cousin replied, "Oh my. Put his ass in a nursing home."

Let's be clear. Neither my sister nor I would ever intentionally leave a dog to starve or freeze, let alone a human being. We took care of our father for two reasons. First, because our mother asked us to and second, because he was a person. The fact that he was our father was entirely irrelevant. On the surface, it sounds like a horrible thing to say but it is simply the truth. It mattered to us that we at least tried to do the right thing. It was very difficult to try to look after him, feed him or even have useless conversation because my sister and I, like everyone else couldn't stand his abrasive personality.

Any time I tried to have meaningful conversation, he changed the subject or diverted my attention elsewhere. I had known for what seemed like an eternity that my father was a liar. His verbal response to any question was minimal, unsubstantial and ultimately frustrating. I always thought, "Why doesn't he just answer a question like a normal human being?" He spoke in riddles in order to be intentionally ambiguous. It worked on my mother and older sister and almost everyone else he knew. It did not work on Cindy or me. We understood far more than he believed and were far more intelligent than he would ever give us credit for.

It was clearly by accident, while talking with this Texas cousin, that Cindy stumbled on yet another cryptic aspect of

Lou's life. We felt that we could ask her anything. The problem was really that Cindy and I could not be very specific. We had to hope through a morbid cat and mouse game that information would just spill out of her mouth.

Our Texas cousin was not shy or guarded when she spoke. This seemed to be a family trait. While Cindy went on and on about how impossible our father was and how cruel he could be they both arrived at the same question. How did Mom survive 50 years with this man? Our mother, a relatively old woman when she died, made it to the finish line. It was while discussing this that our Texas cousin said, "Well, she fared better than his first wife."

Cindy said, "What?"

"Yes, his first wife. She lasted a lot longer than her."

Cindy said, "What did you say?!"

The cousin repeated herself again, "Lou's first wife! He married her in Kentucky."

There was a long pause. "He was married before? What was her name? You're not kidding, are you?"

"No."

We found out from our Texas cousin that this first wife of his was really very nice. She was single with three children. They married in Kentucky and moved to Cleveland after the Korean War. The cousin said she knew this for a fact because they all shared a duplex. My dad, his wife and her kids lived in one side and the cousin and her family lived in the other. What was alarming about this relationship he had was that we never knew anything about it. Our cousin said, "One day she was there and the next she wasn't." She lived with him for roughly a year. After she left, our cousin said our father never talked about her again.

With the miracle of the internet, Cindy and I were able to find out enough information that we could approach our father with at least a little ammunition. We found out her name was Elizabeth and that they did live on a small side street in a western Cleveland suburb. We could never find a death record or what happened to her and children.

The curiosity was killing me so I told Cindy we would catch Dad off guard and ask him some leading questions about his past. Over coffee, we began our investigation. Cindy was trying to be subtle, asking questions about where he lived after the war, who lived with him, etc. He was not taking the bait. I said, "This is bullshit." I looked right at him and asked, "Were you ever married before?" I wish I had a camera to freeze that look on his face. Shock and indignation. He must have wondered how we found out and where we got the balls to ask him such a thing.

He had this nasty smirk on his face and said, "Yeah. So what?" He always said, "so what" when he was backed into a corner. Cindy sat there waiting for the bomb to explode but it never happened. He said that it was his business, no one else's and then said, "Who the hell told you?" I informed him his cousin told us but was very confused as to where his new bride and stepchildren had disappeared. He said, "Don't worry about it. She's gone. I got rid of her."

Cindy finally found her voice and said, "What the hell did you just say? You got rid of her? Where?!"

Before Cindy or I could imagine him throwing her and her children all off the ninth street pier or burying them in the woods somewhere, he said, "She missed her family in Kentucky and wanted to go home. So, I divorced her and sent her back." Well, there seemed a lot wrong with his story, but I just let it go. I knew how my father uses people so I had confidence that the real reason he took a young woman with three children from Kentucky as his wife would materialize before my eyes. I knew I wouldn't see it coming.

I wanted to know if our mother knew he had been married before and he said she did know but I didn't believe him. She told us a lot but never let this monster cat out of the bag. On the surface it's not a big deal, but when you take a closer look, he married my mother, a widow, with three young children. Who does that twice in his life unless he's looking for an opportunity? Our Texas cousin said when he met our mother, he latched on and never let go. She had property and a little money and he wanted it for himself. He dropped anchor and never looked back.

Three or four years passed before the issue of this previous marriage surfaced again. If you have never filled out applications for veteran's aid and assistance, count your blessings. It is a sea of paperwork that only those who totally have their shit together can conquer. As annoyed as I was, it was because of this application that I was forced to dissect his DD214 papers. These are the Department of Justice discharge papers that provide dates and reasons for separation from the service.

When I looked closely at his discharge dates it would have been from the Korean War in roughly 1952. His marital status said "married" so I knew this had to be his Kentucky bride. However, the reason for separation and release from service was listed as, "hardship." The date of discharge was roughly a year from when he got married. At the time the only people he would have had to take care of would have been his mother or his new wife. Since his mother was never sick a day in her life and not incapacitated in any way, I thought, "who the hell is he running home to?"

"Oh my God," was all I said to myself. He married this young woman while he was stationed in Kentucky, brought her and her three kids back to Cleveland and then told the war department he needed to go home to take care of her and them. He married her to get out of the Army! Boo-ya, touchdown, three-pointer, goal, score, game, set, match! I now had the information I needed to accuse him of being a low life. I was going to do just that.

I showed him his own DD214 papers and asked him point blank, "Did you marry this woman and use her as an excuse to get out of the Army?"

He said, "She knew."

Cindy and I both proudly called "bullshit" and told him he was a low-life snake. There is no way a nice woman who has a family to help her would agree to marry someone, move out of state and pull a fast one on the U.S. Department of Defense. Cindy said, "You fucking lied to her to get something you desperately wanted without giving two shits about her kids." It worked for him because he never had anyone watching him or calling him on his bullshit—ever. Either no one cared, or they were terrified of him. I am shocked though that in all of my 50+ years with him I never heard him slip about a "first wife" or anything. If our mother knew anything, she kept her mouth shut.

I have no idea whatever happened to Elizabeth or her children. He had no idea either and if he did, he wasn't saying a word. He got what he wanted. In my heart, I have to believe she figured out the scam all on her own and ran back to Kentucky. I am certain she is dead now and that her children have no idea who our father was or what he did to their mother. If they had any memory, hopefully she lied about Louis to cover up for the enormous mistake she made. At least she got out and away from him after only one year.

I would have liked to have seen a picture of her or her kids. What I hope and pray for is that Elizabeth found a nice, new husband who married her because he loved her. Not because he needed a valid code for separation from duty from the Army.

I know in my gut that there was much more to this story and I will never know what it was. I like to share my stories, especially with my family. I want them to know who I am and how I arrived at this moment in my life. Hopefully my successes and my mistakes have helped me be a better parent, a better wife and a better friend. After all that's where wisdom comes from; gaining knowledge over time and having the capacity to make good use of it.

i need a new head

How should this story end? How will it end? The saying goes, "Life is stranger than fiction." My life with Lou was a dysfunctional soup. Some may take great pity toward my father and excuse his behavior because they believe he needed forgiveness and understanding. Some may be filled with hatred towards a man who had the power to do so many good things yet chose a self-destructive, self-serving existence. Yet still, some may feel sad for me, my siblings and my mother. What I do know is that there is a little bit of all of us in this story.

There is also another expression that goes, "Laughter is the best medicine." Now, during family dinners, my sister and I talk about being sent away from the table for laughing, our father wearing a skirt and high heels, the night I was mauled by our family dog and how she crumpled under the pressure and the day my father's pants fell around his ankles in the midst of one of his famous temper tantrums. We talk about how he unintentionally killed his own dog by scaring it to death or that we thought he had a "thing" with one of his male tenants. Our conversations will never be about our great childhoods or the vacations we took as a family. That's the tragic part. We just sit around now making jokes about the stress and pressure he created as the head of our family.

What shocks me is that when I speak to my children or to anyone, I often hear him loud and clear. I absorbed much of his style and language. It shocks me because I made a declaration long ago to never be like him. It's a thought I refuse to give too much attention to, however, since it turns out I was actually capable of raising decent human beings in spite of all the bullshit.

2014 would be the beginning of the end; a downward spiral for our father that would surely end his life. Cindy and I could feel it with every stumble he had and misstep he took. Even though all we had to do was stand back and let it happen, Cindy and I forced ourselves deeper into a relationship with our father that, given enough time, would surely kill us. There was a chance he might outlive us both.

I used to have a dream as a small child that involved me sitting at a table with Cindy standing nearby. Paralyzed with fear, we both stayed perfectly still while something the consistency of wet dog food slowly covered us both. The pressure I felt from this dream was immense. I woke up crying every time I had this nightmare. I was told many years later that the dog food represented my father and that he was the source of my fears and anxieties. No kidding. But, why dog food? Couldn't I have dreamed up a frosty from Wendy's instead?

The anxiety we felt as children turned from nightmares to panic attacks and restlessness as middle-aged adults. Our fear was that we would never fully escape the profound effect he had on us both. Like some weird black fog, or wet dog food, our father's legacy just keeps changing shapes.

The beginning of 2014 was the same as previous years. Our father was old, but he was moving about and eating on his own. He managed to write down a grocery list every few weeks but there was a significant change occurring. He appeared confused. His thought processes were muddled and he would call me or Cindy and ask the same question over and over again. Questions like, “What is your address?” or “When are you going to the store?" or "When is my next doctor's appointment?"

The death of my mother, his devoted wife, surely made an impact on him, but I struggle to imagine exactly what that might be. He only ever said, "I think your mother was pissed at me when she died." And that he wanted to sue the hospital for poisoning her. He did not seem terribly broken up about her death or really lonely after she passed away. If he was, he kept it to himself.

Cindy and I felt compelled to watch after him more closely simply because it was what anyone else would do with someone who was living alone at 90 years old. It was at this moment that I felt real pressure. The kind that feels like an elephant is sitting on your chest. I would have taken the wet dog food at this moment in time.

Cindy and I fed him and checked on him regularly no matter how mad he became. We washed his dishes and took out the trash while he threatened to break our backs for being intrusive. We were still afraid of him and his temper but together, we could keep going. We continued to ignore our instinct to run and believed that the end of his life was fast approaching. We basically said to ourselves, "We've done it this long. What is the worst he can say to us now? We're at the finish line and we can look after him even though he hates us with an unparalleled passion." Basically we were thinking, "In spite of our own sanity, we're going to do what was right even if he tried to take us down with him."

In April of 2014 he was tripping and stumbling around his house ignoring every plea we made for him to stay off the stairs. If he made it up the stairs would he fall coming down? Cindy and I were certain we would find him in a crumpled heap at the bottom of the basement stairs. It was no surprise that he called one day to say he was sitting on the edge of his bed and couldn't walk.

This one seemingly benign event was the light at the end of

our tunnel. Once we knew he could not walk, we could rightfully move him into an assisted living facility and have him properly cared for. Make no mistake, this also meant that Cindy and I were officially off duty. Because he could not stand on his own for no apparent reason other than he was old and weak, he spent three weeks in a skilled nursing facility. He was so rude and such a liar while he was there that he was released to go home at the exact second his insurance ran out. Cindy and I also knew he could never go back to that place.

He lied about his living conditions and the size of his house. He said he was cooking for himself (if you count heating dinner from Cindy in a microwave "cooking"). He said he had help taking care of himself and help with his house. That may have been true but what he lied about was how he behaved like a spoiled rotten brat towards his own children. What he lied about incessantly was how combative he became at not being allowed to drive; when he tried to open the door of my car and throw himself onto the pavement while I was doing 35 mph; at threatening to have Cindy and me jailed for elder abuse. It was exhausting to listen to his bullshit and totally embarrassing to watch him carry on like a lunatic. My heart was breaking because I knew Cindy and I were trying our best to care for our father, while he was literally lying to every human being within a ten-mile radius. He lied about us to the point that sometimes he told people he had no children at all.

When the staff at the nursing facility sent him home, he was elated and surely felt vindicated once again. The truth is that he was such an asshole that he was kicked out for being too difficult to care for. Cindy and I felt defeated and would have to wait until the next moment that would seal his fate and get him away from us. He needed to fall at home and break something and then be chemically controlled by an army of people who understood exactly what and whom they were dealing with.

He had to have known it was only a matter of time before he would be forced to leave his house. He was fighting like an animal and lying out his ass to be able to stay there. He surely wasn't going to die there. Karma would not allow that to happen. His own doctor said he would never die from a heart attack. In that regard, he was stronger than an ox. I told Cindy that, as depressed as we were in having to take his shit day after day, his journey in life was not over yet. I also said, "This fucker is not going to die any time soon. He is not done making us miserable."

For 15 years our father was told what would happen if he lived long enough. None of us needed a crystal ball to show us what waited around the corner for him. He would eventually go deaf and blind and lose his ability to function on his own. He would be stripped of his freedom and his dignity. That wasn't because anyone would treat him poorly. It would be because he thought he would never die and if he did, angels would sing and carry him to the afterlife on a bed of goose feathers. He refused to acknowledge what Cindy and I knew; what his doctor knew. We all knew Lou would leave this world pissing himself, spitting at the nurses and carrying on like a lunatic. The question was, "When?"

He was sent home from yet another skilled nursing facility. He managed to break free again and leave Cindy and me holding his bag of bullshit. We had to try to figure out his meals again, home health care again, doctor's appointments again; all while fighting the urge to poison him. As harsh and as crazy as that sounds, we were desperate for peace and quiet and wanted off this merry-go-round. After 52 years, we were out of energy and patience. We deserved a break from the stress and pressure that sat on our backs day in and day out like a two-ton truck. We cried together because we did not know what to do except get up every day and do it again.

It had taken all of 93 and 5/6th years for him finally experience the feeling of being controlled by others. He lost his ability to freely go about his day unchecked and unencumbered. He had babysitters now. And a lot of them. Our day for a little reprieve came in April 2014.

He was finally forced into an assisted living facility after proving over and over that he simply could not manage to live alone any longer. Cindy and I had a long-standing joke about how long his morning newspaper sat on the front porch. We knew that if he didn't get it by a certain time that something was wrong. This actually wasn't funny, really, but we simply had no other way to determine his condition on a daily basis—depending on the location of the daily paper, was he alive or dead?

When Cindy called me one afternoon to say that the newspaper was still sitting on the porch, my knee-jerk reaction was to tell her to leave it alone. "So what," I said. That is a horrible reaction as I wouldn't leave an injured dog on the street. What was I thinking? But we are talking about a man who made everyday living impossible. Honestly, as my heart was racing, I thought that this might be the day he finally died in his sleep or fell down a flight of stairs and broke his neck. When he came home from his last three-week stay at a skilled nursing facility, all we asked was that he stay off the stairs. I was specific when I said, "Stay out of the basement. That is going to be your coffin if you don't use some common sense."

To which he said, "Mind your own goddamn business."

"Ok," I said. "It's your funeral."

When people ask, "What's in the basement? What does he need in the basement? What is so important in the basement?" I tell them the only thing I know. There were 19 cans of mandarin oranges, 12-year-old mushrooms, two refrigerators, 60 gallons of old paint and a table-full of carefully sorted screws, nails, pins and empty jars. 400 empty cardboard boxes, pictures of naked women and a whole dining room set. Two eight-foot picnic tables with four benches, eight toolboxes, 600 books and his mother's report card from 1904.

See what I'm getting at here? There's nothing down there worth two broken legs and a smashed in face. Honestly, why did I care if he fell down and killed himself? But I knew that karma would intervene and he would not die immediately. We would be left to watch him die in a hospital bed from infection, pneumonia or any of the unfortunate results of lying flat on your back for months. In April 2014 we finally had a real opportunity to end it all.

Since Cindy lived directly across the street, she was aware of my father's habits which included closing his front curtains before he went to bed. In the morning he would open them again and grab the newspaper off the front porch sometime before 10:00 am. On this particular day, Cindy was worried and called me around noon to say the curtains were still closed, the newspaper was still laying on the porch and he wasn't answering the phone. I told her to wait until I arrived and we would go in together, but she was certain something was wrong and ventured to his house alone.

When Cindy went into the house that fateful day in 2014, she said the television was blaring and she could only hear static noise. She quietly walked through the house looking for any sign of his demise. The lights were on and at first blush, he was nowhere to be found. Since we knew he insisted on regularly going to the basement, it was the next place to look. The basement in his house was dark and dingy and when you look down the stairs, it looked like a black hole. My legs work just fine and I don't like going down those stairs. I feel like I am going to fall at any moment and the only thing to catch me at the bottom is 20 paint cans and a concrete floor.

When Cindy got to the bottom, she could hear him making unrecognizable noises. She saw his cane and slippers but no sign of him. She saw tipped over paint cans and broken glass. To her it looked like he had been in a barroom brawl. Of course, the truth was that he was down there alone and was pulling items off of shelves and tipping things over in his attempt to get off the floor.

She walked toward the animal-like groans and grunts and found him wedged between the washer and dryer in the back corner of one of the rooms down there. Somehow, he managed to scoot, crawl or drag himself to this unfortunate spot and got stuck flat on his back, face up with his head jammed against the wall. He looked like a half-dead turtle stuck on its back, gasping for air. His arms were covered in second and third degree burns and he looked ashen and most certainly dead.

When she called me, all I could think was, "What the hell are we going to do with him now? Seriously! Now what!?" We both thought for a brief moment that we could leave him and he would eventually die. Cindy and I both knew that he would never agree to a more appropriate living arrangement so leaving him to die right in that spot was actually kind. I was pissed that he had not died. We both had our chance to turn our backs and walk away. Looking at him, we knew he was far from dead and once the fireman pulled him out of the basement, he would never go back there again. Call 911 or turn our backs and walk away. We paused for only a split second, while faced with the actual life or death dilemma. We could not leave him there to die. Cindy picked up the phone. Regardless of how many times we said we would just leave him to die, she promptly called 911. This was one of those water-shed moments that would change our lives. How he would die was not up to either one of us.

When I met her at the hospital he was strapped to a back board with his head in a cervical collar. Other than the burns he sustained (he kept touching the steam pipe that heats the house in an effort to pull himself off the floor), there was absolutely nothing wrong. He must have been on the basement floor for 24 to 30 hours and suffered nothing more than a few burns and a little dehydration. How was that even possible? I could not believe that he would survive this. The worst thing now was that Cindy and I would find ourselves in another epic battle of right versus wrong. It was going to be a fight for supremacy and vindication until the day he died. It was still two against one and Cindy and I worked together like a well-oiled machine. Cindy handled the intake at the hospital and I quickly got moving on making arrangements for a nursing home.

He survived the fall and did not get sepsis from the burns on his arms. He came through an accident that would have killed a mere mortal. I don't recall ever seeing him sidelined by illness or injury, so I was not surprised at all that he came out of this ready to once again tackle the world. However, he would have to take on the world from a wheelchair at a nursing home.

Over my own dead body would I even remotely consider allowing him to go home one more time. I didn't care what it was going to cost. Cindy could not babysit him another day. He was slowly killing her with his demanding bullshit, just like he did our mother. Cindy is so much like our mother. She is kind and considerate and accommodating to a fault. She was willing to feed him, drive him to the doctors, hire caregivers and listen to his never-ending diatribe of how his own daughters were conspiring against him. I, on the other hand, was not motivated to help him stay in that house for another day. His care was over my head, Cindy's head and anyone else whom he might charm for five minutes.

Lou was finally moved into the same assisted living facility where our mother had been. He was told a flat-out lie that his stay was temporary and that he needed some therapy. In the background, Cindy and I were making his arrangement permanent. The same nurses that cared for her would now have to care for him. That is why when my father was permanently relocated to his new home, I felt guilty. I knew that he would test their patience and professionalism like never before. They would have to drag this old goat to the dining room and on field trips. They would have to listen to him bitch and complain that they were hurting his precious asshole when they would be forced to clean it. They would have to repeat themselves over and over again because he would not wear his hearing aids. Most offensively, they would have to endure this day after day. On the bright side, they got paid to do this. Cindy and I were happy that the job of taking care of him now belonged to someone else.

After six months, they were all passing with flying colors. The nurses and aides constantly met his demands, listened to his rude comments and managed his daily care better than I ever could. One question that kept surfacing in one form or another from everyone that worked there was "What is wrong with him?" Cindy and I told all of them to pay attention because they would never come across another human being like this again in their lifetimes.

The only answer we could succinctly provide was to tell his caregivers to read up on "sociopathy." At first his nurses were surprised by that response because most people think sociopaths are serial killers. We know that this is not true. After a few months they completely understood what I meant. Cindy and I tried to explain that his issues stemmed far beyond normal frontal lobe dementia. He certainly had dementia, but he had other issues that made the nurses struggle with him often. In addition to all the medical terms you could slap on his chart I said, “He is just an asshole.”

Among many other things, he continually insisted on going home. He was very persistent on this issue. He insisted he was being held against his will. He insisted he could cook for himself and take care of his personal needs. He claimed to be much better since his fall and could manage on his own. He even asked for occupational therapy. The nurses and staff were very sweet when they told him he was out of his mind to think he could be alone. They nodded a lot and smiled and stalled him until another day. I know they didn't believe that this old man had enough gas in his tank to badger them until the very end. They underestimated the willpower of a mentally ill person.

I know that he sat in his room there and wondered for hours how the hell this happened to him. He wanted to be at home with the freedom to cause his usual trouble. He wanted to be at home so he could look at all of his stuff and covet what he managed to collect and hoard throughout his life. That is, in part, what makes this story so sad. He only loved three things; his stuff, his dogs, and the only thing he loved more than those—his freedom, which was now gone.

At home he had a stack of phone books and brochures from which to choose. He loved to make calls to people or organizations and explain his plight. What he was hoping for was three-fold: he wanted others to take pity on him, he wanted whatever he could get for free and he wanted to have his daughters arrested. Cindy and I found numbers at his house and even at the nursing home for elder abuse and personal injury attorneys, free legal aid, subsidized housing, at-risk homeless programs, public assistance programs like food stamps and any other agency that was available to the disenfranchised and the poor. The problem was that he was neither. Every time he made a call, we would have to make three to explain that he suffered no plights whatsoever. What he suffered from was dementia, paranoia and an exaggerated sense of entitlement. He got so pissed every time we thwarted his efforts, but with a clear conscience, we refused to allow him to keep sticking his hand out for whatever free service he thought he was entitled to. And we did not really wish to defend ourselves in some kind of legal matter. Every time I told him he had been foiled again he would say, "You are going to regret this until your dying day." Not so far, big guy.

While he was incarcerated, we cleaned his house. We found boxes inside boxes; a landfill's worth of plastic and metal recycling; mountains of all kinds of paper including 40-year-old tax returns, newspapers articles and medical receipts. Along with names and phone numbers we also found endless notes he had written about what horrible children he has. He would get in some kind of manic rambling episode and vent all his frustration and displeasure on paper at the only two people left in his world; Cindy and me. When people tell us he never meant anything he said we respond in unison, "Yes he did." When you consider a person with no conscience and no regard for anyone or anything, you must understand that no one individual is relevant. My father used people. He used them up. He used their things. He preyed on their pity, kindness, ignorance, stupidity, loyalty, or whatever else makes a human being vulnerable.

One weapon he possessed was the ability to shock with his language. His was a cunning, masterful linguist. We collected and saved many of his handwritten notes, including four small sheets of paper where he called Cindy and me the following:

Ignorant
Inappropriate
Sneaky

Derisive
Asinine
Greedy
Insulting
Dictatorial
Weak
Stupid
Spiteful
Mean
Omnipotent
Thieves
Holier-than-thou
Ridiculous
Uncooperative
Sick
Smug
Malicious
Crooked
Arrogant
Stubborn
Recalcitrant
Intolerable
Obtuse
Intrusive
Acid-mouths
Obstinate
Shrews
Shallow
Pervasive
White trash
Selfish
Parsimonious

Truth-stretchers
Condescending
Penurious
Back-stabbers
Greedy
Vindictive
Defiant
Incorrigible
Extravagant
Deceitful
Dead-beats
Despicable
Conceited
Spend-thrifts
Narrow-minded

Cindy and I made a point to keep many of these notes and put them in what we call the "shit box." One day when the dust has settled and I don't feel as though I need proof to convince the outside world that he really was that twisted, I will burn all of it.

On top of all of that he called us both "fucking bitches" to our faces. While in the nursing home, he hung up on me after he crudely announced he could no longer stand our "holier-than-thou asshole attitudes." That was most likely due to the fact that he could not tolerate or fathom that his daughters continued to out-maneuver him. There have been other vile threats like breaking our backs or necks and punching us in the mouth. He threatened to have us arrested and locked up in prison. He also hoped we would experience unpleasant end-of-life maladies like being blind, penniless, bored, sick or meet a nasty end like being flattened by a car and left to die.

As time moved at a snail's pace, our visits to him were fewer and farther between. Cindy and I did an occasional drive-by to drop off medication. We took him starlight mints and cheese puffs. We sat with him on occasion while he ate his dinner. Cindy cut up his meat and put sugar in his coffee. There was no conversation unless he was demanding something from us like the keys to his house, bank statements and his freebies from Publishers Clearinghouse. Tiny flashlights, nightlights, letter openers, lanterns, pill boxes and screwdriver sets. He referred to these things as his "man goodies," a term I cannot easily choke back.

Even after everyone who cared for him at his new home agreed that he should not have a phone book, he still managed to get the name and number of a personal injury attorney. Luckily this guy quickly sized him up over the phone and declined to assist him in his pursuit of legal action against his daughters. What could my father have said to try to convince a perfect stranger that he suffered some kind of physical or emotional abuse as a result of a specific act or neglect by me? He suffered no losses, unless you consider his freedom, which was his own doing. Essentially my father was trying to prove he suffered damage to his body, mind and/or emotions. Was he serious?

When I think of personal injury cases I think of medical malpractice, libel or slander, dog bites or car accidents. Stepping over his almost-dead body in the basement to leave him to die might have qualified, but it would have been tough to prove once he died and could no longer speak in his own defense. We saved our father and relocated him to a place well-suited for his ailing mind and body. It was there or a hospital with restraints and rubber walls. He should thank us that it wasn't the latter.

The stunt of trying to find an attorney so that he could fully educate himself of his rights was just another of many to inconvenience us and make us squirm. He enjoyed that immensely. We might as well have been the ant he was trying to burn up with a magnifying glass. When I asked my father what he was doing and why he was speaking with a lawyer, he said nothing. After a few seconds of silence he said, "the guy can't help me anyway. So what?" He completely missed the more obvious point in that he made the call in the first place.

This is how it went for several months. The aides forced him to eat in the dining room and assist with his own care. No one, except Cindy and me, went to visit him. He continued to call us regularly to harass us and remind us both we were going to rot in hell for what we were doing to him. We had specific instructions to leave his paperwork alone and if we wanted something from the house like the furniture or dishes, we had to pay him for it.

Each time we went for a visit we could see a noticeable decline. He was eating and speaking less. The nurses commented that he seemed to be sleeping more to which I said, "when he's sleeping, his lips aren't moving. That's a good thing."

As summer passed and we moved into fall, he began to experience periodic low-grade fevers. Remarkably, he was as agitated as ever. To show his disdain for his predicament, he spit his food at the nurses on occasion and tried to stop using the toilet. Thankfully his aides were experienced with this behavior and patiently maneuvered him around. As I sat with him, I had to dig deep to find any sympathy for my father. I was numb as I watched him slowly dying and told myself I would somehow have to find compassion for the troubled soul sitting before me.

Three days before Christmas, Cindy received a call from the nursing home that he had fallen and broken his hip. We were finally out doing a marathon shopping trip for Christmas gifts and were only one hour into our excursion. "Goddamn it," I said. His timing was unbelievable. We left the store and headed for the hospital again. This time we both knew this was it for him. He would never walk again and would painfully suffer until his life was over.

After three days in the hospital, he was sent back to the nursing home. He refused to acknowledge that he would lie in bed until he was dead. He would be moved around in excruciating pain, with a catheter and half out of his mind on painkillers. His dementia was far worse than I imagined. I had to believe he was losing his mind when he kept insisting we help him stand up to walk. Even at this stage he was combative and hateful towards my sister and me. Regardless, we brushed his teeth and fed him pureed food. We wiped his face for him and changed his socks. This was a human being that needed kindness.

Over our Christmas holiday, our father slipped further and further away. As he declined, we found ourselves spending more time at his bedside. He was quiet, though not peaceful. His facial expressions were filled with frustration and anger. There was nothing we could do except wait and pray that he would simply not wake up in the morning. That may have been more for our benefit. Would God take pity on my sister and me now and have him die in his sleep?

After two and a half weeks he stopped eating. He was allowed water if we put a thickening agent in it. It was like cornstarch and made his water the consistency of honey. He didn't drink his water through a straw; he ate it off of a spoon. It smelled like cooked pasta. I hated the way the plastic spoon sounded as it scraped against the Styrofoam cup. To me, it will forever have the same effect on my nerves as fingernails on a chalkboard.

We were told that a person who has stopped eating and drinking eventually moves to a state of euphoria. They lose the sensation of being thirsty and hungry and start to hallucinate. At this point, a person preparing to die usually ends up in a coma. Like my mother, this would be a kind transition. However, our father was not like anyone else and he would not slip away quietly.

In typical fashion, our father was going to fight and carry on until the very end of his life. 2015 had just started and the kids were back in school. Our entire Christmas break was filled with worry and stress. It had been explained to him many times that there was nothing anyone could do for his broken hip. Cindy and I promised that he would be comfortable and well taken care of. He wanted no part of that conversation. He was pissed that we had power of attorney over his health care and accused us of pretty much signing his death warrant.

The last few days were very quiet. The only words we understood were "water, pain and help." With his head in his hands, the last sentence he uttered was, "Oh goddamn it. I need a new head." It was sad to see him so frustrated at not being able to think and speak clearly. He had never been at a loss for words. For a brief second, I believed he realized he was losing his mind and his life. I could not help but cry.

I never thought I would see the day when my father could not speak. He used words brilliantly all his life. The day had arrived, and Cindy and I panicked. If he could not speak, we now realized that he would never be able to say what we waited our entire lives to hear. It was a sobering moment. With heavy hearts, she and I sat quietly at his bedside for hours, feeding him water and asking the nurses for more pain medication.

We contemplated the fact that he was really dying and we would never hear him say, "I love you." I wanted to hear him say, "thank you" for never leaving his side. I wanted him to tell us to enjoy the rest of our lives. I especially wanted to hear him say he was sorry. Cindy and I sat there for hours looking at him and each other, trying to reconcile 52 years with a father who made us feel so badly. We were raised by a mentally ill person and we just had to live with the fact that he was never going to say what we needed to hear, even if he had to lie to do it. We left late that night and the nurses told us not to worry. They assured us he would be well taken care of and that they would call us if his condition deteriorated further.

Twelve hours later his day nurse called and said we should hurry...

the cold truth

Realizing that someone very close to you has a major personality disorder is very scary. I spent half my life thinking one thing and then at the flip of a switch my opinion changed. I had spent too much time reading about mental illness. I was simultaneously sad at what I had discovered and relieved that I now knew he was sick. I did not ever want to admit that my father was an amoral, joyless, insensitive prick. In fantasy land he was Captain Stubing from *The Love Boat* or Blake Carrington from *Dynasty*. I needed my father to be kind-hearted and jovial or rich and powerful. He was neither. He could even have been Fred Sanford. Poor and living in a junkyard would have been okay as long as he was loving and appreciative. He was neither of those.

I ended up with a father who was cunning and ruthless. He could spend minutes to years on one scam or trick without ever weighing the outcome. He went to bed every night plotting revenge and woke up each morning with seemingly harmless money-making schemes. Meaning, he never thought what he would do if something went wrong or that he might suffer some real consequences. My father, like a lot of sociopaths, had no real societal link and used the people and circumstances around him to rise above others. Everything is always about themselves, which is why a sociopath goes through life saying, "Why do I have to give a fuck?" They generally don't give a damn about normal social behavior, about people and their feelings or circumstances or consequences which is why sociopaths don't feel anxiety, guilt, remorse, compassion or love.

Cindy and I had labeled him and we were not sure how to feel. Did we have any right to pick him apart? I believe we did. Fifty-plus years of witnessing his behavior and experiencing his wrath made us the only people left alive who had that right. My father was an enigma and we were ill-prepared to deal with a guy who could at any moment smack your ass because you were not standing up straight or hit you with a spoon because you were leaning over your cereal bowl.

I would have loved to call him "Daddy" and know in my heart I could count on him for love and support. What I learned was that he loved no one in the sense that healthy minded folks do. He pretended to love like normal people. He pretended to care like normal people do. He pretended to work like normal people do. The cold truth was that he was acting. Over time he learned what it looked like to show compassion or empathy, but in his gut and his heart, he probably felt nothing. He went through life faking emotions so that no one knew that he really felt nothing more than gas and hunger pains. The reality is that the only thing that motivated him to get up in the morning is that he discovered another social coffer he could stick his hand in. Or that he had to pee.

He never questioned his own motives or had any regard for the looming responsibilities of marrying a young widow with three children. Which he did twice. He never asked himself if he would put his family in jeopardy when lying to get government support. He never asked me how I felt about living with a dog that tried to kill me. He never asked any of us if we could afford to pay rent when we had just gotten our very first jobs out of college. He never asked my mother what she wanted to do with her life aside from waiting on him hand and foot. Did he ever ask if the two guys who mistakenly delivered carpet to his rentals would get fired or arrested for a B & E? Did he ask himself if repeatedly sticking his hand out to get government freebies he wasn't entitled to was simply wrong? The answer was “no” to all. He was not driven in life to make decisions using a normal person's moral or ethical compass. He never asked himself any probative questions, because his brain lacked reasoning abilities. When faced with a fork in the road he chose the path that had a personal payout at the end. Screw everyone else. He was driven by the game and his trump card was pity.

Lou's game was two-fold. Initially the game begins in how he can position himself to win by getting people to feel sorry for him. We all like to win but what price are we willing to pay? Most of us would never think of lying on a job application or throwing a co-worker under the bus. Most of us would never lie to get food stamps or discounted medical care. Even worse, would you ever try to convince your kids you were on the verge of homelessness just to scare them? Lying and keeping everyone on edge was part of his method. I can tell you, it worked. As a kid, I was kept awake at night thinking about how I would tell my wealthy friends we were eating oatmeal for dinner and would soon be living in a duplex.

This was precisely how he would spin his stories. If he was trying to get food stamps his speech might go something like this, “I have three young daughters at home who are hungry. I can't help it if no one is willing to pay fees for my services. If you allow me into the program, I won't be forced to send my sick wife back to work.” He always talked about falling on hard times and he desperately needed anyone to give him a break. He wanted pity and free shit from wherever he could get it. He tried to get free chocolate for a year from a very popular local candy store. On his entry form he wrote, “93. Widow. Hoping.” Did he think someone would read that and say, “Of course we should make this poor old man who lives in a giant house, owns rental property, has five kids and fourteen grandchildren the winner. What else does he have to live for?” Oh, I know the answer! He said after our mother died, “The only thing I have to live for anymore has four legs.” He was referring to his dog.

Each game he played could take anywhere from a day to several years to pull off. He chased a guy through the courts for ten-plus years because this degenerate owed him rent. My father tried to tell the court that the amount was somewhere over $12,000 because of late fees and interest. Mind you, at the time he had no tenants in his units. It would have been a much more logical decision to forget about one tenant and get six more. I am sure he was pissed because this guy got the better of him. This dumpster-diver beat him at his own game. This guy ended up in one of his units because my father saw him picking through garbage on the tree lawn and thought he could barter with the dude by getting him to paint in exchange for free rent. Nothing ever got painted. He disappeared in the middle of the night one weekend and ended up in Florida. Let this be a lesson to you. Someone picking through garbage cannot afford to pay $800 a month in rent. This person will not make a reliable tenant. Let him or her take away the free junk and leave it alone.

The ultimate game was suckering my mother out of pity for 50 years. That was worth more to him than any amount of money he could get from anyone or any place. That was probably worth more than the free carpet, free refrigerator, tools or clothes. How horrible must it have been to live like that? My mother's extreme morals, sweetness and sense of empathy held her prisoner for more than half of her life. She feared the unknown of leaving a man who was bankrupt of decency. He convinced her from the beginning that no one cared about him and that's all she needed to hear. She jumped into the rabbit hole and never looked back. It was only when she died that I believe he may have realized he was almost completely alone. The only thing now to keep him company was his dog and the woman who dropped off his meals-on-wheels three days a week.

He was never motivated by thoughts of love for any of us. Anyone he came in contact with was a pawn to be taken advantage of and discarded. However, he could not get rid of my sister and me. When he told us we were the worst things that ever happened to him I am certain he meant it. He knew we were watching him. The funny part is that he would tell us most of the time what he was up to in hopes that we would say, "That is fucking brilliant. Teach me how you do it!"

Unfortunately for him we started to thwart his efforts at gaining sympathy and thus getting discounts or vouchers or whatever else he believed he was entitled to just because he was almost 94. After we stopped him from getting housing vouchers, he told us, "You two are nothing but miserable, nosy bitches."

The cold and scary truth is that we were raised by a sociopath. It is very troubling to know you spent fifty-plus years in the midst of a person who was completely bored with his family and only exhilarated by risky behavior. I cannot tell you when Cindy and I realized that our father was mentally ill. Was it when he hid from us in our own house or when we first noticed he took pleasure in degrading and embarrassing us? Was it after we had just broken up our sixth dog fight or when he would send us away for laughing during dinner? Was it when he told us we could only have two ice cubes in our drink or when he made us vacuum in squares? Was it when he told my mother to stop chewing her words or when we realized he was a transvestite? Dressing like a woman and walking around the house not knowing when your kids would barge in must have been the ultimate aphrodisiac.

Any advice we were ever given, whether by our husbands, friends or trained professionals, was to run and never look back. My sister and I were handcuffed because we knew in our hearts we could never leave our mother. Trust me, we were ready to leave at 15. She thought he was so pathetic that she allowed him to get away with anything he wanted. He may have never murdered anyone, but he created carnage nonetheless. He expected my mother to keep all his terrible secrets and at the same time allowed him to emotionally fuck us all at every turn. She did so because she was confused and afraid and she did her best to smooth it over when he wasn't looking. To her he was a skillful liar and she never truly realized she was married to a nut-bag.

His first wife must have figured this out, which is why she disappeared after only a year. He said they divorced because of "irreconcilable differences." I am certain that was true. He wanted to dress like a chick and she didn't agree. His friends knew there was something wrong, his brother-n-law knew it and his kids knew it. My mother seemed defenseless and Cindy and I never convinced her to leave, because as she said, "If I don't stay with him, who will?" Sadly this left us no choice but to continue with "the game" because at the end of the day our loyalty to our mother outweighed our instinct to run.

Knowing what I know now about mental illness, which is limited at best, and applying a few simple words and phrases to his behavior over the years I am confident that what I have believed since I was a small child is absolutely true. My father felt no obligation to anyone, not even his wife and children. He was emotionally unattached because his brain had faulty wiring from the beginning. I will never truly know what flipped his switch and caused him to choose a loveless, joyless and isolated existence. As I stated before, I believe it was a combination of having no father from a very early age and a mother who openly wished for a daughter. Of course, he might have had no choice at all as his psychosis was simply a matter of defective brain matter and environmental influences. He did not know any better and survived in society according to his rules. We just happened to get in the way.

If you asked a hundred people if they would rather go through life with no conscience, driven solely by the thought of winning at all costs or have a life filled with love, compassion and respect what would they choose? The answer is "love" of course. Is money or fame or, in my father's case, a few trinkets and my mother's pity enough of a holy grail to sustain a daily life? I believe that for my father it was, because he didn't want love and he couldn't give it. It played no part in his heart and soul, which was really sad. It is amazing that such a small number of conscienceless people can do so much damage to the rest of us.

My mother overlooked his sinister ways. He had her convinced that he had been victimized his entire life by his family, employers, the government, even his children. Because of the perceived misfortune he regularly encountered, everyone around him should feel sorry for him. There are plenty of people who do not regularly try to rob the system and may truly need a break. They need the government cheese, the free healthcare and section eight vouchers. My father made sticking his hand out in the guise of desperate survival a full-time job when he had never really experienced gut-wrenching hardship in his life.

I hope that when you are out in the world you can give back to others just because it makes you feel good. Having a conscience doesn't mean you have to sacrifice your soul, your time or all of your money for the good of others. What it means is that you give a little to get back a lot. What it means is that you are not motivated by a "me first, so what, fuck everyone else" attitude.

Take a minute to hug your children, work hard, save your money, donate a little of your time, mind your own business, say thank you, call a friend, pay your fair share, adopt a pet, adopt a kid, don't hurt anyone and stay out of trouble.

I would like to think that in some small way my father was being punished with loneliness for having emotionally damaged his wife and his children. Can a sociopath feel this way? There is a saying that goes in part "hell is here on earth." Was my father at all reflective of the damage he had caused with his selfishness and total disregard for the normal order of society? Did he, in his last moments on earth, feel guilty for having caused so much pain?

The cold truth is that my father, like other sociopaths, did not care at all what the rest of us thought or how we felt, as desperately as we wished him to. The cold truth is that we are, all of us, unwilling participants in a sociopath's game and to win we must remember to love others unconditionally and not discount our own intuition. We are surrounded by people who don't care about anyone but themselves. We are exposed daily to people who might look at us as their next meal ticket or scam and they might be as close as a neighbor, a co-worker, a family member or the little old man in the doctor's office.

I have come in contact with plenty of people who made my skin crawl. Unfortunately the person who tried to cripple me emotionally and the person whom I could not seem to escape from was the person who made me. We all wanted his unconditional love but never got it, which is why I think Cindy and I tried so hard for so long to live up to his expectations.

So, why am I so pissed? Is it because I had a father who didn't give a fuck about anyone but himself? Is it because I am of such high moral fiber that the mere presence of my father and all the things that I know about him annoys me? Am I jealous? If so, of what? Our father lived a guiltless existence for most if not all of his life. Can you imagine how free you would feel if you never had to think of consequences, morality, compassion, empathy, the law or someone's feelings? You could literally say or do whatever you wanted and never experience a sleepless night. Think about your life and all of the questionable experiences, people, jobs or opportunities you passed on because of your conscience. Where would you be now if you said "yes" to all?

epilogue

I would love to have my mother back so that she could see her grandchildren, especially the younger ones, grow and progress into adults. I miss her because she was simply one of the sweetest people I have ever known. It plainly was not meant to be. She could not fight her illnesses or our father any longer. What I had always wished for my mother was peace and harmony and that would only have happened if she divorced him, killed him or out-lived him. She was too nice to take either of the first two options and her body gave out from being worn down by stress and illness before the third. When she died, I was consumed with dread. I wanted my father to have died before her so that we could all be left alone. The stark reality was that Cindy and I would have to take our mother's place in his life.

It is clear to me now that as much as I tried to make this journey with my father all about me, it was really all about him. When I wonder why my sister and I were left to manage our father's life, I have to remind myself that this is the journey he was meant to take. We just happened to be along for the ride. He was a menace to everyone he ever came in contact with including doctors, nurses, laborers, social workers, family members, tenants and his children. He was a master at creating discontent and vitriol wherever he went. He controlled every conversation and if he could not control someone's actions or feelings, then that person was discarded.

I said before that words were his weapon. He was a master at knocking you back with one sentence and he did it over and over again. It was so ironic that at the end of his life he could not speak. When the nurses called us and said they thought he was at the end, we quickly dropped what we were doing and headed to the nursing home like bats out of hell. Cindy and I needed to be there for him and for us. The curiosity of his death-bed scene was a morbid thought I played out in my mind a thousand times. When it actually came, I was terrified.

When we walked into his room, Cindy sat on the bed immediately. He grabbed onto her hands and wrists as though she was his life preserver. In our lifetime I do not recall him ever trying to hold our hands or embrace us whatsoever. Cindy recoiled for a moment when he touched her hands and then quickly realized he was completely terrified. For both of us, the thoughts we carried throughout our lives of what a mean and manipulative son-of-a-bitch he was were set aside. With tears in our eyes, we sat there watching him gasp for air while trying to speak. I never thought I would see the day when my father could not spew his venom, but here we were.

We had no idea what he was trying to say. His mouth kept moving like a baby bird looking for food. His gray eyes were wide open. I don't know if he could see us, but I guarantee you he was seeing something. I never saw my father afraid, but he was frightened of something or someone. His hospice nurse looked at him and us and was utterly confused. I know he should have been in a coma at this point so all I could say to the nurse was, "What the hell is this all about? Have you ever seen anyone behave like this when they're about to die?"

She said, "Almost never."

To which I said, "What do we do now? He needs to settle down. My sister and I cannot watch this for very long."

She said he was pissed. She also said he was battling unresolved issues. She asked, "Does he have unresolved issues or conflicts?" My sister and I said, "They are a mile high and there isn't enough time left for him to resolve any of them. He is going to have to take his baggage with him."

The nurse said he was dying how he had lived. After the nurses had given him another dose of morphine to calm him down, it was my turn to sit with him. I looked at him with a million thoughts running through my head. I was trying to find the right words; kind words to ease his conscience and would allow him to die. For a few minutes I spoke to him like a child having a temper tantrum. I said things like, "calm down and relax." I said, "It's time to accept what's happening." I told him, "You're just making yourself feel worse." Then I realized how stupid I must have sounded. My father was never calm. He never thought that what happened to other people would happen to him. He had a look of desperate indignation. He was looking at me to give him his final pass. I had to tell him what he needed to hear.

So, with a quiet resolve I took his hand in mine and with tears running down my face I told him it would be alright. I looked him in the eyes and told him I understood what he was trying to say. I said, "Whatever you've done, you will be forgiven. Don't be afraid. People that love you are waiting for you. Go find Luba. Go find your father. Mom will help you. It's time to have faith and let go."

I sat with him for roughly 30 minutes. He calmed down slightly but never stopped staring at me while trying to speak. His gray eyes were seeing something from another dimension. Whatever he was reacting to was not unicorns and rainbows. Maybe he had a conscience after all, and he realized he might have to answer for a lifetime of deceit. I have to admit that I did not see his death coming so quickly. I watched him curiously as he tightened up his face and that was it. I felt his life slipping away. Cindy and I couldn't save his soul at the end and I have no idea if what we said brought him any peace.

For now and for who knows how long, she and I can quietly

sift through our parents' belongings and decide at our own pace what we will keep. The rest will be donated, recycled or sold. As my brother said, "Turn it into cash!" That was easier said than done as Cindy and I were handcuffed by the thought that we might inadvertently sell something for $1 that was worth $1,000. However, if we did unknowingly pay it forward, so be it. His stuff was his stuff. It was never mine and I didn't want any of his possessions to remind me that he loved his shit more than he loved me. And in all seriousness, I doubt how much truly belonged to him. There was never a story attached to any item in the house.

As I have said before, our father loved to write down what he was feeling about everything, especially what he would have liked to say to someone. Cindy and I found tons of handwritten notes on invoices, newspaper articles, spiral notebooks and scraps of paper. I found a letter he had written, and it was lovely. It was not until the end that I realized for whom these words were intended.

"I stayed in this house to give you a happy secure home we both could enjoy and feel safe. We were devoted to each other. No doubts, no questions, no disloyalty. We shared everything; love, affection, understanding, bed, food, companionship. Everything. I'm not sure how I can handle this devastating loss or for how long. Time may or may not tell. What's next? I am numb with grief.

I'm left with fond memories and heart breaking, bitter tears. I've lost my true, unbiased companion and devoted friend. I hope we meet together in the here after, god willing. I loved you with all my heart and soul. Thank you for being so wonderful, like no other. I will grieve over you and my loss through eternity. Good bye. I will see you again."

That heartfelt prose was written to his dog after she died in 2013. We never found a single, kind word he had written to our mother. Every thought he put down on paper about Cindy and me was full of hate.

His journey was now complete. At the end of his life, Lou lived in a controlled environment with almost no way to cause trouble. He was alone with his thoughts and no one to abuse but the people charged with feeding and bathing him. In his mind my sister and I took his money, his property, his goodies and his freedom. I guess that's true. He believed it was for one reason; we know it was for another. For him the ruthless existence of a nursing home must have been torture. We had to keep rescuing him over and over so that the end of his life would be what is was meant to be. My sister and I were not meant to intervene or change how the story would end.

I believe that a lot of good can come from tragedy. In life you are given lemons, water and sugar and you had better figure out how to make your own lemonade. My sister and I accepted our challenges and met them head-on with determination and grace. Our greatest batch of lemonade took 18 years; the time it took to raise each of our children. Our father, on the other hand, let his lemons rot. He never found the good in anyone or anything. He never found joy and it was all around him. That's tragic.

Our relationship with our father was always dysfunctional. I hated it. Cindy hated it. He said he hated it, but I didn't believe him at all. I think he loved the controversy and discontent he stirred up all the time. We were his unwilling sparring partners; an activity I am afraid I became addicted to. I can only guess that his contempt for his daughters and most everyone around him far outweighed whatever love and kindness he should have possessed. What shocked me was that I continued to keep going back for more.

I never really respected him or held him in any kind of special regard. He was someone I was forced to deal with, so when I finally said "fuck you" to him for the first time in my life I was just shy of 52 years old and it was three months before he died. Saying that to him had been on the tip of my tongue for so long it became a permanent bitter taste in my mouth. I told him that the next time he called me he had better say something nice to me. He drove me to those horrible words for implying again that he didn't care about my kids. I said it because he said he didn't care about me or what I was trying do to with my life, which at the moment was just to be the best mother I could be. I said it for all of the pain he had caused to me, my sisters and my brothers. I said it because I know he married our mother for money; an opportunity to dig his claws into whatever she had.

Lou woke up every single morning of his empty life trying to find an angle for more free shit and went to sleep at night plotting revenge against those who prevented it. My sister and I were the only two on whom he had his cross-hairs continually focused. I thoroughly believed him when he said he would do everything he could to take us down with him. That was not going to happen. Cindy and I learned a long time ago how to survive the likes of him. We learned how not to become one of his victims by watching our mother. We learned how to defend ourselves using language and well-thought-out arguments. It took a long time not to give him the power to dictate how Cindy and I would feel about ourselves as women, wives, mothers, friends, athletes or employees. Fuck him and all of his baggage and twisted thoughts. I am strong and confident and know what I am doing and who I wish to spend my time with.

That is how his journey ended. He was finally out-numbered and out of control and there was not a single human being left on this planet who would entertain his craziness. Not a lawyer. Not the police. Not his doctors and nurses. Not his kids. No one. At times, I felt cruel for what I had to tell him at the end. No bullshit. No sugar coating. Get to the point. I learned to do that from him. Besides, he did not understand long, drawn-out anecdotal lectures. "You are not going home," was all I said when he was finally wheeled through the front doors of a nursing home. I must admit, however, that Cindy and I got a perverse amount of pleasure knowing he was finally getting a dose of his own medicine. Paybacks are a bitch. We learned this from him, too.

There will never be a time when I won't wrestle with my feelings for a man who did a lot right when it came to raising kids, like making sure we walked without dragging our feet or spoke without raising our voice at the end of a sentence. He made sure we spoke clearly and did not litter our language with "like", "you know", and "um". He made sure we had impeccable table manners and taught us how to stand up and fight for ourselves. I am certain that all of that training made Cindy and me better mothers and valued employees. What I cannot escape however, is that I know how unkind he was to the people around him and that's what makes me sad. My mother, his step children and his daughters never felt important.

But as I write this, sitting at a cottage in Lakeside, Ohio, my heart overflows with gratitude. I've pushed the thoughts of my father Louis to the back of my mind and remember that I am worthy of love and kindness. And in spite of him, I am capable of giving the same. It's a warm Labor Day weekend. I am having a drink, relaxing and watching the wind rustle the leaves in the trees. My brother is playing his guitar and singing a few of my favorite songs. I am thinking of our mother Marie, whose thoughts and unselfish acts guide me daily to love my children as I know she loved all of us. I hope Marie is with us in spirit this weekend. This is the part of life she missed.

Made in USA - Kendallville, IN
1208800_9781948613101
12.16.2020 1545